The Logic of
Anarchy

Neorealism to Structural Realism

New Directions in World Politics

Helen Milner and John Gerard Ruggie,
General Editors

The Logic of
Anarchy

Neorealism to Structural Realism

BARRY BUZAN

CHARLES JONES

AND

RICHARD LITTLE

COLUMBIA UNIVERSITY PRESS

NEW YORK

Columbia University Press
New York   Oxford
Copyright © 1993 Columbia University Press
All rights reserved

Library of Congress Cataloging-in-Publication Data

Buzan, Barry.
The logic of anarchy : neorealism to structural realism
Barry Buzan, Charles Jones, and Richard Little.
p.   cm.—(New directions in world politics)
Includes bibliographical references (p.   ) and index.
ISBN 0-231-08040-9 (CL: acid-free paper).
—ISBN 0-231-08041-7 (PAPER)
1. International relations—Research. 2. Realism.
I. Jones, Charles A., 1949–   . II. Little, Richard. III. Title. IV. Series.
JX1291.B89   1993   327′.072—dc20   92-31656
                                        CIP

∞

Casebound editions of Columbia University Press
books are Smyth-sewn and printed on permanent
and durable acid-free paper.

Printed in the United States of America
c 10 9 8 7 6 5 4 3 2 1

Contents

□ Contents □

Preface

This book began to take life in 1986, when Barry Buzan proposed to the others a collective volume that would try to extend the existing framework of Neorealist theory. Before that it had simply been a set of attractions, dissatisfactions, and questions in Buzan's mind arising from his encounter with Waltz's work while preparing the 1983 book *People, States and Fear*. After that it became a genuinely joint project, with an agreed division of labor, and extensive comment and cross fertilization between the drafts. After a longish period of gestation, reading, and discussion, Buzan's first draft came out in 1988, serving in part as an exegesis of Waltz, while Jones and Little produced a ground-clearing draft on structuralism. Their two sections followed on in 1989–90. We first went public with the project at a panel for the BISA/ISA Conference in London in March 1989. As is evident from differences of style, each of us has taken the prime responsibility for writing one of the three main Sections. But there has been an immense amount of constructive interplay, and some direct "hands on" inserts, with the result that the text as a whole represents a high level of integration and consensus. The Overview and Conclusion chapters were written collectively. Although we are leaving our names on the Sections in the text, we present the book as a jointly authored whole.

We would like to thank Ken Waltz for taking an interest in the project at an early stage, and for being willing to answer questions and comment on ideas; and Hayward Alker, Ole Waever and Alex Wendt for reading and commenting on the whole text. Barry Buzan would like to thank the many people who made thoughtful and helpful comments on earlier drafts of Section I, and particularly Kjell Goldmann, Bob Keohane, John Ruggie, and Ken Waltz for taking the time and trouble to give detailed written responses. Charles Jones would like to thank Robert Skidelsky, Paul Chilton, and Martin Hollis for comments on Section III, and the classes at Warwick University with which he used *Theory of International Politics* as a discussion text. Our thanks also to Frances Pinter for helping us to connect to Columbia University Press, and to the referees and series editors for Columbia for their helpful comments on drafts of the whole manuscript.

BB, CAJ, RL

The Logic of
Anarchy

Neorealism to Structural Realism

CHAPTER ONE

Overview

REALISM AND NEOREALISM

Since the publication of Kenneth Waltz's *Theory of International Politics* (hereafter *TIP*) in 1979, Neorealism has become a dominant school of thought in International Relations theory. It is no exaggeration to say that *TIP* shaped much of the theoretical debate during the 1980s, and that positive and negative reactions to it still reverberate in the literature of the 1990s. By developing the idea of a structural explanation for the logic of power politics, Waltz revived the flagging fortunes of the Realist tradition. In the first place, by attempting (albeit unsuccessfully as we shall show later) to place Realism on a secure scientific footing, he generated interest in the philosophical foundations of International Relations theory. It is now beginning to be recognized by analysts such as Ashley (1982), Walker (1987), Wendt (1987), and Spegele (1987) that these foundations are much more complex and eclectic than was previously thought. In the second place, Waltz provided a theoretical framework that proved sufficiently robust for others to apply some empirical cladding. One of the reasons why *TIP* made such an impact was that it changed the theoretical orientation of the discipline.

His book inspired a critical literature, best exemplified in Robert Keohane ed., *Neorealism and its Critics* (1986), Spegele "Three Forms of Political Realism" (1987), R. B. J. Walker, "Realism, Change and International Political Theory" (1987), and Alexander E. Wendt, "The Agent-Structure Problem in International Relations Theory" (1987). It also gave rise to some interesting attempts at application, including Robert Gilpin, *War and Change in World Politics* (1981), Stephen Walt, *The Origins of Alliances* (1987), Michael Mandelbaum, *The Fate of Nations* (1988), Barry Posen, *The Sources of Military Doctrine* (1984), and Christensen and Snyder, "Chain Gangs and Passed Bucks: Predicting Alliance Patterns in Multipolarity" (1990).

In the decade before the appearance of *TIP,* the hold of post-1945 Realism on the study of international relations had finally looked as if it were about to be broken. From the late 1960s onwards it began to be argued and accepted that the methodology and theory associated with Classical Realism were anachronistic. Cobwebs rather than billiard balls now appeared the appropriate metaphor for international politics and the theoretical foundations of Realism were coming under increasing attack (Burton 1972). At the same time, behavioralists were arguing that, in spite of their insistence on "eternal laws" of international politics, the work of Classical Realists did not satisfy the canons of scientific investigation. Waltz acknowledged that Classical Realism was indeed open to theoretical and methodological attack, but not on the grounds claimed by mainline critics. He insisted that these authors had failed to identify the basis on which international relations could be developed scientifically. Whatever might be its own shortcomings, this critical breadth would ensure that *TIP* caused heated controversy (Kaplan 1979; Rosecrance 1982).

But it is hard to believe that *TIP* would have provoked such enduring discussion had it not appeared at a moment peculiarly propitious for a restatement of Realism. At the end of the 1970s, detente gave way to a second Cold War, and advocates of interdependence and transnationalism, still confidently generating explanations premised on the progressive redundancy of force in international relations and the fragmentation of state power, were caught off balance (Keohane and Nye 1977). By contrast, Waltz's theory took the ability of the state to survive as axiomatic. Partly because of the sweeping nature of the attack on the discipline and partly because Waltz's theory resonated with the times, the ideas underpinning *TIP* circulated very rapidly and Waltz was soon seen to provide a serious challenge to alternative theoretical perspectives. Work emerging from those perspectives in the 1980s in many instances bore traces of theoretical and methodological reassessment deriving from Waltz's critique.

Although Waltz undoubtedly rekindled interest in Realism, he intended in *TIP* to distance himself from the older traditions of Classical Realism. For this reason he was happy to identify himself as a Neorealist. The older tradition had dominated the theory and practice of international relations after the Second World War when an influential group of writers including Morgenthau, Carr, Aron, Niebuhr, Kennan, Herz, Wight, and Kissinger produced major texts on the subject, with Kissinger going on to become an important decisionmaker. These writers styled themselves as Realists on the grounds that they were willing to look at things as they were rather than how they might like them to be. But *TIP* provoked two incompatible responses to the marked distinction it created between the Neorealism of Waltz and the Classical Realism of Morgenthau and the others. The first response was to identify a core of ideas common to Classical Realism and Neorealism. For many, Waltz was only the latest contributor to a coherent tradition of thought that could be traced back through Hobbes and Machiavelli to Thucydides. No other tradition of thought in the field of International Relations can begin to compete with the distinguished pedigree claimed for Realism. It is now also possible for specialists in International Relations to draw on an expanding literature in the history of ideas which is in the process of tracing the lineage of realist writers and exploring, for example, the links between Thucydides and Thomas Hobbes, who made the first English translation of *The Pelopponesian War* (Brown 1987, 1989).

A second and more muted response to the distinction between Classical Realism and Neorealism stressed the disparity between the two schools. Ashley was quick to point out that while the Classical Realists drew on a rich hermeneutic tradition, the Neorealists were relying on an arid and now discredited structuralist tradition. This defiant attack gave way to a much more measured and sympathetic assessment by Walker, who denied, in the first place, that there was a coherent theoretical position running through political Realism. Instead, he depicted Realism as the site for some of the most significant philosophical debates in Western political thought: more battlefield than school. The contemporary divide between Classical Realism and Neorealism appeared, in this view, to be no more than the latest stage in a continuing debate that could be traced back to arguments amongst Greek political thinkers about the relationship between identity and difference.

Walker observed how the Classical Realists had focused on the constant flux of political reality and stressed the contingent nature of political events. The Classical Realists, as a result, were regarded as predisposed to a historical approach to analysis. They accepted that the nature of social reality could undergo fundamental change and that the world could be understood only by examining the evolving practices of social actors. By contrast, Walker argued, Neorealists saw a more stable and structured reality, where social action was amenable to scientific analysis. Walker concluded that, without dismissing the importance of social structures, it was vital to give priority to the social practices responsible for bringing them into being in the first place. From this perspective, therefore, agency is privileged over structure. Walker's justification for his position needs to be more fully worked out because the complex and contentious relationship between agency and structure has now become quite a central theme in the social sciences (Cerney 1990, Clegg 1989, Layder 1989). The issue is examined in more depth in chapter 6. What is worth stressing here is that the dual response to Waltz has begun a post-Neorealist debate characterized by a three-way tension between structure, agency, and historical contingency.

Those most sensitive to the internal inconsistencies and eclectic character of Realism have stressed the need to look carefully at both Classical Realism and Neorealism. Neither is considered to provide an adequate foundation on which to build a theory of international relations. They have argued, as we will, that the foundations of Realism need to be extended (Spegele 1987; Walker 1987). But so far this has been very much a minority response. As Walker makes clear, it is much more common in the discipline simply to gloss over the tensions that exist within Realist writings, appealing to a continuing broad consensus.

As noted earlier, the agreed tenets of Realism have been articulated on many occasions during the 1980s. Often this was done to distinguish Realism from the brand of neoliberalism or new institutionalism which had become its major contender. Oversimplifying somewhat, it is usually argued that Realists focus on conflict within the international system while neoliberals stress cooperation. The next step is often to suggest the need to integrate or reconcile the two approaches (Niou and Odershook 1991), a process already visible in the work of writers such as Keohane and Gilpin. In fact, a clear distinction between the two can be sustained only by defining Realism in very narrow terms. The difficulty becomes apparent when attention is focused, for example, on the work of Hedley Bull (1977), who describes the anarchic international system in terms of a rule-governed society. The emphasis on anarchy is seen to place him in the Realist camp, whereas his emphasis on rules has meant that he is also rightly associated with the new institutionalists. It is not surprising, therefore, that the literature in International Relations at this juncture often seems confused.

This confusion may in part account for frequent complaints of lack of progress. Many International Relations theorists have claimed that the discipline has lost its sense of direction and is in a state of disarray (Holsti 1985:1–2; Ferguson and Mansbach 1988; Onuf 1989:8). Reactions to this assessment have varied. One has been to argue that the discipline has been overambitious and that the quest for rigorous theory was misguided (Ferguson and Mansbach 1988). Another has been to insist that the proliferation of contrasting approaches should be seen as a necessary and desirable consequence of the demise of positivism and the emergence of a post-positivist era. Any complex social reality, it is argued, needs to be seen from a variety of divergent perspectives. But Lapid, who has developed this argument, surely displays a closet positivism when he concludes that as epistemology advances we will move toward a better and more coherent understanding of social reality (Lapid 1989). A third response has been to argue that the loss of direction experienced in International Relations has occurred because the discipline as a whole has been working on an erroneous premise. It is denied that anarchy is the central and defining feature of international relations (Onuf 1990:14). Onuf has developed a sophisticated attack on the use made by International Relations theorists of anarchy, which he sees as an empty concept. His attack threatens the very foundations of the Neorealist framework by dissolving the distinction between International Relations and Political Science.

TIP AS A STARTING POINT FOR A THEORY OF INTERNATIONAL RELATIONS

Given the confusion and conflicting positions in International Relations, it is necessary to explain why we have decided to use *TIP* as a jumping off point rather than beginning from a broader conspectus or starting from scratch. In general, we took the view that it is better to focus debate on a real representative figure, and on widely read texts, than to hack away at some amorphous composite labeled Neorealism, where private interpretations would inevitably sow the seeds of misunderstanding. Waltz filled this bill nicely. More specific motives for

5

working thorough *TIP* lay partly in the attractions of some of Waltz's fundamental definitions, and partly in dissatisfaction with his theory and his critics. Like Waltz we accept that International Relations constitutes a legitimate and independent field of inquiry. Our discipline confronts the uniquely difficult question of how to theorize the totality of intersocietal relations in all their forms. Although we disagree with many of Waltz's positions on epistemology, structure, and consequence, we take the view that his basic conception of structure offers a solid foundation for this task. It is attractive both because of the penetration of Waltz's original insight into structure, and because it provides an intellectual framework that has become part of the standard equipment of the profession. For more than a decade *TIP* has been shot at, embellished, misunderstood, and caricatured, but never quite displaced. We think it is now time to build a new structural theory of international relations to replace *TIP,* but acknowledge that Waltz's work still provides some of the foundations for this enterprise.

Along with many of his critics, we are not entirely satisfied with Waltz. We find flaws in his logic, epistemology, and conceptualization of the field. We find him taking an unnecessarily narrow, static, and political perspective on what can and should be a much more comprehensive theory of international relations. We chafe at an ahistorical approach to theory. Our dissatisfaction with his critics stems from their misunderstandings of *TIP,* from their own very different, but equally obstructive, flaws and obscurantism in logic, epistemology, and vocabulary, and from the preponderance of destructive over constructive criticism.

As we have already noted, there have been attempts to apply Waltz's theory, attempts to debunk it, and some sympathetically critical attempts to defend it. But so far there has been surprisingly little sustained attempt to develop it. This book is not, like the 1986 Keohane volume, a collection of disparate commentaries. It is a systematic attempt to rebuild Structural Realism along much more open lines than Waltz's project, and to begin extending its logical framework outward to link up with other areas of International Relations theory. It dismantles and redesigns the philosophical framework of Waltz's analogy with economics, and opens up the historical and sociological dimensions of structuralist thinking about the international system.

We want to identify the useful core of Neorealist theory, and then use it as a foundation on which to construct a more solid and wider-ranging Structural Realism.

We appreciate that "structuralism," even more than "realism" itself, is a word drained of energy by excessive use. It is possible, at one extreme, to make reference to structural functionalism as developed by Talcott Parsons in the 1950s, and, at the other, to the poststructuralism of the more recent past. There can be no question of surveying the complex history of structuralism here. Those in search of a more comprehensive introduction should turn to Lane (1970), Robey (1973), or Skinner (1985). But the thread which runs through the twentieth-century preoccupation with structure is a belief that to understand human behavior it is necessary to transcend the self-conceptions and conscious motives of the individuals under investigation. All structuralists have believed, in some way or another, that they had gained access to a level of understanding that is superior to anything offered by the human "objects" under investigation, and that offered, in addition, a causal theory of aspects of human behavior sufficient to justify some form of therapeutic intervention or social engineering. What you cannot immediately perceive in your unconscious mind might be reached by Freudian analysis; what formerly appeared to be one damned thing after another can be seen by the Marxist as the dialectical unfolding of an orderly human history based in material conditions, to be helped upon its way by conscious political action. There is, in short, a broad family resemblance between Freud, Darwin, Marx, Classical economics, and linguistics after Saussure.

For the natural scientist, the claim that there may be some order of a general nature beneath the flux of appearances is routine and relatively unproblematic. But it has long provoked fierce debate among social scientists. On one side, those working in hermeneutic and historicist traditions have believed it fallacious to search for any objective general theory of society. To do so, they insist, necessarily involves moving away from how social action is understood within a specific group. Moves of this kind are attributed to inappropriate pursuit of the style of explanation proper to the natural sciences. There it is perfectly acceptable to assume, say, that the behavior of a molecule has no intrinsic meaning. Investigators may attach whatever meaning they find useful and consistent with experience. In the search for general theory, it is argued, social behavior is necessarily treated as though it were reducible to physical movement. Its essential meaning, as intentional action, is thereby lost.

Structuralists, by contrast, insist that social science must move beyond self-conceptions and motives because individuals are constrained by structural forces over which they have no control and of which they may possess no knowledge. Language provides a classic example often used to illustrate this point. In linguistics, it is invariably accepted that no individual or group of individuals ever sat down to construct and then impose the grammatical rules that establish the structure of language. Indeed, when we apply such rules, we may not be aware that we are doing so; nevertheless, these rules constrain us at every point when we endeavor to communicate verbally. It is further argued by some that beneath the surface structure of grammar, which varies from one language to another, there is a genetically coded deep structure that ensures we can all use the grammatical rules of the language we first encounter. It would appear that the act of speech draws on the deep structure and thereby reproduces the surface structure of language.

Using language as a metaphor for society, it is often suggested that although surface rules, sometimes also denoted as structures, may diverge markedly from one society to another, there is a deeper set of structures that accounts for how these surface rules are reproduced. Surface structures may play an important role in the description of society, but to explain how these structures are reproduced it is necessary to identify the existence of deep structures which provide the "underlying generative mechanisms which give rise to certain observable manifestations" (Layder 1981:3). Briefly, international law and diplomatic procedures are seen, in a structuralist approach to international relations, as surface structures dependent for their reproduction on the bare bones of an anarchic state system.

Much more might be said about structuralism as a movement in twentieth-century social science. Part of the reason for the controversy surrounding *TIP* has indeed been that Waltz advanced a structuralist theory of international politics at a point when many considered structuralism to have been buried under the weight of critical literature. We remain committed to a form of structuralism that we have called Structural Realism. But it is a form of structuralism that hopes to retain the explanatory power of radical abstraction in social science while avoiding the role structuralist theories have traditionally played in extending to the therapist, the policymaker, and social engineers of every kind a spurious legitimacy for their will to power. Instead, it will be argued here that it is necessary to find some means of reconciling the hermeneutic and the structuralist traditions. Proposals for integration developed by Giddens and others will be explored and modified. It will be claimed that, in the international system, structure and agent are mutually constitutive.

At this point some clarification of terms is in order. Waltz adopts the term "Neorealism" to label his own position, preferring it to "Structural Realism" (1990:29). This usage of "Neorealism" to encapsulate Waltz's theory is widely understood and accepted as indicating both his continuity with, and distinctiveness from, the "Classical" Realism of Carr and Morgenthau (Keohane 1986:15–16). We intend to respect it. Keohane prefers "Structural Realism," but uses it merely as a synonym for "Neorealism" (1986: 17, 160). This seems wasteful. Our intention is to reserve "Neorealism" for Waltz's narrow theory of international politics but take "Structural Realism" as our label for the much more wide-ranging theory of international relations we intend to construct. "Neorealism" emphasizes backward-looking links to "Classical" antecedents: it bespeaks simply a new, or renewed, Realism. The term "Structural Realism" more accurately emphasizes the method that lies at the heart of the new theory. The distinction between Structural Realism and Neorealism can be clarified in a preliminary manner by looking at the commonly accepted tenets of Realism. Gilpin (in Keohane 1986:304–5) suggests that three assumptions about political life are common to all Realists:

1. The nature of international affairs is essentially conflictual;
2. The essence of social reality is the group rather than the individual, and particularly the conflict group, whether tribe, city-state, kingdom, empire, or nation-state;
3. The prime human motivation in all political life is power and security.

Keohane (1986:164–65) identifies the following hard core assumptions of Classical (i.e. mid-twentieth century) Realism:

1. States are the most important actors in world politics;
2. States are unitary rational actors, albeit operating under conditions of stress, uncertainty and imperfect information;

3. States seek power and calculate their interests in terms of power.

Waltz builds a structural approach on the primacy of conflict groups or states, and uses this to generate the other assumptions. This innovation eliminates the problematic necessity to found Realism in conservative assumptions about human nature and the nature of states ultimately rooted in early modern philosophical psychologies promoted by Descartes and Hobbes. It moderates the power motive (though not the conflict assumption) by emphasizing security, and hugely simplifies and clarifies the logic of power politics.

Both Classical and Neorealists also assert the autonomy of the political from the economic and the societal and seek to construct theories on that basis (Morgenthau 1978:5–8; Waltz 1990:24–29). Waltz is particularly insistent on this point: "Theory isolates one realm from all others in order to deal with it intellectually. To isolate a realm is a precondition to developing a theory that will explain what goes on within it. . . . neorealism establishes the autonomy of international politics and thus makes a theory about it possible" (Waltz 1990:26, 29). Note the pointed title of his book: *Theory of International Politics*. While we would dissent from the conventionalism of this view we, too, wish to argue for the primacy of the political.

Robert Cox (in Keohane 1986:211–14) sees Neorealism as an American phenomenon reflecting the particular conditions of the Cold War. He argues that Neorealism uses the power, rationality, and structural assumptions to construct an ahistorical mode of thought. By doing this it commits the error of "taking a form of thought derived from a particular phase of history (and thus from a particular structure of social relations) and assuming it to be universally valid." Similar objections to Waltz's delinking of structure and history are made by Walker (1987). How does Structural Realism differ from this, and what continuities remain to justify the continued association with Realism?

Three elements mark Structural Realism as an extension of the Realist tradition. First is a continued insistence on the primacy of the political sphere. By this we mean that the anarchic political structure of the international system is to be regarded, in terms that will be developed in Section III, as a necessary rather than a contingent anarchy. Primacy, however is not privilege. We do not say that anarchy is ineradicable or that politics trumps economics, ideology, or any other facet of society. Quite the contrary. Section III argues that the primacy of the international-political can best be developed and humanized by dropping older Realist claims for the superiority of political over economic competition or rival systems of belief, realms every bit as anarchic as the world of international politics. This approach retains the possibility of meaningful argument by analogy between different social sciences, and hence facilitates the formulation of a theory of international relations that avoids isolationism and confinement to the political. However, it does draw attention to the ultimate need to ground such analogies in real structural resemblance rather than notions of supposed theoretical maturity or superiority, and it suggests that the safest way to proceed toward this goal is to accept rather than suppress the rhetoric of the social sciences, the necessarily rhetorical character of any analogy, and the influence of such rhetorical devices upon policymakers. Very much in the tradition of Carr, we allow "power over opinion" back in. Very much at odds with Waltz, we deny the reducibility of all forms of power to political power.

The second feature which places Structural Realism in the broad Realist tradition is its focus on the state as the most important defining unit of the international system. Once again we want to emphasize that this neither closes the theory to other units nor constitutes a privileging of the political. States, contrary to the purest ideals of liberalism, have always exerted power in manifold forms.

Third is the acceptance of Waltz's basic definitional framework for international structure, albeit with very substantial changes to his specific formulation. These three elements are closely interlinked. The Waltzian notion of structure is, as has often been pointed out, derived from the units. It is not, as in some of the more metaphysical versions of structuralism in linguistics, a preexisting force that generates the units and interactions. Rather it is generated by the interaction and arrangement of the units. This close linkage between units and structure not only defines the continuity between Structural Realism and the traditional Realist assumptions, but also opens the way to a much more fully systemic and multisectoral theory than that offered by Neorealism.

There are three key differences between Structural Realism and Neorealism. First is that a much more comprehensive and more open definition of structure is deployed, and one that can be applied well beyond the confines of the political sector. Second is that structure is not seen as the only systemic-level factor in play. Key elements of interaction also have a systemic quality, and one that radically affects the development and consequence of structure. These arguments are elaborated in Sections I and II. They affirm the centrality of anarchic structure and security motives, but they do not always or necessarily generate a dominating logic of power politics. Pursuit of their logic involves a multisectoral approach to the nature of international interactions. Third is that Structural Realism does not rest on the positivistic analogy with microeconomics that informs Waltz's theory. It uses instead a more linguistic approach to analogy, developed in Section III.

The combined effect of these differences opens four possibilities not available to Neorealism. First is that structure becomes a way of addressing history, and not something detached from it. We aim to meet both of Cox's charges by presenting a structuralism that is neither slave to nor master of a particular historical period, and can engage with all of human history. Crucial to this is the second possibility, which allows the explicit linkage of units and structure through the logic of structuration. The redefinition of deep structure undertaken in Section I and unfolded in Section II leads to the third possibility, which is to break out of the narrow logic of political interaction that dominates Neorealism and to look at the whole range of interactions (economic, societal, environmental, as well as military and political) that have shaped both the units and the structures of the international system. A fourth possibility, arising out of our revision of the philosophical posture of Realism, is to facilitate a clearer understanding of the relationship between the study and the practice of international relations by exposing the rhetorical character of discourse, academic as well as official, which can then be seen to be action as much as or more than knowledge. We will argue in Section III that a position of this kind can be maintained in conjunction with a philosophically realist methodological position which mitigates the binds of relativism and reflexivity that have restricted so much self-proclaimed postmodernist and poststructuralist work.

In our view, structural logic leads much more naturally to the discussion of history, including contemporary history, than to the detailed discussion of current policy. By definition, structural logic is at a higher and more abstract level of analysis than specific policy questions. Structural logic can certainly be used to shape and inform the analysis of foreign and domestic policy, as we try to show, but it is mostly too abstract and large scale to be used prescriptively. Between history, especially grand history, and structural analysis, the levels are much better matched. Our Structural Realism offers a synthetic method in which structure can be used to interpret history, and in which history is necessary to understanding the consequences of structure.

The task of developing a theory of Structural Realism needs itself to be set into context. Both the historical and the intellectual milieus for this enterprise are strikingly different from those prevailing when Waltz wrote during the late 1970s. The historical context for *TIP* was a confrontational world, dominated by the Cold War rivalry between the superpowers, and heavily shaped by configurations of opposed ideology and military power. It was a world fixed by the historically unusual bipolar structure. Despite worries about American decline, this structure had enjoyed a remarkable continuity, and looked set to continue for the forseeable future. It did indeed roll on largely undisturbed for another decade. Its end in 1989–90 came swiftly, and took most observers by surprise.

The historical context for *Logic of Anarchy* (hereafter *LoA*) is much more open. The collapsing power, ideology, and political framework of the Soviet Union, and the growing cohesion of the European Community, have opened the way, not toward a unipolar system but toward the more traditional multipolar structure. This time, however, multipolarity is occurring on a truly planetary scale, and there are strong signs that the substantial ideological harmony among the major powers will serve as the foundation for something like a global concert. Military power has lost prominence as the key shaper of international relations among most of the great powers, though as the second Gulf War illustrated, not among the states of the periphery, or between them and the core powers. Economic, environmental and societal factors have risen in importance. The United States is worried less about its military and more about its economic competitiveness, and the ideological landscape is dominated by the relative success of market economics and pluralist politics.

TIP thus spoke to a world whose problem was how to manage a continuing Cold War. *LoA* speaks to a world whose problem is how to manage a twenty-first century and third millennium international system in which there is more change than continuity, and in which there is a lack of clear vision about both structure and direction.

As noted above, the intellectual context of *TIP* was set by a vigorous academic assault on the Classical Realism of Morgenthau coming from those concerned with interdependence, political economy, and transnational relations. A brief recapitulation of that story is necessary to contrast the contexts in which *TIP* and *LoA* were written. The assault included an attack on the centrality of the state and military power in Realist thinking, accused Realism of being unable to deal with either the issues or the character of international politics in an interdependent world, and denounced the logic and the morality of its normative bias toward conflictual assumptions. Among other things, all of this was in part aimed at reducing the status of American power, adding to Realist worries about the loss of American nuclear superiority over the Soviet Union. There was also a pervasive fashion for "science" in the form of positivist methods left over from the behavioral "revolution" of the 1960s.

TIP was the most successful of the Realist counterattacks in this intellectual joust. It reasserted the logic of power politics on firmer foundations than Morgenthau's resort to human nature, and it exposed the partiality of the interdependence view of international relations. It also reaffirmed the primacy of American power in the international system. Indeed, almost the entire last third of *TIP* is taken up with these rather polemical issues. Chapter 7 is preoccupied with rebuffing the thesis of rising interdependence, while chapters 8 and 9 are largely concerned with the virtues of the United States' role in a bipolar system. These concerns go some way to explaining both the wide interest in Waltz's theory and why its operational side, which is ostensibly what these chapters are about, seems relatively poorly developed and eccentric.

By contrast, the intellectual context of *LoA* is considerably less burdened. The advocates of power and interdependence have by and large made their peace, so that the two concepts are now generally seen as complementary rather than mutually exclusive. It is no longer odd to talk of writers such as Gilpin, Keohane, and Strange in terms of a Realist International Political Economy. The epistemological straitjacket of empiricism has been loosened, and the field is now informed as well by more philosophically open tendencies. Neorealism has established a secure place despite continuing dissatisfactions with it, and a fair measure of downright hostility. Its preoccupation with anarchy as the central political condition of international relations has been widely taken up in writings about cooperation theory, game theory, regimes, and international society.

Although concern with American decline is still on the academic agenda, it is not on ours. We write from outside the United States, and we have no interest in becoming part of an Anglo-Saxon tradition that stretches from E.H. Carr to Kenneth Waltz, in which theoretical discourse is used to mask prescriptive arguments about the contemporary policy problems of hegemonic powers, respectively Britain and the United States. To the extent that it is possible, our aim is to use this period of relative historical openness and intellectual calm to push forward the development of Structural Realism as a coherent theory of the international system. Any hidden policy agenda in this book is hidden as much or more from its authors as from its readers. We try to make explicit the extent that advocacy of any form of Realism is in itself a political position.

THE STRUCTURE OF THE BOOK

The book consists of three main sections and a conclusion. The main sections are closely interlinked, but they do not form a cumulative linear progression of argument. Instead they form a series of complementary excursions, each spiraling outward from the same core. Each Section uses Waltz's text as a starting point, demolishing, rebuilding, and adding as necessary, and then building outward from the new core in such a way as to integrate other areas of International Relations theory into Structural Realism. It is the common critical relationship to *TIP,* and the common purpose of constructing a more comprehensive and better founded structural theory that unites them. Because the three sections start from different parts of Waltz's theory, and are aimed at different areas of International Relations theory, they necessarily differ markedly in style and approach. Their purpose is to construct a series of widenings each developing from a different part of a common center, and connecting to diverse areas of theory.

Section I begins with a detailed exegesis of Waltz's structural theory (principally chapters 5 and 6 of *TIP*). Buzan reconstructs the central logic and vocabulary, examines flaws and criticisms within the theory, and misunderstandings of it, and develops some key reformulations and extensions. In particular, he argues for a major revision to the definition of deep structure, the refurbishment and reintegration of the unit level, and the addition of a wholly new interaction component to the theory. With these additions, Neorealism becomes Structural Realism, making connections with the literatures of international political economy, interdependence, international history, international society/regimes and strategic studies.

Section II takes off from the revised definition of deep structure in Section I, and pursues the logic of the Ruggie/Buzan amendment to Waltz's second tier of structure. The two Sections are thus closely connected, but in Section II Little moves considerably further away from Neorealism. He reconstructs the theory not only in the light of international history and world system theory, but more particularly in terms of the agent-structure debate, and recent literature on the structuration approach to social systems. This approach exposes an implicit theory of the state in *TIP,* and demonstrates, in line with structuration thinking, that the state and the international system are mutually constitutive. This insight makes it possible to overcome Waltz's ahistorical assessment of the anarchic system, and to establish the historical credentials of Structural—or possibly Structurational[1]— Realism. It also opens the way to a systematic linking of the unit and structure levels of analysis, revising the structural framework so as to expand its potential for interpreting both continuity and transformation in the international system. The expansion and contraction of the Roman Empire is used as a case study to illustrate the circumstances under which system transformation takes place, and to exemplify the historico-structural method of analysis.

Section III starts not from Waltz's theory as such, but from the methodological prologue offered in chapters 1–4, and less directly 7, of *TIP.* It might logically have been placed as the first Section, but this would have forgone the benefits of opening with an exegesis, and thrown readers straight in at the deep end. Coming last, its purposes are to investigate the alleged positivism of Neorealist theory and to criticize the analogy between balance of power and microeconomic theory that informs Waltz's approach. Jones then proceeds from this critique to reconstruct on firmer ground the philosophical foundations on which Structural Realism stands, and on which the arguments in

Sections I and II ultimately rest. He seeks a more open and plausible basis for relating economic theory to international relations by way of metaphor and postmodern methods of analysis. He offers a restatement of international political economy in Structural Realist terms, focusing particularly on the implications of a distinction drawn between necessary and contingent anarchies, and on the disaggregation of power.

The Conclusion summarizes the main arguments, and sets out the implication of these discussions for the application and further development of a Structural Realist theory of International Relations. We outline research programs suggested by the arguments in the three main Sections, drawing particular attention to the need for further thinking about: how systems are defined; how functional differentiation can be operationalized; and how the full dynamics of a system can affect the relationship between units and structure. We do not pretend to be offering a fully developed theory of international relations. What we hope we have accomplished is to have laid the foundations for such a theory, to have built, and in a few cases occupied, some of the lower floors, and to have indicated the main lines along which the construction might be continued.

Note

1. We are grateful to Morten Kelstrup for this idea.

I

Rethinking System
and Structure

BARRY BUZAN

This section of the book undertakes the first stage of transformation from Neorealism to Structural Realism. The method is to work through Waltz's logic in its own terms, suggesting reformulations where it is weak or defective, clarifying it where it is unclear or underdeveloped, and pushing it further where it has stopped short. The spirit of this approach is in line with the conclusions reached by both Ruggie and Keohane (but probably not by Waltz), that Waltz's theory is best seen as a beginning rather than as a finished product (in Keohane 1986:152, 191).

The title of his book (*Theory of International Politics*) is studiously noncommital on whether it is *a* theory or *the* theory, though he is clear that it is a theory of *politics*. Our intention is to construct *a* theory of international *relations,* which we call Structural Realism. By seeing it as *a* theory we assert that Structural Realism is an extremely interesting and useful way of understanding the international system. But it is only one theory among many, and we make no claim that it is the only valid way of conceptualizing the international system. It is simply one way that strikes us as being useful, not least because it can be made complementary to other perspectives, serving as a firm foundation on which to integrate many other elements of international relations theory. By focusing on international *relations,* our aim is to begin drawing structural theory out of its narrow political domain, and to start interweaving it with the more socioeconomic concerns of liberal thinking about the international system. In this respect, we are in complete sympathy with the desire of Keohane and Nye to fuse Neorealism and liberalism into a full system theory that incorporates process as well as structure (Keohane and Nye 1987:747). Toward this end, our aim is to extend the logical reach of the theory so that it can more easily be connected to the study of specific situations and cases.

Chapter 2 looks briefly at Waltz and his critics. It relates Waltz's theory to the level of analysis problem, and looks at the criticisms that it is too narrow, too static, and too restrictive of other types of system analysis. Chapter 3 reconsiders the foundations of a structural theory of international relations. It begins with the general idea of the international system, examines the consequences of restricting the inquiry to the political system, and then goes into a detailed investigation of the logic underlying levels of analysis. Chapter 4 departs completely from Neorealism, taking up the issue of interaction as a key element in system theory, and looking particularly at the quality of capabilities across the system as a whole. It shows how variations in interaction capability determine the very nature, as well as the consequences, of structure.

Care is taken throughout to preserve the distinction between structural theory and system theory. Confusion about this important distinction seems to underlie much of the discussion of Neorealism, including that by Waltz himself.

CHAPTER TWO

Waltz, His Critics, and the Prospects for a Structural Realism

Waltz's theory develops from the level of analysis problem in the study of international relations. Waltz himself explicitly used a "levels" approach to analysis in his 1959 book *Man, the State and War*, and the term "levels of analysis" was later given prominence by David Singer (Singer 1961:77–92). Singer's concern was to raise awareness of the need to distinguish between what he labeled state and system level explanations in the analysis of cause and effect in international relations. Waltz's purpose in *TIP* was to advance system theory down this path by showing how to differentiate clearly the system from the unit level. His method was to construct a definition of the system level in terms of structure that is precise enough to identify the boundary between unit and system factors. To facilitate this task, Waltz narrowed his focus down to the international *political* system, which enabled him to devise a neat, but very sparse, definition of system structure. This approach captured Singer's system level and made it available as a distinct basis for explaining part of the nature of international relations. As Waltz puts it:

> Structure has to be studied in its own right, as do units. To claim to be following a systems approach or to be constructing a systems theory requires one to show how system and unit levels can be distinctly defined. Failure to mark and preserve the distinction between structure, on the one hand, and units and processes, on the other, makes it impossible to disentangle causes of different sorts and to distinguish between causes and effects. Blurring the distinction between the different levels of a system has, I believe, been the major impediment to the development of theories about international politics (Waltz 1976:78).

There is little reason to criticize Waltz's decision to focus on system structure. The relative simplicity of structure in comparison with the messy diversity at the unit level made clear identification of structure much the easiest approach to defining the boundary between the two levels. Waltz was fully aware that a structural theory would by definition focus mainly on the continuities in the international system. "Systems theories explain why different units behave similarly. . . . Political structure produces a similarity in process and performance so long as a structure endures" (Waltz 1979:72, 87). "Structures never tell us all that we want to know. Instead they tell us a small number of big and important things. They focus our attention on those components and forces that usually continue for long periods" (in Keohane 1986:329).

Waltz was also fully aware that structural causes could never offer more than a partial explanation of international outcomes. "The weight of systems-level and of unit-level causes may well vary from one system to another," and it is important "to keep open the theoretically interesting and practically important question of what, in different systems, the proportionate causal weights of unit-level and of systems-level factors may be." (Waltz 1979:48–49) "One must ask how and to what extent the structure of a realm accounts for outcomes and how and to what extent the units account for outcomes." "Structure operates as a cause, but it is not the only cause in play." (Waltz 1979:78, 87) "Neither structure nor units determine the outcomes. Each affects the other." "Structures shape and shove. They do not determine behaviors and outcomes, not only because unit-level and structural causes interact, but also because the shaping and shoving of structures may be successfully resisted." (in Keohane 1986:328, 343) His many statements on this point have not prevented the emergence of a widespread and mistaken perception of him as a structural determinist. This is a worrying development for anyone trying to pursue cumulative scientific understanding in the field, and particularly for those trying to develop structural theory.

Waltz's theory made three major contributions toward a system theory of international relations.

1. It succeeded in defining system structure in a way that allows it to be used as a discrete explanation for some of the behavior of units in the international political system.
2. It thereby created a firm structural basis for the logic of power politics. This structural basis amplified and clarified the much vaguer notions of structure present in Classical Realism,

strengthening them to the point where they render unnecessary the controversial normative foundations of power politics in human nature and the internal dynamics of state politics: thus the label "Neorealism."

3. It exposed an area of theoretical bedrock which can serve as a solid foundation for further development of international system theory. Waltz's accomplishment was to identify important durable elements in a field where development of scientific analysis is everywhere hampered by the apparent universality of change.

On the negative side, Waltz seemed insensitive to the difficulties created by his very tight definition of system structure for other systems analysis approaches to international relations. He defined a system simply as "composed of a structure and of interacting units" (Waltz 1979:79; and in Keohane 1986:327). This dyadic approach strongly reflected both his earlier division of the universe of international political theory into reductionist and systemic categories (Waltz 1979:18), and his concern to identify the boundary between system and unit levels of analysis.

It is this part of Waltz's approach that created difficulty. The logic is as follows. First, he divided the universe of system into structure and unit levels. Second, he took structure to represent the system level of analysis. Third, he defined structure in highly restrictive terms. By this method Waltz could not avoid pushing a vast array of causes and effects down to the unit level. In addition, as Waltz's prime purpose in establishing the unit-system boundary was to elaborate theory at the system level, he naturally paid little attention to unit factors once he had banished them beyond the realm of his structural definition. He was always aware that unit causes played an important role in outcomes, and that "any theory of international politics requires also a theory of domestic politics." (in Keohane 1986:327, 331) But since the emphasis of his analysis in *TIP* was on system structure, he was simply not concerned to investigate what went on beyond his definitional boundary.

The consequence is that Waltz's definition effectively (but as will be shown in chapter 4 mistakenly) appropriated the whole content of the system level for his own narrow definition of structure. In the process, he forced down to the unit level all other attempts to conceptualize the international system in general terms. Many acknowledge the analytical centrality of his ideas on structure, but few are comfortable with his conclusion that all else is thereby relegated to the unit level. As Keohane and Nye argue it, "making the unit level the dumping ground for all unexplained variance is an impediment to the development of theory" (Keohane and Nye 1987:746). Consequently, there has been continuous pressure to push what Waltz counts as unit level factors back into the structural level. Waltz acknowledged "how difficult it is to keep the levels of a system consistently distinct and separate" (in Keohane 1986:328), but uncompromisingly defended his strict boundary. This struggle over the boundary has too easily ignored the possibility that Waltz's mistake lay not in the placement of the line between structure and unit levels but in the assumption that there is nothing else but structure in the system level.

This tension over the nature and placement of the boundary between the system and unit levels sets much of the tone of response to *TIP*, as indicated by the title of the 1986 volume, *Neorealism and its Critics*. Two lines of criticism stand out: one, that Waltz's theory is too narrow, the other, that it is too static. The complaint of narrowness has three sources. Firstly, and most broadly, criticism has occurred because of basic methodological differences between Waltz's positivist, structuralist approach, and the relativist, historicist positions of some commentators, most notably Cox and Ashley.

The second and third sources of narrowness arise from Waltz's restriction of his inquiry to the international *political* system and, within that confine, to his sparse definition of structure. In combination, these two restrictions exclude, or marginalize, a range of factors that others see as being: (1) "structural," (2) important to outcomes, and/or (3) lying both beyond a strictly political domain, and above a strictly unit level of analysis. Ruggie focuses on "dynamic density," defined as "the quantity, velocity and diversity of transactions that go on within society" (in this case world society) (in Keohane 1986:148). Keohane looks at richness of information, rules, and institutions in a similar light (Keohane 1986:190–97). Keohane and Nye highlight "non-structural incentives for state behavior" and "the ability of states to communicate and cooperate." (Keohane and Nye 1987:746) Both Ruggie and Cox also want to bring socioeconomic factors into the analysis: Ruggie draws attention to the linkage of property rights and capitalism to political sovereignty, while Cox wants to include the social forces engendered by the organization of production (in Keohane 1986:141–48, 220).

The charge that Waltz's theory is too static arises partly from the tendency of structuralists to emphasize continuities over change, which some find unacceptable (Ashley in Keohane 1986:265–67). This criticism is easily countered by the argument that one cannot make sense of change without first understanding continuity. Walker, for example, contrasts historicism and structuralism as extremes of concern with change and stasis, but does acknowledge that structure can be used to define change (Walker 1987:77). One merit of a strong definition of structure is precisely that it provides a benchmark with which one can differentiate between significant and trivial change (Jones 1981:1). More seriously, Ruggie and Keohane both criticize Waltz for excluding the sources of systemic change from his theory. As Ruggie puts it: "Waltz's theory of 'society' contains only a reproductive logic, but no transformational logic" (in Keohane 1986:152). This charge stems directly from the narrowness of Waltz's formulation in terms both of its confinement to the international political system, and its sparse definition of structure. In Waltz's scheme, change is either completely absent (the deep structure of anarchy), or infrequent (the single shift from multi- to bi-polarity), and its sources lie outside what is defined as structure (Waltz in Keohane 1986:343). Waltz kept variables to a minimum, and maximized the salience of continuity. Most of his critics want a more richly defined structure that is closer to the dynamics of change.

To some extent, these disagreements simply reflect matters of preference about the focus of analysis. Theory, after all, is nothing more than an abstract construct imposed on a selected body of objects, events, and processes. Provided the logic remains clear and coherent, many such formulations are both possible and legitimate, the choice among them being made on grounds of usefulness (Waltz 1979:8). Though we will have refinements to add in Section III, we take this pragmatist epistemology to be one of the points on which we are in substantial agreement with Waltz. Criticisms of Neorealism that it does not take adequate account of economic structures, that it does not explain change, and that it says little about the unit level, are thus true, but in one sense beside the point. Whether one agrees with his objectives or not, Waltz was primarily interested in identifying continuities of political structure, and in this he substantially succeeded. It is, however, possible to do much more.

The natural tension between the explanation of continuities and the explanation of change has plagued most attempts at the direct, empirical type of structuralism under consideration here, opening them to the charge of intrinsic conservative bias. So long as structural explanations are set within a bounded context of defined conditions, however, the tension between continuity and change does not seem to raise any fundamental intellectual issues. Waltz acknowledges that his structural theory is bounded by historical conditions: thus it is "problem-solving theory" in Cox's terminology (in Keohane 1986:208). The merit of structuralism as an explanation depends significantly on how durable the identified structure is. The salience of enquiry into change will be higher either if the specified structures have a short duration, or if the point of enquiry is close to the decay of a long-lived structure. Waltz's view was that he was dealing with long-lived structures, and that within his theory questions of structural effect were therefore more important than questions of structural change. Indeed, Waltz's deep structure is so durable that it does not seem to be a good use of one's time to be concerned with change on that level. Worrying about the end of anarchy is best left to those future generations who will be closer to it.

Others, of course, would simply challenge the description—or assumption—of continuity. The problem is in some degree linguistic. Continuity is most apparent to those who feel that key terms ("state," "nation," "anarchy") have been referring and continue to refer to essentially similar things over the past few centuries. By and large, status quo theorists, including Waltz, have perceived this to be the case, while revisionist or utopian theorists have repeatedly striven to introduce new vocabulary ("transnational") implying inadequacies in the ability of the existing terms to capture new (and very old) realities. We are aware that the theory of reference has been a lively area of development in recent philosophy, and that any attempt to bring the Realist tradition of international relations within the philosophical fold of a scientific realism of the sort that we sketch out in Section III will eventually have to cross this minefield. In brief, we suggest that the safest path would appear to lie in a causal or social account of reference of the kind advanced by Hilary Putnam, which sits well with political Realism by giving a special place in the division of linguistic labor to practitioners (Putnam 1977:118).

Although these criticisms of Waltz are beside the point in one sense, they nonetheless do define the challenge facing those who seek to develop a structural theory of international relations. In effect, the charge is not that Waltz's theory is wholly wrong (though bits of it are disputed), but that it is incomplete. Waltz's style of presentation exacerbates this problem. He took his *structural* theory to be the *system* level theory of international politics. Although the distinction between a system theory and a structural one may have been clear in Waltz's mind, it was not always clear in his prose. This was partly a problem of vocabulary. Waltz was clearly aware that a system is composed of a structure and interacting units. If this is so, then a system theory must logically incorporate both levels. But his concern to develop a structural theory led him into a terminologically unfortunate distinction between *reductionist* theories (those at the unit level), and *systemic* ones (those about structure). By this route, his usage of terms such as "systems theory" and "systems level" makes the term system effectively a synonym for structure. In confusing system and structure in this way, Waltz made his theory unnecessarily provocative, helping the case of those who wish to dismiss him as a structural determinist.

In their various ways, Waltz's critics all think that system theory needs to contain more than Waltz's structure. This "more" could either be a more comprehensive exposition of structure, or a more integrated theory of the system as a whole. Some want structure defined in more than political terms. Some want more recognition of language as an intervening system that allows no strictly neutral descriptions of international relations while also playing an ineradicable part in their conduct. Some want system theory to contain more linkages between the unit and structure levels. And some want a richer selection of generalizations about the international system to be available between Waltz's sparse conception of structure, at one end, and the densely populated unit level on the other, particularly in the area of process. In the chapters that follow in this Section and the next two, we hope to show how all of these desires for "more" can be met without compromising the basic distinction between structure and unit levels.

CHAPTER THREE

System, Structure, and Units

Neorealist theory is rooted in the basic ideas of system, structure and units. Any attempt to advance from it needs to start with these concepts, clarifying their definitions, and focusing on how structure and units relate to each other and to the broader idea of system that encompasses them.

SYSTEM

In general terms, and also in terms of international relations, "system" refers to a group of parts or units whose interactions are significant enough to justify seeing them in some sense as a coherent set. A group of states forms an international system when "the behavior of each is a necessary factor in the calculations of the others." (Bull and Watson 1984:1) A system therefore comprises units, interactions, and structure. Interaction is crucial to the concept of system, for without it, the term system has no meaning, a point that will be more fully developed in chapter 4 and Section II. A system may be identified specifically in terms of the function of the set as a whole (as in a central heating system), or more generally by an enclosing boundary that contains the whole universe of a specified set of units (as in the international system). The functional approach, which is that of general systems theory, can be rejected as a model for the international system on the grounds that it is too highly structured (Waltz 1979:59). The international system reflects no conscious design, and has no specified purpose or function. But it is a major artifact of human evolution, and the manner of its working is an important element in defining the human condition.

The term *international system* has two senses, and the resultant ambiguity is a common source of confusion. Its first, and most specific, meaning refers to the system of states, and reflects the puzzling, but firmly established use of nation as a synonym for state. This usage confines the idea of system to states (singly as units, collectively as the embodiment of structure) and their interactions. One could more accurately refer to this conception as the *interstate system*. Its second, and most general meaning refers to the totality of human interaction on the planet, and incorporates a range of units varying from individuals, through firms, nations and a great variety of other nongovernmental organizations or entities, to states. This should more properly be called the *interhuman system*, or somesuch, because the term *international*, with its suggestion of interstate relations, contains a strong bias toward an exclusively political interpretation of the total system of humanity.

In what follows, the tension between the interstate and interhuman views of the system plays an important role. The simplicity of Waltz's theory depended in good measure on his use of highly restrictive definitions. His trailblazing cleared a basic path, and allows others to devote more energy to exploring the byways of less restrictive assumptions. Much of the logic of Structural Realism results from shifting away from a strict *interstate* understanding of the international system, and toward an interhuman one. To avoid proliferating terms, we will use "international system," but draw attention to points where the distinction between its two senses is important to the discussion.

SYSTEM SECTORS

It is a common tactic when discussing systems to seek greater specificity by qualifying the identity of systems in terms of particular *sectors* of activity within them (as in "the international economic system," or "the international political system"). This is the approach that Waltz adopts (Waltz 1979:79). In doing so he places himself firmly in the tradition of Classical Realism that asserts the autonomy of the political sphere. (Morgenthau 1978:5) When we refer to more specific sectors of the international system these will also be identified as the international political, military, societal, economic, or whatever, system. This approach is commonly used in academic discussions of the international system, but as a practice, has not itself been much discussed.

The partial systems identified by sectors are not subsystems in the normal sense of a subset of units located within a larger set, and containing fewer units than the whole. Instead, they are views of the whole system through some selective lens that highlights one particular aspect of the relationship and interaction among all of its constituent units. The metaphor of a lens is quite accurate (Manning 1962:2). In the physical world, one can look at an object using many different types of "lenses," ranging from the naked eye and telescopes, through infra-red sensors and radars, to X-ray machines and electron microscopes. In each case the lens is either sensitive to different types, or wavelengths, of energy (e.g., infra-red and X-ray), or else sensitive to the same type of energy in a different way (e.g., microscope and telescope). Thus even though the object observed remains the same (ignoring Heisenberg), different lenses highlight different aspects of its reality. The naked eye sees mostly exterior shape and color. The infra-red sees the pattern of heat. The X-ray sees the pattern of physical density. The electron microscope sees molecular structure. The function of sectors is the same as that of lenses: each one gives us a view of the whole that emphasizes some qualities, and de-emphasizes, or even hides completely, others.

The use of sectors/lenses has the advantage of highlighting, and therefore making easier to see, certain qualities of whatever is being observed. It is a way of unpacking the confusion of the whole. In analytical terms, it confines the scope of inquiry to more manageable proportions by reducing the number of variables in play. Thus the economist looks at human systems in terms that highlight wealth, and justify restrictive assumptions such as the motivation of behavior by the desire to maximize utility. The political Realist looks at the same systems in terms that highlight power, and justify restrictive assumptions such as the motivation of behavior by the desire to maximize power. The military strategist looks at the system in terms that highlight offensive and defensive capability, and justify restrictive assumptions such as the motivation of behavior by opportunistic calculations of coercive advantage. Each is looking at the whole, but seeing only one dimension of its reality. The obvious danger in this method is that the observer will begin to confuse the partial reality of the sector with the total reality of the whole. Sectoral blindness is an occupational hazard of all human specializations. It is a particular disease of an academia excessively blinkered by deeply institutionalized disciplinary boundaries.

In relation to systems analysis, the use of sectors raises two difficult questions. First, it introduces a definitional problem about how the different sectoral "systems" within the total system are to be distinguished from (and thereafter related to) each other. Waltz makes very clear from his title that he is attempting a sectoral theory of international politics. If theory is to be constructed within a sector then the definitional issue is inescapable. But how can one differentiate between the international political and economic systems? Ruggie's discussion of the intimate links between property relations and sovereignty illustrates the difficulty (in Keohane 1986:141–48). At root, the question here is whether a viable theory can be constructed within a sector, or whether to do so inevitably confuses the sector with the whole? In thinking about any given historical event, it is difficult to disentangle the economic, political, societal, and strategic threads that make up the whole. Because each sector is a partial view of the whole, sectors necessarily overlap and interweave. Sectors are not separated by clear boundaries like those between levels of analysis. Indeed, the whole spatial metaphor of separation, boundaries, and the like is simply inappropriate. This is because, as with lenses, the distinction between sectoral boundaries is to be found as much in the equipment of the observer as in the thing observed. By contrast, boundaries between levels of analysis are more wholly within the thing observed, serving to identify distinct elements of causality. We will consider this metaphor further in chapter 12.

Following the sectoral path to theory means assuming that sectors can be made distinct. This assumption raises a question: how do the vertical division of a system into sectors, and the horizontal division of the system into levels of analysis, interact? (See figure 3.1 below.) Do levels of analysis get defined in relation to the whole system, or only in relation to a particular sector? Generally, the definition of system in terms of units, structures, and interactions points to the validity of levels of analysis extending across all the sectors. But while the categories of levels may extend across all of the sectors, their contents may well differ. If sectors can be defined in distinct terms, it is probably by specifying the differences in their units and structures. Specificity, consistency, and clarity of usage are therefore extremely important in discussions involving system sectors.

It might be useful to construct the relationship between sectoral subdivisions and levels of analysis on the assumption that levels of analysis refer to horizontal subdivisions of the "field" of the interna-

	SECTORS			
	economic	political	societal	strategic[1]
LEVELS OF ANALYSIS	system structure			
	unit			

Figure 3.1. Conceptual Subdivisions of the International System

1. The distinction of strategic from political sectors might be controversial. One justification for it goes back to Morgenthau, who took the view that politics was essentially about psychological control, a process that ended when control was attempted by direct coercion. (Gellman, 1988, 252)

tional system, while sectors refer to vertical "subdivisions" of the same field, as sketched roughly in figure 3.1. It is important to understand here that sectors do not represent subdivisions of the whole system, but partial views of the whole.

This scheme enables us to consider levels of analysis either in terms of the international system as a whole (by dissolving the sectoral distinctions), or in terms of specific sectoral subdivisions (by defining the levels in terms that are bounded by one or more sectoral subdivisions e.g., international political system, or international political economy). The question of what the complete universe of sectors might look like for the international system is beyond the scope of this discussion. The four listed certainly cover the main preoccupations of International Relations theorists. Waltz's theory is an attempt to define levels of analysis exclusively within the political sector. One needs to be aware that this confinement is a source of both the strengths and the limitations of Neorealism.

LEVELS OF ANALYSIS

The question of levels of analysis must arise in any attempt to understand behavior within systems because it defines the layers of the system within which explanations are sought. Each level must identify a major source of impact on behavior, and thus an explanation for events, that is distinct from other major sources. Like sectors, the idea of levels of analysis is an abstract construct. Because this is so, the definition of levels contains considerable scope for choice, which again makes clear specification and consistency of usage extremely important. The basic definition of system offers two obvious "top and bottom" candidates for levels of analysis: the structure, representing that collective element of the system which transcends the units, and the units themselves. This is the path that Waltz takes. The unit level of the system he defines as "the attributes and interactions of its parts" (Waltz 1979:18). The system level he defines "by the arrangement of the system's parts and by the principle of that arrangement" (Waltz 1979:80).

To understand why the boundary between these two levels in Neorealism has proved so troublesome to other analysts, one needs to explore deeper into its logic. In doing so, it is worth remembering Singer's conclusion to his assessment of the system and state levels of analysis: "it must be stressed that we have dealt here only with two of the more common orientations, and that many others are available and perhaps even more fruitful potentially than either of those selected here" (Singer 1961:90). In developing Structural Realism, one needs to keep an open mind not only about definitions of the system and unit levels, but also about what constitutes a level of analysis. Are the system and unit levels the only ones in play? (We will argue in chapter 4 that they are not.) Are they monolithic as sources of explanation, or can they be more finely divided into sublevels with distinct logics of their own? (The case for subdivision is made in this chapter.) Is the crude system/unit distinction the most efficient one for a theory of international relations, and how far can the separation of levels be sustained? (This issue is pursued in Section II.)

THE STRUCTURE OF THE INTERNATIONAL POLITICAL SYSTEM

If the idea of system is to represent more than just any selection of parts and their interactions, it must be accompanied by the notion of structure. For Waltz, structure means the ordering principle underlying the way in which the units relate to, and are functionally differentiated from, each other. In this context, "relate to" refers to how the parts are arranged or positioned in relation to each other, *not* to how they interact, which in his terms (but not ours, as will become clear in chapter 4) is a unit level phenomenon (Waltz 1979:80–81). His concern is only with the structure of the political sector of the international system. Two issues arise: (1) how is the structure of the international political system defined, and (2) once a suitable definition has been obtained, how does it relate to other definitions of structure (e.g., economic, societal, strategic) arising either from the other sectors that comprise the international system, or from a holistic view of the system?

These two questions drive in potentially contradictory directions. Seeking a definition for the structure of the international political system means accepting the Realist assumption that one can and should identify a distinctively political sector within the international system. Looking at how a political view of structure relates to notions of structure in other sectors of the international system may undermine the distinctively political emphasis of Neorealism by leading to broader definitions of structure, for example in terms of political economy. In this Section we begin by working with the Neorealist assumption about the primacy of the political sector. Section III explores the wider relationship between political and economic structures.

The problem of defining structure within the relatively narrow sectoral terms of politics is that the core defining feature of politics is itself a matter of controversy. Waltz does not attempt a formal, generalized definition of what the political sector covers, though there is no doubt that he sees the political sector of the international system as defined in terms of states. States are both the units of his international political system, and the foundation of its structure, a linkage that causes Wendt to accuse him of ontological reductionism (Wendt 1987:341). This rather crude delineation of the political sector sows the seeds of subsequent difficulties in his sparse definition of international political structure.

Politics does not have a neat, generally accepted, definition. The essence of it concerns the shaping of human behavior for the purpose of governing large groups of people. This shaping may be done both by the citizens themselves and by their leaders. If one takes government as the key to comprehending the political sector of the international system, then the theory and practice of government can be approached along three main paths, in terms of power, authority, and organization. Each of these approaches identifies a distinct emphasis in the management of collective human behavior: coercion in the case of power, legitimacy in the case of authority, and administration in the case of organization. In practice, however, none of these three can be made more than partly distinct from the others. Power and authority are conceptually distinct, but notoriously hard to disentangle in practice. Both normally depend on some element of organization. The process of government invariably involves a combination of all three. These different aspects of politics open up a variety of possible approaches to the definition of political structure. The problem is that each element taken individually has a logic and a set of applications that extends far beyond the reasonable limits of a strictly political domain. Power, for example, plays a big role in social and economic relations, as well as political ones. Only their combination for the purpose of governing produces a reasonably bounded notion of the political sector.

The Neorealist position is laid down by Waltz in his three-tier definition of political structure as: the organizing principle of the international system, plus the functional differentiation of units, plus the distribution of capabilities across units (Waltz 1979:ch. 5, esp., 100–101). This definition does not clearly enough confront the meaning of politics in relation to the sector of the international system that it addresses. The first two tiers of Waltz's definition are about government, albeit with a tightly restrictive focus on sovereignty. The organizing principle tier captures the distinction between systems with only one sovereignty, and systems with more than one (hierarchy and anarchy). The functional differentiation tier, by Waltz's argument (but not ours, as will be seen in the next part of this chapter and Section II), does not apply to anarchic political structures because all sovereign states are by definition like units. Thus in anarchic international political systems, government is strongly concentrated in the units, and only weakly, if at all, present at the system level.

The third tier, distribution of capabilities, is not about government, but focuses more narrowly on the power dimension of interstate politics, though still deriving directly from the sovereign state structure established by the first two tiers. This change is, by itself, grounds for suspicion in a supposedly integrated definition. Waltz's shift to a narrower approach in the third tier raises three issues. First, his focus on power heavily discounts the authority and organizational dimensions of international politics, an exclusion that seems to bear directly on the criticisms of Keohane and others who think that rules, regimes, and international institutions need to be brought into the definition of international political structure. Second, Waltz's formulation raises longstanding definitional problems about power and how to measure it. Third, his use of the distribution of capabilities across units as an element of structure opens the question of why he confines the principle of distribution to the single variable of capabilities aggregated into power.

The difficulties in Waltz's third tier take on added significance because they occur at the point of maximum controversy in his theory, namely the boundary between the unit and system levels. They are serious enough to require a separate consideration of the placement and nature of the boundary between the system and unit levels. Before taking up this problem, it is helpful to establish firm ground on either side of it. We will therefore consider next the first two tiers of Waltz's definition, which will collectively be referred to using Ruggie's term *deep structure,* (in Keohane 1986:35), after which we will look at the unit level.

DEEP STRUCTURE

In dealing with deep structure it is helpful to fix a firm view of what defines the political sector of the international system. The discussion above pointed to *governing* as the core of what politics is about. In general, governing requires institutions that claim the right to be the makers and enforcers of laws and the executors of policy for a specified people and/or territory. These institutions must possess a sufficient combination of power, authority, and administrative capacity to put that claim into meaningful practice against rivals both within and outside their jurisdiction. The sovereign state is without doubt the hardest and clearest form of government. It is also by a long stretch the most dominant form of government in the modern international system.

But the state is not the only form that government can take. No iron law requires the functions of government to be undertaken only by sovereign entities (i.e., states). As Ruggie argues, there was government without sovereignty in the Medieval political system (in Keohane 1986:141–48). In the contemporary international system, non-sovereign bodies such as the European Community, and even more loosely the United Nations and its agencies, undertake some governmental, or at least government-like, functions. As the strictly governmental function of laws blurs into the rules and norms beloved of theorists of international society and international regimes, one's sectoral perspective begins to incorporate both the international political system and the international societal system (where the emphasis is on cultural and normative determinants of behavior). General awareness of the distinction between the international political and societal sectors is reasonably well established, most notably through Hedley Bull's emphasis on the common rules and norms of anarchical society (Bull 1977, esp. chs. 2,3; Bull and Watson 1984; Manning 1962; Mayall 1990; Wight 1977).

If government defines the makings of political structure, then one can stick with Waltz for at least the first two tiers of his definition (i.e., the organizing principle of the international system, plus the functional differentiation of units). Waltz's first two tiers identify an element of political structure that is *deep* in the sense of representing a basic pattern that is not only durable (on historical evidence), but also self-reproducing (in that the operation of the balance of power sustains the anarchic arrangement—and in Waltz's view also the like units). In Waltz's logic, these two tiers are so closely linked as to be nearly opposite sides of the same coin. Each tier offers two broad structural options clearly defined in terms of government. In the organizing principle tier, the options are *anarchy* (no central government over the units in the system) and *hierarchy* (central government over all the units). There is a possible ambiguity about anarchy in this formulation, since it could refer either to a system with no government at all (individual humans as the basic unit), or to a system with two or more governments controlling different parts of the system. In the international system the former condition never occurs, and is therefore of no practical interest to the theory: international anarchy always refers to a system with two or more governments.

In the functional differentiation of units tier, the options are that the units are *similar* or *different* in terms of the range of governmental functions they claim and perform. *Similar* effectively means sovereign, where all units define themselves as the highest authority in all matters of government over their specified territory and people, including the right to wield power independently. *Different* means that units claim

		ORGANIZING PRINCIPLE	
		Hierarchy	Anarchy
FUNCTIONAL DIFFERENTIATION OF UNITS	Similar	1	2
	Different	3	4

Figure 3.2. The Configuration of Deep Political Structure

sovereignty only over a limited range of functions, as in the Medieval system. Where claims are limited, they must logically produce difference in order for all of the political functions to be covered. A system in which all the units claimed the same limited functions would be incompletely governed, which is why *similar* points strongly to full sovereignty. These definitions are extremely sparse, delineating only the most basic political principles. They specifically exclude societal elements in which sovereignty is seen not just as a function of claim, but also as a function of mutual recognition between states. Because they are so basic, they leave a lot of room for variety within the scope of anarchic structure.

Taken together, the two tiers yield a 2 x 2 matrix as in figure 3.2. By Waltz's argument, however, two of these categories (numbers 1 and 4) are virtually empty because of the existence of strong, two-way interactions between organizing principle and functional differentiation of units. It is worth examining this argument in some detail, for the whole conception of deep structure (and therefore the definition of significant change) hangs upon it.

His argument runs as follows. In type 2, similar units and anarchy are opposite sides of the same coin. If all the units are subject to the survival logic of self-help, then the shoving and shaping pressures on them of life in the anarchy will push their range of governmental functions toward sovereignty. If all the units are sovereign, then the organizing principle amongst them must, by definition, be anarchic (Buzan 1991:ch. 4). Thus anarchy tends to generate like units, and like units, by pursuing sovereignty, generate anarchy.

Under anarchy, the logic of survival dictates that units are subject to the pressures of socialization and competition (Waltz 1979:76; Ikenberry and Kupchan 1990). In historical terms, one can easily see how both of these pressures work to produce homogeneity of unit type. Socialization works by the demonstration effect of the most successful units, which encourages others to copy them. In the post-war period, the former Soviet Union has been a model for some, the United States for others, and more recently, Japan has set the pace as a model of economic efficiency and prowess. The collapse of communism in 1989 not only removed one demonstration model from the system, but also illustrated the powerful socialization effect of more successful units as much of the ex-communist world struggled to adopt the forms and practices of the West. The effect of competition is rivetingly demonstrated by the period of European imperialism. The stronger European states simply took over weak units, eventually releasing them by decolonization only after they had been remade (often badly) into copies of European territorial states. Those Asian nations not colonized, such as Japan, Thailand, and China, had quickly to remake themselves in the European state mode in order to avoid becoming victims of European power.

Similarly, the Second World War allowed the victors to restructure in their own image the domestic politics of the losers. As Waltz puts it: "the close juxtaposition of states promotes their sameness through the disadvantages that arise from failure to conform to successful practices" (Waltz 1979:128). Quite so, and this logic can work as strongly for commercial relations among merchant states as for strategic relations among warrior ones. In this way, socialization and competition should push strongly away from any durable manifestation of category 4 (anarchy/different). In striving for survival and security, units will tend to converge on the model of the most successful and powerful of their number, thus moving the system toward type 2.

It must be pointed out that Waltz's logic on this point relies on the transfer from microeconomics into international politics of a very specific, and very partial characterization of competition. All the emphasis goes to the way in which competition leads to imitation—all family cars become the same style, all tomato soups adopt the same taste, and all states become centered on sovereignty, power, and security. This view discounts another side of the analogy from economic behavior, which is the search for market niches, where differentiation of function provides (temporary) refuge from the full pressure of competition. These two dynamics are not mutually exclusive, and taken together allow the dynamics of convergence to work simultaneously with those of differentiation. This view opens up the possibility of a type 4 deep structure in a way that Waltz's narrower logic does not allow, and we will make more of it in Sections II and III.

There is a matching logic in Waltz's theory that ties together hierarchic organizing principles and functionally differentiated units. In a hierarchic structure, the imperative for units to specialize is driven by the efficiency logic of the division of labor (Waltz 1979:106–7). If the organizing principle is hierarchy, as most clearly illustrated by looking at an individual state as a political system, then units within it are strongly pressured to make themselves functionally different. This is evident from any organizational chart of a national government or any bureaucracy. Indeed, there is virtually no sense in having a hierarchic structure unless the units have differentiated functions. Here the processes converge on type 3 (hierarchy/different), and away from type 1 (hierarchy/similar). The logic that pushes toward type 3 is clear if one starts from hierarchy, but is harder to illustrate if one starts from differentiated units. If units are functionally dissimilar in terms of government (i.e., claiming not full sovereignty, but only the right to govern over selected aspects of law and behavior), then their specialization must create interdependence in order to fulfill the basic requirements of governing. Because specialized units by definition do not fulfill the whole range of political functions, they must depend on each other for mutual support in relation to the political environment as a whole. Since order is a prime political value (Bull 1977:ch.4) security needs will drive differentiated units either to the collective safety of hierarchical structure, or back to self-help (and thus back to similarity, sovereignty, and anarchy). Perhaps the only strong historical case covering this point is the transformation from the Medieval to the modern system in Europe, where the choice was for anarchy, on which we will have more to say below.

Waltz's scheme identifies compelling linkages within a political system between organizing principle and differentiation of units by function. Among other things, this linkage points to an incipient theory of the state in Neorealism (on which more in Section II) that has been overlooked by some of its critics (Walker 1987:78). Yet within this logic of deep political structure Waltz takes what seems an unnecessarily extreme view in asserting that an anarchy *must* have like units, and that if units cease to be alike, then anarchy ends (Waltz 1979:93; in Keohane 1986:323; and interview). This rigid stance is not required by the logic of his theory, and does not follow from the essential defining condition of anarchy, which is the absence of central government. Its apparent source is Waltz's strict adherence to the "interstate" meaning of international system. If the international system is conceived purely as an interstate system, then non-sovereign, and thus non-like and non-state units simply fall outside the definition of international system. Because he puts too much emphasis on sovereign states, and too little on governing, Waltz's theory is simply unable to deal with type 4 systems (unlike units in anarchy). Waltz seems prepared to abandon a massive area of political reality in the international system in order to hang onto this definitional nicety. This seems to be a serious and unnecessary mistake, with pursuit of parsimony leading him to trade a small gain in definitional neatness for a large loss in the relevance of the theory to the international system.

Waltz's stance provokes Ruggie's justified riposte that the history of Medieval Europe provides a case where units that are not sovereign— and that therefore *are* differentiated by function—exist without having a hierarchical structure, and therefore in an anarchy (in Keohane 1986:141–48). At a very minimum, Ruggie's demonstration that type 4 has historical content supports Waltz's point that structures "do not determine behaviors and outcomes" and "may be successfully resisted." (in Keohane 1986:343) At a maximum, as has been hinted at above, and as will be seen in Section II, it points to a radical widening of the practical possibilities for the nature of units under anarchy.

But this point need not disturb Waltz's theoretical assertion that the logic of political structure in the international system will, over time (perhaps a long time, the theory gives no prediction about this), *tend* to bring organizing principles and differentiation of units into line. In interpreting his own theory too statically, Waltz seems to lose sight of his argument that structure shapes and shoves rather than determines (Waltz 1979:73–74). The power of his idea is nonetheless demonstrated by the current configuration of the international system, in which the superior power (in terms of competition) and attractiveness (in terms of socialization) of the sovereign state have virtually eliminated all other forms of government from the system. Since 1945, the system's units have become more functionally similar than ever before.

Within a Structural Realist framework, explanations for type 4 cases of functionally different units without a central government (as in Ruggie's argument, or in the more extreme views of contemporary transnational developments) can be sought in at least three ways. First, a manifestation of type 4 can be seen as a transition phase, in either direction, between anarchy and hierarchy. In the case of the Medieval system the transition could be placed historically between the long hierarchy of the Roman Empire and the long anarchy of the modern European state system. The differentiation among Ruggie's Medieval units may have reflected the collapsed hierarchy of the Roman Empire that preceded them, but in the self-help context of anarchy, the imperative governing their behavior was more "take care of yourself," than "specialize." Over the centuries, self-help security logic thus pushed the direction of change toward like units in the form of sovereign states.

Second, it can be explained as a deviation from structural norms (the anarchy-sovereignty and hierarchy-differentiation imperatives) due to the intervention of countervailing factors on the unit level. In the Medieval case these factors might include a shortage of political resources at the unit level. Small, weak units scarcely generated enough interaction in the system to drive the homogenizing logic of socialization and competition with any urgency. This question of how much, and what kind of interaction is required in order for a system to operate in Neorealist terms is vital to the theory, but as yet little discussed, and will be taken up in detail in chapter 4 and Section II. Third, it can be explained as a consequence of intervening, or overlapping, effects from other sectors within the international system. In the Medieval case, the obvious candidate is the international societal system. The existence of the Roman church as a strong, system-spanning societal entity might have helped to sustain the otherwise unstable type 4 mix. In the contemporary international system, high levels of economic interdependence and the emergence of an international society are the prime candidates for this cross-sectoral effect.

Wherever the correct historical answer lies, Ruggie is right to argue that differentiation of units remains open as a source of structural change in the international political system: type 4 systems are an area in which variation of second tier deep structure is possible. Anarchy may remain constant, but units can shift into and out of alternative patterns of differentiation of function. Both type 2 and type 4 anarchies are possible. This point does not require revision to the argument that type 4 political arrangements exist against the grain of deep structure forces. The appropriate Structural Realist hypothesis here is that type 2 structures should be more stable than type 4 ones. Type 4 should exist only when the logic of deep political structure is either overridden by forces arising in other levels or other sectors, or weakened by low levels of interaction. This reasoning significantly alters Waltz's causal nexus. The issue is more than just whether units or structures dominate outcomes within the political sector. There are also questions about the autonomy of the political sector, and the need to judge the effects of political structure against conditions in other sectors that may countervail against the narrow political logic of anarchy.

If the second tier is opened as an area of possible change, then there is a need for some definitional work to clarify the boundary between clearly similar units (no differentiation) and clearly different ones (where a principle of differentiation is in operation). This question is taken up in Section II. Waltz closed this area off, treating all sovereign states as like units. This strategy favors rather undemanding criteria for similarity, like those in such categories as fruit and mammal. Only then can all states over the modern period be treated as essentially the same type of unit. Ruggie wants to differentiate between these and the less exclusive, more overlapping, units of the Medieval system. Others might want to open up type 4 systems, and give better handles on questions of change, by arguing for tighter classifications of similarity (apples instead of fruit, humans instead of mammals). Robert Gilpin's work leans in this direction (Gilpin 1981:41–42).

It could be argued, for example, that there was a significant differentiation of units during the colonial period, with the system divided between sovereign states and varying degrees of less than sovereign vassals, ranging from colonies, through protectorates, to Dominions. If this was accepted, then decolonization, during which colonies changed into states, would mark a structural shift from a differentiated to an undifferentiated structure. Similarly, political economists might want to toy with the distinction between liberal and mercantilist states as a differentiation of function. Liberal states effectively renounce control of the economy as a function of government, turning it over to civil society, albeit remaining significant regulatory players. Mercantilist ones, especially of the socialist variety, claim the whole economy as a central function of government. Shifts in the composition of the international system between these two types might count as a second tier structural change for political economists.

The evolution of the European Community as a *sui generis* entity with some actor qualities perhaps also poses a challenge to the notion that the system is composed of undifferentiated units. The EC could also be seen simply as illustrating the socializing pressure of anarchy as the European states, finding themselves too small to function efficiently as major powers, seek a way to copy the power and security eminence of semi-continental states. In Waltzian terms (Waltz 1979:107), one of the fascinating elements in the European Community is how the states within it are torn between the anarchic imperative "look after yourself," and the hierarchic one "specialize." But the EC may not be simply a new state in the making. It may be a new type of semi-sovereign entity, binding together, but not replacing entirely, a group of states (Buzan et al. 1990:ch. 10).

If type 4 systems are to be made operational as part of Structural Realist theory, then their logic, dynamics, and classifications must be systematically developed. This is a major theoretical undertaking, at which we can do no more than hint here. It seems likely that the dynamics of a type 4 system would be more complicated than for type 2. Differentiated units would be more subject to interdependence, and perhaps, as in the example of colonies, to elements of hierarchy. Although balance of power might still operate strongly among subsets of like units within the system (e.g., the colonial powers) it might well be much less influential between functionally differentiated units. The relational dynamics of a type 4 system would also be much influenced by the nature of the forces preventing a reversion to type 2. A type 4 system made possible by weak interaction (thus emasculating the effects of socialization and competition) would be quite different from one in which functional specialization was supported in a high interaction environment with a strong international society among the units.

In investigating type 4 systems, it is important to be clear about the idea of function. Waltz uses it in the sense of function as a unit. He argues that all modern states function similarly as units because sovereignty imposes a similar range of governing tasks upon them. The pursuit of similar functions often leads to similar internal structures, as any comparison of states as organizations will show. This process is also encouraged by the homogenizing effect of competition and socialization under anarchy. But it is also possible to read function as including the different roles that states play in the international system. Some would like to push the idea of differentiation down this path by having it include role differences such as great and small powers, neutrals, allies, hegemons, and suchlike. This temptation should be resisted. Differentiation of function refers to function as a unit, and only in that sense does it link to the essence of deep structure, which is about government. Differentiation of roles is best dealt with at the unit level.

Given the modern history of the international system, this leaves us looking mostly at deep political structure defined in terms of the organizing principle of anarchy (types 2 and 4). Since there are no global cases of hierarchically structured political systems, types 1 and 3 are of interest mainly to those who either want to speculate about the character of, or the process of transition to, a world government, or those who want to think about the subglobal "world empires" of premodern times.

For practical purposes, anarchy thus remains a constant feature of the international system. But as revised along the lines pointed to by Ruggie, even deep structure offers interesting and accessible insights into change. Change in the first tier of structure will by definition be massive, extremely infrequent, and on the rare occasions when it occurs, extremely interesting. There has never been a global system change in the first tier, though analogous shifts from anarchy to hierarchy (the Roman and Chinese Empires) and from hierarchy to anarchy (the decolonization of South Asia, China's warring states periods) have occurred within regional subsystems. Change in the second tier is more easily accomplished than change in the first, and is historically more frequent. How much more frequent depends on what is accepted as a definition of "functional differentiation," as discussed above. Where first tier political structure operates strongly, second tier change is heavily constrained and conditioned by continuity in the first tier. Second tier change might be interesting as an illustration of first tier pressures at work, as in the twentieth-century move toward a uniform state system. But it is more likely to be interesting as an illustration of the political impact of forces from other sectors and levels overriding the narrow logic of the purely political structural theory. For those interested in first tier change, change in the second tier may also be an indicator of which way the wind is blowing. Opening up the second tier allows us to reject the argument that "structural Realist theory treats the internal character-istics of nation-states as given" (Mastanduno et al. 1989:461), and to accept, at least in part, the argument that the domestic character of states needs to be included in conceptions of international system structure. (Ruggie in Keohane 1986:147–48; Rosenberg 1990:299–303)

THE UNIT LEVEL

The second arm of a pincer approach to the area between deep struc-ture and the unit level is the unit level itself. Waltz does not say much about this. His clearest positive statement is where he defines the reductionist approach as understanding the whole "by knowing the attributes and the interactions of its parts" (Waltz 1979:18). This is reaffirmed in the negative when he says that "definitions of structure must leave aside, or abstract from, the characteristics of units, their behavior, and their interactions" (Waltz 1979:79). However, Waltz later slips into a tendency to deal with the unit level by exclusion, treating it as a catch-all for everything that falls outside his definition of structure: "structure includes only what is required to show how the units of the system are positioned or arranged. *Everything else is omitted*" (Waltz 1979:82, our italics). This questionable practice arises from both his preoccupation with structure, and his acceptance of a rigid two-level model of the international political system. It emerges most strongly in his response to Ruggie, and is implicit in such statements as:

> Clean and simple definitions of structure save us from the pernicious practice of summoning new systems into being in response to every salient change within a system. They direct our attention to the units and to unit-level forces when the particularity of outcomes leads us to search for more idiosyncratic causes than are found in structures (in Keohane 1986:329).

Structural Realism requires a tight, positive definition of the unit level as a counterpoise to the structural one. A full system theory requires one to be as explicit about the unit level as about the system structure. Simply defining the unit level by exclusion, once a definition of structure is in place, lacks sufficient rigor to give proper definition to the unit level in its own right. It also forecloses the questions raised by Wendt (1987) about the relationship between agent and structure (which we take up in Section II).

According to Waltz's formulation, the unit level as a source of explanation for behaviors and outcomes in the international system, consists of two distinct components: *the attributes of the units, and the interactions among them*. Explanations in terms of attributes seek to understand the behavior of individual units by examining their domestic characteristics, components, and processes. Foreign policy analyses where outcomes are interpreted in terms of such factors as bureaucratic process, leadership personality, the organization of the government, and the organizing ideology of the state, all illustrate this method. So do theories of war which suggest that certain types of state—autocratic, fascist, capitalist, communist—are likely to be more aggressive than others because of the domestic dynamics generated by their mode of social, political, and/or economic organization. Attempts to explain behavior in terms of the preference functions of units—whether they seek power, security, welfare, or cultural values as their prime objective—also fall within the unit attribute mode of analysis.

Explanations in terms of interactions among units—often referred to as *process* (Keohane and Nye 1987:745) seek to understand behavior and outcomes in terms of the ways in which units respond to each other's attributes and behaviors. As such, they are heavily conditioned by deep structure. One would not expect the process manifestations of anarchy and hierarchy to be similar, nor would one expect process to be unaffected by the difference between like and unlike units. These are essentially action-reaction theories, in which the key element is a dynamic of stimulus and response. Many recurrent patterns have been found in these often very complex dynamics, and it is the elements of consistency in these patterns that inspire attempts at theory. The best known of them include war, alliance, the balance of power, arms racing and the security dilemma, and the whole range of international political economy patterns arising from protectionist and liberal policies on trade and money. Buzan's concept of regional *security complexes* also belongs in this category, since it is based on durable, but not permanent, patterns in the degree of amity, enmity, and indifference with which states view each other (Buzan and Rizvi 1986:chs. 1 and 9; Buzan 1991:ch. 5), as does Bull's concept of international society

(Bull 1977), and the related idea of regimes. Here also lies the often confusing, but important, distinction between the structural feature of *polarity* (the number of major powers in the system) and the process feature of *polarization* (the number of opposed coalitions in the system) (Rapkin et al. 1979). These patterns are the focus of much theoretical enterprise aimed at finding ways of mitigating or controlling negative effects by constructing countervailing patterns. Regimes, for example, are proposed as a way of stabilizing trade and financial relations, and interdependence is offered as a way of muting the security dilemma. Generalized theoretical conceptions such as Choucri and North's idea of "lateral pressure" are aimed at understanding system process (Choucri and North 1975).

Because these process patterns do exhibit some consistency—for example the beggar-thy-neighbor logic of protectionism, the self-defeating logic of the arms dynamic, and the anti-hegemony logic of the balance of power—they give rise to the tendency deplored by Waltz to identify them as structures. The common sense logic here is based on an interpretation of "structure" to mean simply any pattern that either endures or recurs. Despite their persistence, Waltz is logically correct to count these patterns as unit level explanations and to reserve the term structure for the positional relations of the units. Yet there is no doubt that unit attributes and process are quite different types of explanation. Some analysts see them as different enough to justify calling them separate levels of analysis (Goldmann 1979:1–2). The choice here is between elevating process to the status of a level of analysis, or establishing a strong boundary within the unit level (between attributes and process) along the same lines as that between Waltz's first two, and third, tiers of structure. The analytical consequence of this choice is not large, and for the sake of consistency we will stick to Waltz's scheme. Waltz is at fault in this area for constructing an unbalanced systems theory by developing a highly elaborate definition of structure, while leaving the unit level as an indifferentiated mass about which it has been all too easy for confusions to multiply. The error is especially damaging, not only because it draws too hard a line across the agent-structure debate, but also because it is precisely through elaboration of process that change can best be dealt with in the context of structural theory.

To relieve the pressure on the term structure, and to differentiate process explanations from the attribute mode of analysis, some other label is needed to identify the patterns arising from the interactions of units. Given the fashion for using "structure" in a loose way, and the absence of obvious alternatives, this is no easy matter. Simply qualifying the term structure (as in "process structures") has the appeal of ease and convenience, but fatally blurs the distinction between the unit and structural levels. The word "formation" is perhaps an acceptable substitute, maintaining both the distinction from structure, and the sense of durable or recurrent patterns in behavior at the unit level. These patterns can be referred to as *process formations*.

It is beyond the scope of this section to delve into the labyrinths of theory at the unit level. It is important, however, to establish that the unit and structural levels are linked. Since the two levels are in some ways mutually constitutive, Structural Realism is able to serve as a theory of the international system as a whole. On this point, it is possible to agree with Wendt that agents and structures should be seen as mutually constitutive, while disagreeing with him that Neorealism simply generates structures from units (Wendt 1987:359–61, 340–44). Waltz also too easily forecloses opportunities here by arguing in favor of de-linking theories of the state from those of the international system (in Keohane 1986:340).

One of the attractions of Structural Realism's approach is precisely that it does neatly incorporate the mutually constitutive relationship between unit and system. Anarchy and autonomy are opposite sides of the same coin. As has been shown in the discussion of deep structure, structural forces play a major role in constituting sovereign states. Anarchy equals self-help (with or without states), though it does not preclude cooperation. Self-help generates a competitive and sometimes conflictual system. Competition leads toward like units by the mechanisms of copying and coercion though still leaving open strategies of differentiation as suggested above. Structural Realism certainly does not assume that states are constructed entirely by forces generated from within. Because this is so, it can and should serve as a linking framework for theories at the unit and structural levels, a theme taken up in Section II. Making this link explicit is one way to release Structural Realist theory from the high level of generalization to which Waltz has largely confined Neorealism.

BETWEEN THE DEEP STRUCTURE AND THE UNIT LEVEL

In Waltz's scheme, the only occupant of the space between deep structure and the unit level is the third tier of structure, the distribution of capabilities, which he sees as an integral part of his definition of structure. It plays an important role in Neorealism because, within it, change is frequent enough to bring the theory into some contact with the universe of policy problems. Without this level, Neorealism would be completely static on a timescale of millennia, particularly since Waltz closes off the second tier. It would retain only the (still considerable) value of its deep structure insights into what conditions behavior in the international system. Two issues need to be considered in order to clarify the logic of this area: (1) the soundness of the principle of distribution as an element of system structure, and (2) the validity of aggregating plural "capabilities" into singular "power."

The Principle of Distribution

In Neorealism, the principle of distribution is a system level element because it comes within the general definition of structure as being about "how units stand in relation to one another, the way they are arranged or positioned" (Waltz 1979:80). Even though the principle refers to unit characteristics, it hinges on their distribution, a property that fits into the concept of "relation" seen in positional terms (Waltz 1979:79–82, 97–98). This argument seems sound in itself, and provides a clear way of drawing the boundary between the structure and unit levels.

In relation to deep structure it can be argued that the distribution of capabilities derives directly from the organizing principle of anarchy. A fragmented political structure, mediated by a diverse geography, necessarily and automatically generates a pattern in the distribution of capabilities. This pattern could, in theory, be one of even distribution, but in practice it is almost certain to be uneven, and probably very uneven. Historically, the political units within the system have distributed themselves across a range of capabilities covering several orders of magnitude: the United States at one end, Vanuatu at the other. This uneven distribution will occur no matter whether the fragmentation is based mostly on territory, as in a type 2 structure with sovereign states (anarchy/similar), or more on organization, as in a type 4 structure like Ruggie's Medieval system (anarchy/different). It underlies and motivates many of the process formations at the unit level, which gives the theory *some* generative standing inasmuch as each tier within it strongly conditions the one(s) below. In this type of structuralism (i.e., where structure is defined by the arrangement of the units), it is impossible for structure to act as an ultimate generative source, as it does in some other (e.g., linguistic) conceptions.

In relation to the unit level, the principle of distribution clearly represents a different and higher type of generalization than either type of explanation within the unit level: "capabilities are attributes of units, the distribution of capabilities across units is not" (Waltz 1979:98). Explanation of behavior in terms of possession of a capability by a unit is quite different from explanation in terms of the distribution of capability within the system. In power terms, the fact that any single state has many capabilities is a different type of explanation for how it behaves than is the fact that the system contains only two great powers. Distribution of capabilities is also logically distinct from the action-reaction patterns that were labeled *process formations* above. Distribution patterns may underlie process formations, but they are not the same thing. Interaction process focuses on the action-reaction dynamics of unit behavior. Distribution patterns are about the positional logic of how units are ranked in terms of their capabilities.

Since the logic of Waltz's boundary between the system and unit levels seems sound, the main question that arises here is whether his single, but multi-tiered, definition of structure is the most useful way of presenting his ideas. The case for lumping all three tiers together is that they all conform to the logic of structure as positional relation, which is what differentiates them from the unit level. But within that logic, there are sufficient differences between the third tier and the first two to make a good case for putting more emphasis on the sub-boundary between them. Two differences stand out, one major, one minor.

The major one is that tiers one and two are connected by a powerful logic (discussed in the fifth part of this chapter) that does not extend to tier three. Tiers one and two are both concerned with "positioning" in terms of the principles of political organization. It is on that basis that the tier one logic of basic ordering principles, and the tier two logic of the functional differentiation of units, interact so closely (virtually to the point of merger in Waltz's narrow formulation). Tier three is not affected by this logic. Indeed, it is not specifically about political organization at all, but mostly concerns the relative weight of resources available to the political units within the system. The link lies in the fundamental Realist axiom that anarchic deep structure makes power the *ultima ratio* of international relations.

The minor difference is the relative depth of the structure identified by tiers one and two as opposed to three. Tier one is relatively deep, in the sense that major change is infrequent and has large consequences for political behavior. In Waltz's formulation tier two is closed and so doesn't count. Reopening it, as we have done, raises the question of how frequent change within it is. The answer to that question depends on the yet-to be decided matter of what qualifies as a change in differentiation of function, on which see the discussion above, and in Section II. Tier three is much shallower, in that change is more frequent and can be of low consequence. Changes in the distribution of capability may have little impact if they are simply from one high degree of diffuseness to another. A shift from a seven to a six power system might well be only of local interest. The significance of change rises as the number of powers gets smaller, and Waltz argues that only changes between one and four are significant enough to be called structural shifts (Waltz 1979:163). On this logic, the most significant shift would be one from bipolarity to unipolarity. A unipolar power structure could, but would not necessarily, trigger a deep structure shift from anarchy to hierarchy. It might equally trigger frenzied balancing attempts to stave off the final move from hegemony to world empire. There is thus a different, and less compelling logic linking tier three to the deep structure, compared with the way that tiers one and two are linked together. Like the first two tiers, however, tier three is also a useful tool for static analysis. When change is not the issue it is a fruitful source of insights into how structural continuities condition the behavior of units.

The extent of these differences between the first two tiers and the third has already meant that the terms "structure" and "structural change" cannot sensibly be used with a single meaning. In discussing political structure, whether in terms of its effects, or in terms of changes in it, one is forced to qualify which sublevel one is referring to. For this reason, it seems sensible to keep the unity of the term structure, but to distinguish within it between *deep* structure (tiers one and two), and *distributional* structure (tier 3). This distinction is within the framework of Waltz's logic, and clarifies the usage of structure. The case for identifying a sub-boundary between deep and distributional structure is reinforced when one questions the validity of aggregating "capabilities" into "power."

The Aggregation of "Capabilities" into "Power"

The second step in Waltz's logic of distributional structure is a complicated one. He aggregates his originally plural formulation of *capabilities* into the singular concept of *power*, and then restricts the application of the distributional principle exclusively to the distribution of power (Waltz 1979:97–99). His reasons for proceeding in this way are neither clear nor convincing. His formulation seems to place unhelpful and unwarranted restrictions on the application of the principle of distribution, and so on the application of the theory. He is aware that he is venturing onto boggy terrain by abstracting so closely from unit level attributes, but establishes firm ground with the principle of distribution. His tactics raise the question: why is the principle of distribution only to be applied to power? This question has two overlapping components: why must plural capabilities be collapsed into singular power; and why are attributes other than power excluded from the principle of distribution?

On the first question, Waltz's eagerness to end up with power is understandable. Because he has closed off the second tier, he needs the power dimension as a way of classifying and differentiating the units within anarchy: "the units of an anarchic system are functionally undifferentiated. The units of such an order are then distinguished primarily by their greater or lesser capability for performing similar tasks" (Waltz 1979:97). With the second tier of structure now opened, this rationale vanishes for Structural Realism. Waltz also wants to connect to the central concept in Classical Realist analysis, and makes the point that he is simply restating formally the emphasis on great powers that has always marked the study of international relations (Waltz 1979:97).

The principal justification for collapsing capabilities into power stems from the competitive self-help imperatives of anarchic deep structure:

> States, because they are in a self-help system, have to use their combined capabilities in order to serve their interests. The economic, military, and

other capabilities of nations cannot be sectored and separately weighed. States are not placed in the top rank because they excel in one way or another. Their rank depends on how they score on *all* of the following items: size of population and territory, resource endowment, economic capability, military strength, political stability and competence (Waltz 1979:131, his italics).

Is this aggregation necessary to the theory? If not, is it the best way to apply the theory? The obvious gain is that it enables Neorealism to pose as a highly parsimonious grand theory. But we will argue that aggregation often misleads more than it informs, and that under many circumstances it simply cannot be made to work at all. Grand parsimony is only occasionally available, and for the most part little is lost and much gained by treating power in terms of separate capabilities.

On the question of why the principle of distribution is confined only to power, Waltz's first justification is a technical one. He chooses power because it "is estimated by comparing the capabilities of a number of units" (Waltz 1979:98). In other words, the choice of power is made initially simply because it fits with the requirements of the principle of distribution. The key distinction here is between, on the one hand, distribution of attributes seen in direct, absolute terms (e.g., 15 democracies, 12 communist states, 30 military governments, etc.), and on the other, distribution of attributes seen in relative terms (e.g., not how many states with armed forces and GNPs of specified sizes, but how many great powers). It is the *relative* measurement of power that makes its distribution a structural rather than a unit level feature. This logic is sound, but it does not seal off the possibility that other attributive elements of states could also be cast in distributional terms.

Waltz recognizes this, and in his response to his critics, he argues that power is selected simply because it is a more important determinant of behavior than other characteristics of states. This reasoning harks back to Morgenthau, and the traditional Realist aspiration to derive an autonomous theory of political behavior similar in form to economic theory. Where the economists defined interest in terms of wealth, and assumed a principle of utility maximization, Classical Realists defined interests in terms of power (Morgenthau 1978:5), and many of them followed the economic parallel by assuming a motive of power maximization. While Waltz is careful to dissociate himself from the power-maximizing school of Realists, he chooses power because he takes it to be the dominant factor, not because it satisfies criteria of logical completion within categories.

> In a self-help system, states are differently placed by their power. . . . State behavior varies more with differences of power than with differences in ideology in internal structure of property relations, or in governmental form. In self-help systems, the pressures of competition weigh more heavily than ideological preferences or internal political pressures (in Keohane 1986:329).

This at least makes the reasoning clear, and Waltz tries to reinforce it with a plea for "clean and simple definitions of structure" (in Keohane 1986:329). The resulting formulation is not logically complete, and in Waltz's reasoning does not need to be. The issue here cannot be separated from his decision to collapse capabilities into power. The principle of distribution does not, in itself, require such aggregation. Nor does the theory require confinement to an erstwhile dominant element. Even if power was the most important variable within the distributional tier of structure, that would still be a weak reason to exclude other variables that meet the logical requirements of the theory. The Neorealist focus on aggregated power is neither the most logical nor the most effective way to deploy structural theory in an international system context.

Disaggregated Capabilities and the Application of Structural Realism

The arguments above make two points. First, the principle of distribution is solidly established as an element of structure. Second, neither the aggregation of capabilities into power, nor the restriction of the principle of distribution to power, necessarily follow from the logic of the theory. The question is whether aggregation and restriction best serve the utility of the theory, or whether a wider and more useful range of applications can be opened up. Two issues need to be considered: the case for reversing the aggregation of capabilities into power, and the case for de-restricting the application of the principle of distribution exclusively to power. In both cases the logic of sectors developed above under System Sectors and to be expanded in chapter 12, points to the utility of differentiated power. Indeed, there is nothing new in this idea in itself: discussion of disaggregated power has been a feature of the literature on interdependence for many years (Baldwin 1980; Keohane and Nye 1977).

Aggregation across a wide range of capabilities absorbs attributes into the catch-all of power that there may be good reasons for considering separately. Waltz's list of six components of state power (Waltz 1979:131) is not a mutually exclusive set. The three most complex and organizational components are also the most interesting candidates for separate treatment—military strength, economic capability, and political stability. They largely incorporate the three simpler, and more purely physical components—population, territory, and resource endowment. Waltz's explicit rejection of the separate treatment of attributes (Waltz 1979:130) seems to stem almost entirely from his concern to keep structure simple. It does not follow from the principle of distribution. Within that logic, aggregation of diverse capabilities into the gross category of power is simply one of several possible ways of proceeding. Theories are judged by their usefulness, and it is on that basis that aggregated versus disaggregated applications of the principle of distribution should be assessed. Both fall clearly within the logic of system structure as defined above.

How useful is the aggregation of capabilities into power? Although it does produce a sparse version of distributional structure, it also creates several problems. Like Morgenthau, Waltz cannot easily escape the difficulties of treating an elusive concept like power in scientific terms (Keohane 1986:10). Waltz acknowledges the difficulty of measuring the diverse and shifting components of power in any definitive way, but contrives an escape from this dilemma by appealing to a kind of mass common sense: "historically, despite the difficulties, one finds general agreement about who the great powers of a period are" (Waltz 1979:131). It is not clear whether this general agreement is thought to have existed at the time or only in historical retrospect, a point of some importance for the applicability of the theory to the present. Nevertheless, by this generalizing device Waltz seeks to preserve the aggregation of capabilities by avoiding the very serious difficulties that confront attempts to devise objective measures for state power.

Here he walks into a trap of his own making. Having derided well-informed and thoughtful individuals such as Kissinger, who have sought to disaggregate capabilities (Waltz 1979:130), he is not well placed to appeal to common sense as a means of overcoming the ambiguity of power. The fact is that under present conditions, the application of common sense produces hopeless confusion in any attempt to deal with power in aggregated terms. When the different components of state power don't line up, the aggregated category collapses. What in the late 1980s was one to make of an ostensibly bipolar system in which one of the two "superpowers" had only the third largest economy in the system, and the other had the biggest debt? How did one weigh the relative importance of the Soviet Union's large territory and endowment of resources against China's large population and ethnic coherence? How does one weigh China's nuclear weapons against Japan's wealth? At what point did the economic and political disintegration of the Soviet Union outweigh its large military power sufficiently to disqualify it as a pole? How does common sense enable one to assess polarity in the fluid conditions of the 1990s when plausible arguments can be made for unipolarity, bipolarity and multipolarity all at the same time?

Waltz's appeal to the analogy of oligopolistic markets to support the legitimacy of his aggregative approach actually supports the disaggregative case. He implies that oligopoly analysis is simply about how many major firms populate a sector of an economy, and that power analysis is therefore similarly appropriate for the international political system (Waltz 1979:131). Leaving aside the difficulty that the "sector" referred to by economists is merely a small subsector of an economic system, and therefore a much narrower construct than the political sector of the international system, the fact is that oligopoly theory has itself had to tread the path of disaggregation. Markham argues that "oligopoly is far less homogeneous than the term 'few sellers' might imply," and that theorists need to break down "an unsatisfactory and meaningless aggregate into classes useful for analytical purposes" (Markham 1968:288–89). Mainstream analysis has already made progress down this path by dividing oligopolies into "concentrated" (deriving from economies of scale), "differentiated" (arising from economies of specialization), and mixed types (Sylos-Labini 1987:701). In addition, static approaches to oligopolistic competition have been challenged by more dynamic ones, which accept as systematic, rather than merely accidental, observed oscillations of competitive and collusive behavior (see Section III).

Tellingly, a review of Waltz's applications of Neorealism in chapters 6 to 8 of *TIP* reveals that aggregation is not a necessary condition for *any* of his major observations (leaving aside the question of whether or not one agrees with his applications of the theory, particularly his controversial interpretations of bipolarity and interdependence). His insights deriving from deep structure are unaffected by how distributional structure is treated. Those on the balance of power could just as well be discussed in terms of the distribution of military strength. The full meaning of military strength anyway takes in many of Waltz's components of power—and poses similar difficulties of assessment. His arguments on economic effects could just as well be discussed in terms of polarity defined by economic capability. If this were done, his bipolar case would become theoretical rather than empirical, because the contemporary international system has never displayed economic bipolarity except perhaps briefly right after the end of the Second World War. Although the use of aggregated power did enable Waltz to say something interesting about superpower relations, it did so only at the cost of missing both most of the economic reality of the contemporary international system, and most of the substance of the interdependence argument. The Neorealist approach offers no insights that could not have been gained using disaggregated power, which largely removes the rationale for a highly parsimonious theory.

Disaggregating capabilities thus seems to have few costs and many advantages. Waltz notes, but does not pursue, the idea that "distinguishing between anarchic structures of different type permits somewhat narrower and more precise definitions of expected outcomes" (Waltz 1979:70). Any move from simple toward complex has to be justified against the general rule that parsimony is preferable to elaboration in the construction of theory. Waltz is very strict on this point, but it may well be that he has pushed the pursuit of parsimony too far in some places, with results that limit the utility of Neorealism. Disaggregation does increase the diversity of what counts as structural change. But it does so firmly within the bounds of distributional structure. It does not affect the simplicity of deep structure, and it does not invite spillovers from process formations at the unit level. In addition, there are not all that many attractive candidates for defining different types of distributional structures: neither massive nor uncontrolled proliferation of system types is a problem.

One advantage of disaggregation is simply that it reduces the confusion caused by trying to use undifferentiated power, and so produces a clearer analysis. Separating military strength and economic capability, for example, gives a much more accurate characterization of distributional structure than attempting to work with an extremely unwieldy aggregate. Military and economic hypotheses can be pursued within the two resultant distributional structures, and an additional area of insight is generated by the study of situations in which these two distributional structures do and do not line up. Where they do coincide, aggregated analysis may be the most appropriate formulation. Where they don't, the interplay of the disjunctures is itself an important structural datum. Disaggregation offers scope for a wider variety of hypotheses than is possible in Neorealism. One could investigate, for example, whether increases in polarity are less likely, and decreases more likely, to trigger system-wide wars; and within that question whether military or economic polarity change accounts for more violence, or whether it is the combination of them that matters.

A second advantage of disaggregation is that it enables structural theory to be connected in a constructive way to the mass of work on process formations. A good chunk of this is taking place under the heading of interdependence (or Neoliberalism), and one key to it has been the disaggregation of power along issue lines as a means of making sense of outcomes in an interdependent international political economy. Caution is required here, because analysis is poised on the boundary between the structural and unit levels of analysis. As Keohane makes clear (Keohane 1986:182–97), the disaggregation of power, and the abandonment of the Classical Realist assumption that power (broadly conceived) is fungible across issues, is not without problems. The point is not to try to blur the boundary between distributional structure and the unit level analysis of interdependence, but to set them into a clear and complementary relationship with each other, and to place both in the context of the interaction component of system discussed in chapter 4. Waltz is right to stress that theory does not need to describe every detail of reality, and should not be judged by how accurately it does so. To push theory in the direction of describing reality is to defeat its purpose, which is to provide generalized explanations for outcomes (Waltz 1979:6–9). But maintaining theory as an abstraction does not mean that it has to be disconnected either from reality or from other levels of theory. A theory increases in usefulness to the extent that its explanations can be related both to empirical observation and to other areas of theory.

A disaggregated distributional structure can both preserve a clear boundary between itself and unit level analysis, and at the same time provide a framework within which the unit level analysis can be organized. For example, a description of distributional structure in degrees of polarity can result from analysis either in terms of economic capability or military strength. Polarity defines the distributional structure in terms of a specific capability. The degree of polarity may range from unipolar to diffuse, and structural hypotheses can be generated for the range of conditions that result. These hypotheses can serve as a foundation for unit level analysis without causing confusion or trespass between levels of analysis. Structures define the environment that conditions and constrains unit level causes.

Illustrating this approach in more detail leads to disaggregation's third advantage: it allows more finely tuned structural hypotheses. Waltz made only limited progress toward operationalizing Neorealism by generating hypotheses from it. His thoughts about the behavioral consequences of deep structure have proved quite acceptable, whereas those about distributional structure have been more controversial, not least because of his attempt to work with an undifferentiated concept of power. Trying to think in terms of aggregated power has led, *inter alia,* to the overambitious and inconclusive debate about polarity and war (Deutsch and Singer 1964; Rosecrance 1969; Thompson 1986; Waltz 1964) and to Waltz's interesting, but rather tangential analysis of interdependence (Waltz 1970; 1979, ch. 7).

Analysis in terms of specific capabilities opens up clearer possibilities for a considerable range of more precisely defined structural hypotheses. In relation to military strength, for example, variations in degrees of polarity generate a host of important "shoving and shaping" forces (Buzan 1987). The logics of deterrence, arms control, arms racing, and alliance all vary sharply according to degrees of polarity. Deterrence requirements and logic are transformed by the differences between unipolar, bipolar, and multipolar systems. An example of the possibilities here is provided by the work of Intrilligator and Brito, who calculated the deterrence consequences of nuclear polarity from unipolarity up through successive additions of nuclear powers to a full multipolar system (Intrilligator and Brito 1979). Arms racing is more complex in multipolar than in bipolar structures. One could begin to construct systematic theory in this rather poorly developed area by starting analysis with a specification of military polarity. One hypothesis connecting distributional structure to process formations is that, under bipolarity, a strong pressure is created for the two principal powers to engage in an arms race. Military polarity is similarly important to theorizing about arms control. For example the principle of parity in arms control is much easier to formulate in bipolar than in multipolar conditions. Polarity also affects both the possibilities and conditions for alliance making. Alliances are more likely to be rigid and long-lasting in bipolar systems than in multipolar ones. Again, starting with the relevant distributional structure seems a fruitful way to approach this subject, enabling one to construct clear and systematic links between structure and process formations. Just how does military polarity relate to degrees of polarization in the system in terms of alliance coalitions? (Rapkin et al. 1979).

In relation to economic capability, Waltz has already explored some of the logic that arises in a bipolar distributional structure. The logic of unipolarity relates in an obvious way to the study of hegemony, and so offers a connection to the work, among others, of Gilpin, Keohane, Kindleberger and Modelski (Gilpin 1981; Keohane 1984; Kindleberger 1981; Modelski 1978). Disaggregation opens up some particularly useful ground in relation to hegemony. In the military sector, and when using aggregated power, unipolarity is structurally resisted by the balance of power and hardly ever occurs. But it is a fairly common feature in the economic sector, where relational logic is much more supportive of it. Dealing in terms of aggregated power virtually excludes the possibility of discussing hegemony, because it hides economic unipolarity within a balance of military power that is peculiarly resistant to unipolar distributional structure. Again, starting analysis by specifying distributional structure is a useful way to link structural and process/unit factors in a systematic fashion. It might also link to the second tier of deep structure if the difference between liberal and mercantilist states is accepted as a functional differentiation. The difference between economic multipolarity and unipolarity raises well-known questions about system management and the sustainability of liberal economic policies. All of these "shoving and shaping" forces could be cast in the form of hypotheses deriving from distributional structure seen in terms of economic polarity.

The other "capability" liberated from aggregated power is political stability. This can more usefully be cast in terms of political cohesion, states being differentiated along these lines in terms of a spectrum running from *strong* (meaning closely integrated and stable state-society relations) to *weak* (meaning weakly integrated and unstable state-society relations) (Buzan 1988:18–27; and 1991:ch.2). In using these terms it is important to keep clear the distinction between weak and strong *states,* in terms of political cohesion, and weak and strong *powers,* in terms of military and economic capabilities. A weakish state, like Pakistan (or the Soviet Union as it was), might be quite strong as a power, and vice versa.

The variable of political cohesion can be cast in distributional terms, but does not yield structure in the form of polarity. It links interestingly to the definition of political deep structure. How lacking in sociopolitical cohesion does a state have to be before it either meets criteria of functional differentiation, or, in extremis, ceases to count as a unit of the system—for example post-1976 Lebanon? The most useful way of characterizing the distributional structure of the international political system in terms of political cohesion is to ask how homogeneous it is. Are the units all strong in terms of political cohesion? Are they all weak? Is there some mix of weak and strong? Applied in this way the principle of distribution can yield important structural hypotheses about the tendency of relations at the unit level. For example, one could posit that in a homogeneous system of strong states, intervention will tend to have low salience in international relations. In a system containing a mix of weak and strong states, like the present one, intervention by the strong into the weak will tend to be a major and unavoidable feature of international relations. In a homogeneous system of weak states all interaction would be intervention (Buzan 1988:27–31).

The process of disaggregating power liberates most of the attributes of units that are interesting in distributional terms. The remaining case for de-restriction rests on the principle of distribution itself. Logic demands that any attribute which can be cast in the relational terms of distribution be admitted to the theory. Waltz concedes the point that there are additional candidates with his reference to "other characteristics of states that could be cast in distributional terms" (in Keohane 1986:329), even though he has, in fact, buried most of them within his definition of power. In the political sector, the most obvious remaining candidate is the ideology of governments. In distributional terms, ideology can be treated like political cohesion: is a political system ideologically homogeneous or plural in terms of the number of major organizing ideologies active among its units? This question can almost be put into the terms of polarity: is the system ideologically unipolar (like eighteenth-century Europe), or bipolar (1950s), or tripolar (1970s) with the rise of Islamic politics; or, (as in the 1930s) with liberalism, communism, and fascism). Structural hypotheses arising from this variable might usefully address questions about alliance formation (polarization), international society, and system management.

The end result of disaggregating and de-restricting the distribution of capabilities is a fairly limited set of possible distributional structures based on four types of attribute: military capability, economic capability, political cohesion, and ideology. To assess the distributional structure of any given system would involve examining a set of overlapping "shoving and shaping" forces. These can be envisaged as a set of vectors (lines of force) operating within a field. Sometimes their influence would be mutually reinforcing, as when economic, military, and ideological patterns all coincide—as they did briefly after the Second World War. When that happens strong structural pressure on the behavior of units is created. Sometimes the different vectors would work at odds, perhaps canceling each other out, or at least creating weaker, more diffuse structural forces, as in the international system of the early 1990s. This could leave the field relatively devoid of influence from distributional structure, and therefore clear for the operation of unit level and deep structure factors.

Because more variables are in play, a disaggregated distributional structure will exhibit more change than an aggregated one. Any individual element might remain stable for a considerable period, as military strength has done since the end of the Second World War. But all the vectors are unlikely to remain fixed, and the influence of those that do has to be calculated against the shifting influence of those that don't. A political-economy analysis, for example, would need to deal with the increase in economic polarity in interplay with the stasis in military bipolarity. In this way, the powerful positional logic of structural analysis can be brought to bear on a wider range of events within the system. This can be done without transgressing the boundary between the unit and the structural levels. Although somewhat more complex than aggregated polarity, this form of analysis has three advantages: (1) it yields more finely tuned structural hypotheses, (2) it is applicable to a much wider range of conditions within the international system, and (3) it gives a fairly rich and replicable structural framework within which to conduct systematic comparative analysis.

Disaggregation does not lose any of the insights of the more parsimonious approach. The error of Neorealism is to try to universalize the rather special case in which the main elements of power are all distributed in the same pattern. This special case does sometimes occur, but it is not necessarily, or even probably, the normal condition of the distributional structure.

SUMMARY AND CONCLUSION

This move through Neorealism toward Structural Realism has left two basic elements of Waltz's structural theory firmly in place: the first tier of deep structure, and the boundary between the system and unit levels. Four new developments have been sketched out: the clarification of the sectoral boundary of the theory; the elaboration of what the unit level actually contains; the opening up, clearer demarcation, and application of the third tier, relabeled as distributional structure; and the opening up of the second tier of structure (the functional differentiation of units), which will be pursued further in Section II. The opening up of the second and third tiers of structure enormously increases the scope of Structural Realist theory, allowing it to serve as a wide-ranging and integrative general theory of international relations. The vocabulary of Structural Realism is summarized in figure 3.3.

	INTERNATIONAL POLITICAL SECTOR
STRUCTURAL LEVEL OF ANALYSIS	deep structure = organizational principle plus functional differentiation of units
	distributional structure = systemic patterns in the distribution of unit attributes
UNIT LEVEL OF ANALYSIS	process formations = action-reaction relations between units, in particular, recurrent patterns of action-reaction
	attribute analysis = unit behaviour explained in terms of unit attributes

Figure 3.3. The Vocabulary of Structural Realism

CHAPTER FOUR

Beyond Neorealism:
Interaction Capacity

The design of Neorealism tends to blur the distinction between structure and system (Keohane and Nye 1987:747). Waltz constructed it on the basis of two levels of analysis—unit and structure—that were supposed to comprehend the principal features of the international political system. As far as it goes, this logic is correct inasmuch as the definitions of structure and unit levels provide distinct sources of explanation that range from the nature of the political units, at one end, to the nature of the international political system as a whole, at the other.

This logic does not, however, capture all of the main features of the international political system. The criticisms of Ruggie, Keohane, and others suggest that it does not, because their concerns with factors such as "dynamic density," information richness, communication facilities, and suchlike do not obviously fit into Waltz's ostensibly "systemic" theory. With the new formulations developed in the previous chapter to hand, one can now identify more clearly where the problem lies. It goes right back to the basic definition of system as units, interactions, and structures. Waltz sees interactions as part of the unit level, varying according to the dispositions and capabilities of the units as mediated by structural pressures. Many of his critics think that the interaction component of system needs a higher profile in the theory, but are blocked by Waltz's preemption of structure as the sole system level component of Neorealist theory. The argument in this chapter is that interaction cannot be confined to the unit level. There is a massive and vital interaction component that is systemic, but not structural. The identification and explanation of this third level is a major key to the transition from Neorealism to Structural Realism.

Despite its scale and scope, the logical entrance to this level is not all that easy to find. The distinctions involved in identifying it are subtle but important, and require a rather lengthy excursion. As one might expect, they hinge on the question of capabilities, which already lies at the heart of many people's uncertainties about the boundary between the structure and unit levels. Neorealism makes extensive use of capabilities at both the unit and structure levels, leaving no room for doubt that capabilities are a major component of the international political system. In drawing the boundary between the unit and structure levels, Waltz relies heavily on the distinction between the distribution of capabilities, which he argues is structural, and the possession of them by individual units, which is not. This distinction points toward a more general one between *absolute* and *relative* capabilities, and it is this that reveals the missing level. The aggregated concept of power provides a good illustration of the point, and is worth developing in some detail.

DEFINITIONS OF POWER: ATTRIBUTIVE, RELATIONAL AND CONTROL

The meaning of power in absolute terms is derived from the natural sciences, and refers to the capability of units to perform specified tasks as a result of the attributes they possess. In order to avoid the unwanted overtones of extreme political centralism implied by "absolute power," this understanding of power can be referred to as *attributive*. Depending upon their attributes, states either can or cannot do certain things, like building nuclear weapons, or putting 12 million men into uniform. This is the same type of power as one refers to when talking about the horsepower of engines or the lifting power of rockets. In the international political system, as in engineering, attributive power is non–zero-sum. It is open-ended, in that all units can increase (or decrease) their levels of it through such capability-expanding activities as technological development, industrialization, administrative efficiency, and collective identity. In theory, attributive power should be objectively measurable. As it can and does change markedly and rapidly in both quantity and quality, state power, and its implications for international relations, are continuously subject to significant change. Think, for example, of the way the absolute power of states both to inflict damage on each other, and to absorb each other's exports, has increased over the last 150 years. These increases have of course had an impact on the relative power of states, but within the logic of relative power the level of attributive power has been rising steadily.

By contrast, power seen in relative terms is wholly positional and zero-sum, referring only to the pattern of distribution of power amongst the units in the system. This understanding of power can be referred to as *relational*. Relational power takes no cognizance of the open-ended character of attributive power except inasmuch as this affects the zero-sum distribution of power among units. If all units increased their attributive power in the same proportion, there would be no change in the relational power ranking among them, even though their absolute capabilities might have increased enormously. The bipolar distributional structure after the Second World War would have existed regardless of nuclear weapons, but the existence of those weapons made a huge difference to the absolute capabilities of the two superpowers to inflict damage on each other and the rest of the world.

Measuring relational power is extremely difficult. The task can be approached by trying to compare levels of attributive power. It can also be approached, though only retrospectively, in terms of outcomes (*control* power), the ultimate traditional test here being the outcome of war. Using control power creates the widely recognized difficulty of a circular definition (where the erstwhile cause is defined in terms of its effect). Short of the test of war, relational power is highly subject to perceptual variables. Social "facts" may be more important than real ones in determining outcomes: the perceived power of a state, and therefore its ability to determine outcomes, may exceed (or understate) its real capabilities.

In Neorealism, relational power is incorporated in both levels of analysis, but attributive power is found only at the unit level. Relational power defines the distributional structure: "polarity" is simply the label given to the main pattern of relational power. At the unit level, relational power plays a major role in action-reaction dynamics such as arms racing. Waltz acknowledges the importance of attributive power, but assigns it firmly to the unit level.

> In my view, the two biggest changes in international politics since World War II are the structural shift from multi- to bipolarity and the unit-level change in the extent and rapidity with which some states can hurt others. . . . Wars that might bring nuclear weapons into play have become much harder to start . . . A unit-level change has much diminished a structural effect (Waltz in Keohane 1986:327).

The nature of Waltz's definitions excludes attributive power, with its open-ended qualities, from the structural level. Given the overall dyadic construction of Neorealism, this forces the placement of attributive power exclusively in the unit level.

The problem is that this placement does not encompass the full nature of attributive power. Up to a point, Waltz's formulation serves. It does capture the significance of capabilities both in the domestic determination of individual unit behavior and in specific action-reaction dynamics between units such as arms racing and trade wars. Beyond that point, however, there are still substantial elements of attributive power that cannot be located in the unit level without seriously straining the sense of what "unit level" means. In confusing structure with system, Waltz has lost sight of the systemic interaction element that is essential to give the notion of system meaning.

SYSTEMIC CAPABILITIES

This discussion now becomes clearer if we revert to talking about the absolute quality of specific capabilities, rather than power generally. Whether capabilities are aggregated into power or treated separately makes no difference to the logic that brought us to this point.

There are at least two key aspects of absolute capabilities whose very nature, and not just their effects, are clearly *systemic* in character when they are central to the interaction component of the system: one is technological capabilities, and the other is shared norms and organizations. These factors not only affect the ability and the willingness of units to interact, but also determine what types and levels of interaction are both possible and desired. They are systemic even though they clearly fall outside the meaning of structure.

The evolution of technology continuously raises the absolute capability for interaction available within the system. It is true that many extremely important technological factors, especially those relating to military power, can be captured at the unit level in terms of the particular capabilities commanded by individual states, and the way those capabilities affect relations with other states. But in some important areas, most obviously communication, transportation, and information, these capabilities cannot adequately be expressed in unit terms. Communication and transportation technologies are in an important sense system-wide in their deployment, as well as in their effects. Things like shipping capacity and telecommunications are more sys- tem- than state-based. Once developed to the point of cost-effective- ness, such technologies tend to spread quickly throughout the system, just as steamships and telegraphs did in the nineteenth century, and civil aviation and computer networks have done since the Second World War. Although command of these technologies is unquestion- ably an element of unit power, their availability quickly transforms conditions of interaction for all units, and therefore transforms the system itself.

Compare for example a system in which the best transportation technology is horse-drawn wagons and wooden sailing ships, with one in which transportation capability is defined by jumbo jets, high-speed trains, 500,000 ton ships, and trucks using extensive networks of paved roads. Across a wide range, the interaction possibilities—mili- tary, economic, and societal—in the former are vastly more con- strained than those in the latter. Both levels of technology permit an uneven distribution of power, but the quality, quantity, and impact of interaction in the two systems will be radically different. The present day example could itself be compared to a possible future in which "star Trek" technology makes the direct, and virtually instantaneous, transmission of matter (including nuclear bombs) the principal method of transportation. A similar exercise could be performed for commu- nication and information. As technologies in these areas spread, they change the quality and character of what might be called the *interac- tion capacity* of the system as a whole. This is both a characteristic, and an effect that is qualitatively different from the way the particular attributes of particular states affect their interactions with other indi- vidual states.

The other area of absolute capability relevant for the interaction capacity of the system is shared norms and organizations. The sharing of norms and values is a precondition for establishing organizations, but once established, such organizations greatly facilitate, and even promote, interactions that shared norms and values make possible and desired. It is difficult to see global or even subglobal international institutions as unit-based, and easier to see them as in some important sense system-based. Political communication in a system with no such international norms or institutions will be quite different from one that is richly endowed with them. Institutions provide not only more opportunities to communicate, but also more obligations and more incentives to do so. They also prestructure communication in a variety of ways. The interaction capacity of a system not served by such norms and institutions, other things being equal, will be systematically different from one that is well served. In effect, we are talking here about the difference between systems with and without a developed international society (Bull 1977; Wight 1977; Bull and Watson 1984). The interaction capacity of a system with few shared norms will be much lower than one where significant norms are shared widely among the major actors, which will in turn be much lower than one in which shared norms have given rise to the communal institutions and organizations that are the hallmark of a maturing international society. "Lower" here refers to both the quantity and the variety of interactions.

Between the technological and societal elements of interaction capacity the former is both prior and more basic. Technology determines the level of interaction in a very fundamental sense. Without a substantial impact from technology on levels of interaction it is difficult to see how or why common norms and communal institutions could develop other than in geographically limited subsystems. Once they do develop, however, they become an important element of interaction capacity which is quite distinct from technology in its effects.

A proper sense of interaction capacity as a feature of the system as a whole is missing from Neorealism. This causes Neorealists to ignore (or rather to dismiss as unit level factors) the impact of systemically distributed absolute capabilities. As will be expanded upon in Section II, this misclassification causes Waltz to overlook entirely the fact that the whole operational logic of his structural theory depends on prior assumptions about the nature of interaction capacity. These assumptions are never examined in Neorealism.

The systemic, as opposed to unit or structure, status of interaction capacity is easily demonstrated by elaborating the scenario sketched above. Think of two international systems that are identical in both deep and distributional structure, and in unit characteristics, except that the predominant communication capability differs. In the first system, communication capability is defined by the speed and capacity of human messengers using horses or sailing vessels as their means of transport. In the second, communication capability is defined by globally distributed satellite, satellite receiver, and cable networks. The interaction capacity in these two systems is profoundly different for all the units in terms of the speed, volume, and reliability of their communications. Information and communication will move much faster, and in much larger volumes, in the second system than in the first. Add in similar magnitudes of difference in transportation technology and institutionalization, and it is apparent that the whole quality, scale, and intensity of international relations in the two systems will be radically different. Indeed, it becomes impossible to sustain the assumption that the units themselves would be "otherwise similar" in the two systems, a linkage taken up in Section II. Because the differences in absolute capability are system-wide in operation, they can, as will be shown below, serve as a basis for hypotheses at the system level about the impact of this variable on international relations.

These scenarios illustrate a set of variables that clearly belong within a system theory of international politics, but which are neither structural nor unit level in character. They are aspects of absolute capability that transcend the unit level, but which are not structural in the sense of having to do with the positional arrangement of the units. They are systemic not only because they represent capabilities that are deployed throughout the system, but also, and mainly, because they profoundly condition the significance of structure and the meaning of the term system itself. This is a different quality from selective unit capabilities that have system-wide effects, such as nuclear weapons, which Waltz rightly places within the unit level.

Interaction capacity is an appropriate label for this category, distinguishing it from the structure and unit levels as a distinct source of explanation (and thus as a level of analysis), and expressing the idea of a range of system-wide variables that affect the interaction capacity of the system as a whole. Interaction capacity captures the importance of the absolute quality of capabilities as both a defining characteristic of the system, and a distinct source of shoving and shaping forces playing on the units alongside those from the structural level. As with distributional structure, a case could be made for both aggregative and disaggregative conceptions of interaction capacity. Ruggie's concern with "dynamic density," noted above, captures the effect of interaction capacity without specifying the cause, and perhaps captures the essence of an aggregative view. A disaggregative approach would look separately at technological and societal capabilities in the system. One advantage of disaggregation is that it enables account to be taken of the different logistical requirements of interaction in different sectors. Significant societal interactions can take place by the movement of a few individuals carrying ideas. Its logistical requirements are rather low even over long distances. Significant military and economic interaction, by contrast, require major logistical capability, especially over long distances. These sectoral differences reinforce the case for disaggregating power. They also have profound implications for the way in which international systems develop.

The standing of interaction capacity as a third level of analysis is demonstrated by its profound impact on the operation of Neorealism's whole structural logic. As the basic definition of system indicates, the absolute quality of interaction capacity is fundamental to the existence of a system. How much interaction, and of what type, is necessary before one can say that an international system exists? This question has not been addressed in Neorealism. Yet so basic is the effect of interaction capacity that unless its level and type are specified first, one cannot say whether structural logic will operate or not. Units can exist without being in a system if their capabilities are so low as to prevent significant interaction among them. Waltz simply presupposes an adequate level of interaction to make the political dynamics of socialization and competition operate. But if structural theory is to be applied across the whole history of the international system, as it can and should be, then many interesting and important questions about degree and type of interaction arise. We explore some of these in more detail in Section II.

One can start, as Waltz does, with Rousseau-like assumptions of a nonsystemic state of nature in which political units evolved in isolation from one another. An international system comes into being when these units begin to interact. But the studies of international historians such as McNeill (1963) and international historical theorists such as Wallerstein (1974) suggest strongly that, for the great bulk of its history, the international system has not obeyed Neorealist logic, or at least has done so only very slowly and weakly, and on a regional rather than on a global scale. The reason is to be found in interaction capacity. For most of its history, the international system has been characterized by low levels of the technological and societal capabilities necessary for system-wide economic and military interaction. Strategic interaction among the units has thus been poorly developed and highly constrained. When low quality of technological capabilities across the system puts heavy restraints on the speed, volume, range, and reliability of communication and transportation, and hence of the capability and incentive to develop international society, then the strong interaction between organizing principle and functional differentiation of units in deep structure does not operate effectively or rapidly, and may not operate at all except over rather limited distances.

As McNeill tells the story, significant interaction among major centers of human civilization can be traced back to at least 3000 B.C. From the earliest origins of civilization in Mesopotamia, Egypt, and the Indus valley, cultural interaction played an important role in shaping the development of human communities. Technologies, religions, styles, and a limited trade in goods traveled between communities too remote from each other to make strategic rivalry possible. For long periods, civilizations in Egypt, India, China, and the Americas existed in strategic and economic, though not cultural, isolation from other centers of power. McNeill's core theme is that until the expansion of Europe beginning in the fifteenth century A.D., the international system consisted of four largely autonomous civilizations centered in the Middle East, India, China, and Europe. There was enough cultural exchange and impact to support the idea that a weak (i.e., nonstrategic) international system existed. Think, for example, of the spread of Buddhism from India to East Asia, and of printing and gunpowder from China to Europe. But in trade, and even more so in military threats, the overall interaction capacity of this system was low. Only in rather specific situations did strategic interaction occur. Strategic interaction could be intense *within* civilizations, as in classical Greece and ancient Mesopotamia. In addition, all civilizations had periodically to face onslaughts from barbarians equipped with the transportation and military technologies of civilization. In a few places, most notably on the boundary between the Greco-Roman and Middle Eastern civilizations, there was sustained military rivalry between the major centers of power.

But except where adjacency made war possible, the constraints on economic and strategic interaction meant that the structure of international anarchy did not produce the "like units" that Neorealism predicts. Interaction capacity was so low as to prevent the pressures of socialization and competition (discussed in 3.5 above) from working. Because interaction capacity was low, a type 4 system (anarchic, with dissimilar units) could exist in a stable state. Unlike units were under no pressure to conform, because distance and ignorance insulated the weaker from the stronger. Distance could only provide insulation because the absolute capabilities of transportation and communication across the system were low.

Should this be considered to constitute an international system? If a system exists as soon as coaction begins, then the answer is clearly yes, but then structural hypotheses need to be modified to account for the impact of low interaction capacity. If the answer is no, then careful thought needs to be given to how much and what kind of interaction it is that constitutes a system for Structural Realist purposes. Trade and military contact create peculiarly intense pressures between political units, and there is an unspecified but strong assumption in Neorealism that the interaction capacity of the system is sufficiently developed to permit extensive contact of this type.

Wallerstein's idea of world empires suggests one solution to the dilemma of how to deal with the 4,500 years of the international system predating the modern world system. Somewhat like McNeill's civilizations, world empires point to the idea that prior to the modern period, the international system is best understood by posing a regional or subsystemic level between units and systems. Waltz, refuting Kaplan's notion of a "subsystem dominant system" (where "subsystem" refers to individual states), has argued that "a subsystem dominant system is no system at all" (1979:58). But in relation to subsystems *of* states this may be too hasty a judgment. Unless one assumes that an international system has existed only for the last half-millennium or less, the idea of a subsystem dominant system is a precise way of describing most of the history of the international system. It captures rather well the limitations imposed on the system by a poorly developed interaction capacity. In a subsystem dominant system, the subsystems are defined by their internal strategic interaction with its structural consequences, whereas the system as a whole is defined mostly by cultural interaction with its low structural effects.

The image that emerges is one of subsystems in which adjacency compensates for low levels of interaction capability. Within these subsystems, structural logic begins to operate much earlier than it does for the system as a whole. It is for this reason that one can read Thucydides' history of the Peloponnesian War (as a subsystemic strategic story) and still see clear parallels with modern history. The argument is that in order to understand the concept of international system in its full historical context, one must accept the centrality of a subsystem level between unit and system. History did not move directly from a Rousseauian state of nature to a Neorealist international anarchy. Instead, a weakly interactive international system came into being quite early, but for a long period the main force of structural logic worked almost exclusively within regional subsystems. The international system as a whole remained a stable type 4 (anarchy with unlike units), but within the subsystems, the forces of socialization and competition worked more vigorously. In theory, this subsystem dynamic should have resulted either in anarchic subsystems with like units (the Greek and Italian city state systems, the Middle Eastern empires, the European state system), or in unifying "world empires" that took over a subsystem (China, Rome, Persia). As interaction capacity improved, these subsystems increased their range. Contact eventually led to rivalry. The more effective subsystems either absorbed the less effective ones, as Rome did, or entered into long-term strategic rivalry with them, as between Rome and the Parthian empire (see Section II).

At some point, the logic of this progress suggests that interaction capacities must improve sufficiently to end the dominance of subsystems, and shift the structure to one in which the forces of socialization and competition work most strongly at the global system level. This can occur either because several centers become strong enough to bring economic and military pressure to bear on the whole system, or because one center becomes so disproportionately powerful that it is able to impose a higher level of interaction on the rest of the system. World history followed the latter course. The highly competitive internal dynamics of the European subsystem created a developmental hothouse that gave rise to units that were much more effectively organized and better equipped than any others in the system. Between the sixteenth and nineteenth centuries, this European system took over most of the world. In so doing it not only imposed its own form of political organization (the sovereign state) on all of the other units, but also created a truly global system in which subsystem logic became subordinate. By the late twentieth century, this lopsided development had waned. Europe was merely one of several centers of power having global influence, and the foundations were laid for an international system resting on a more even distribution of power and activity. Subsystems remain only as a shadow, though one still strong enough

	INTERACTION CAPACITY OF THE INTERNATIONAL SYSTEM	
	high	low
SYSTEM DOMINANT	modern inter-national system	
SUBSYSTEM DOMINANT		pre-modern international system

Figure 4.1. Interaction Capacity and Anarchic Logic

to have inspired a literature on regional international relations and regional security (Ayoob 1986; Brecher 1963; Buzan 1991:ch. 5; Cantori and Spiegel 1970, 1973; Haas 1970, 1974; Russett 1967; Thompson 1973; Väyrynen 1986; Waever 1989). Regional security complexes identify persistent patterns of relatively intense local security interaction. Although the global system rules, most threats still travel more easily over short distances than over long ones, thus giving regional security relations a particular priority within the broader global pattern (Buzan 1991:ch. 5). The linkage between interaction capacity on the one hand, and subsystem and system level dominance on the other, is shown in figure 4.1.

In historical perspective, the impact of low density on the logic of anarchy thus becomes very clear: the variable of interaction crucially affects the meaning and construction of the system. When interaction capacity is low, even the existence of a meaningful international system is in question. Structural logic is suppressed by the overall thinness of interaction, operating mainly at the subsystem level. In some middle range of interaction capacity subsystems decline in importance, and interaction is sufficient to support the structural logic across the system as a whole. The international system has been within that range for several centuries, and still is.

The argument that interaction capacity crucially conditions structural logic can also be cast in a future where it is much higher than at present. For this purpose one can hold the structural logic constant by assuming that anarchy continues to define political relations in the international system. The question then becomes what impact does high interaction capacity have on the logic of anarchy? Put in other terms, how do the logics of anarchy and interdependence interact?

This question puts into Structural Realist terms the feelings of many enthusiasts for interdependence and world society. It avoids the rather silly issue of choosing between either interdependence or anarchy, and asks instead what kind of dialectic emerges when both fragmenting anarchic and integrating market logics are powerfully and durably in play. Structural Realism provides a basis for synthesizing the Neoliberal and the Neorealist approaches to the study of the international system, as called for by Keohane and Nye (1987:747), opening the possibility of transforming a theory of international *politics* into a theory of international *relations*. The proponents of interdependence and world society are essentially supporting the systemic hypothesis that high interaction capacity profoundly conditions the logic of political structure. One early attempt to think through the logic of anarchy under conditions of high interaction capacity is Rosenau's *Turbulence in World Politics* (1990), which puts an interesting focus on the impact of a better educated, more aware, more critical, more engaged, and more networked global citizenry.

When interaction capacity moves from middling to some higher level, it does not seem unreasonable to hypothesize that the interaction variable might once again begin to override structural effects in the overall logic of the system just as it does when it is low. In other words, when the volume, speed, range, and reliability of interaction become sufficiently high, they might begin systematically (and systemically) to override the deep structural effects of anarchy. They could override the tendency for similarity of units to foster low interdependence, as already seems to be the case among the leading capitalist powers, which are becoming simultaneously more similar and more interdependent. They could erode the anarchic imperative of "take care of yourself," by allowing some units to survive and prosper through specialization. That trend would eventually regenerate a type 4 system (anarchic, with functionally differentiated units), though on a very different basis from the type 4 system created by the weakly interactive international system of premodern times. Some see a development along these lines in the current rise of multinational corporations. It might also be indicated by the ability of Japan, Italy, and to a lesser extent Germany, to play a significantly specialized role in the system for an extended period, by keeping their military and political power much lower than their economic strength could easily support. A type 4 system, if it proved stable under these conditions, could pave the road for an eventual deep structural shift to hierarchy, or if not that, then to a system in which political logic took a back seat to economic and societal structures.

Here is an issue where theory really matters if the theoretical assumptions of policymakers breed self-fulfilling expectations. If Japanese statesmen side with Waltz they will see their strategy of these past four decades as one of delaying the evil day when they have once again to grapple with being a great power; if they accept the argument made above, they might abandon thoughts of having eventually to convert economic into military power in order to compete in terms of aggregated power, seeing their specialized economic role not as a stopgap, but as a viable long run strategy.

There is a strong case for saying that interaction capacity ranks alongside structure as a "shoving and shaping" force on the interactions of the units throughout the system. It provides the essential third leg of a full system theory (units + interaction + structure). One of the challenges of interaction capacity is that it generates a rather difficult requirement for indexes of measurement. This, however, is a technical rather than a theoretical problem, and one that is already familiar to the behavioral side of International Relations. It may be an obstacle to the mechanical operationalization of the theory, but it does

	INTERNATIONAL POLITICAL SECTOR
STRUCTURAL LEVEL OF ANALYSIS	deep structure = organizational principle plus differentiation of units
	distributional structure = systemic patterns in the distribution of unit attributes
INTERACTION LEVEL OF ANALYSIS	interaction capacity = absolute quality of technological and societal capabilities across the system
UNIT LEVEL OF ANALYSIS	process formations = action-reaction relations between units, in particular, recurrent patterns of action-reaction
	attribute analysis = unit behaviour explained in terms of unit attributes

Figure 4.2. The Vocabulary of Structural Realism

not stand in the way of the basic conceptualization. Measuring inter-action is no more and no less difficult than measuring power. One of the great advantages of interaction capacity is that it meets the require-ment of so many of Waltz's critics that structural theory somehow be more sensitive to the dynamics of change. Because it expresses the absolute quality of capabilities, interaction capacity is highly sensitive to the dynamics of change. It is by definition open-ended, and its largely technological, normative and organizational determinants are rooted in the main drivers of change for the international political system. Adding in interaction capacity as a third level of analysis is thus a major step from Neorealism to Structural Realism.

If all this is acceptable, then figure 3.3 needs to be extended as in figure 4.2.

II

—

Rethinking System Continuity and Transformation

RICHARD LITTLE

The initial aim of this section is to take stock of the theoretical and methodological implications of Structural Realism. The developments made in Section I are substantial, but they remain compatible with Waltz's idea of establishing a general and parsimonious theory based on the structure of the international system. Nevertheless, they do complicate the Neorealist design, and what follows here makes it clear that the conception of Structural Realism established so far needs to be further extended. As in the previous section, it proves useful to begin this exercise by reconsidering certain aspects of Waltz's argument.

The center of interest in this section focuses on the relationship between system transformation and system continuity. Neorealism presupposes that the historical record provides no evidence of system transformation; it follows that world history can be analyzed in terms of a persistent and unchanging anarchic arena. Even sympathetic critics have found this position unsatisfactory and in the previous section, although it was accepted that world history has been conducted within a continuous anarchic arena, it was also argued that the structure of the arena has undergone major transformations which must be accounted for in any general theory of the international system.

By building upon that analysis, attention is drawn in this section, first to the way political units in the international system have evolved, and second to the process whereby the international system itself has moved from a condition of subsystem dominance to one of system dominance. An important implication of these two factors is that anarchy needs to be treated as a differentiated structural property which can undergo transformation. A further distinction is made between a structured anarchic system which is system dominant and an unstructured anarchic system which is subsystem dominant. Substantial discussion is necessary before the significance of this distinction can be demonstrated. In Neorealist theory, undifferentiated sovereign units operate within an international system defined by a rigid and unchanging anarchic structure. As a consequence of these restrictions, the theory is unable to entertain the possibility of either differentiated units or an evolving international system. In the past, there has been little interest shown in such refinements at least in part because of a persistent failure to adopt a world historical perspective in the study of international relations. Attention has been focused almost exclusively on the contemporary international system. To the extent that theorists in International Relations have taken an interest in world history, they have tended to project the prevailing conception of the contemporary international system onto earlier periods. As in the previous section the analysis made here further elaborates and loosens the unduly rigid Neorealist framework.

We proceed simultaneously on two fronts in this Section. On one front, we seek to locate Structural Realism in the context of the debate surrounding the "agent-structure problem." This methodological problem has arisen because social scientists so rarely develop explanations that take account of both the structure of a social system and the agents operating within it. Waltz, for example, is considered to be a prime target for criticism because it is claimed he has self-consciously developed an exclusively structural based theory of international politics. As a consequence, his critics argue that he is a structural determinist who can account only for continuity in the international system, leaving no room for the idea of system transformation. Since Structural Realism is designed to provide for system transformation, it becomes of crucial importance to see what light the debate surrounding the "agent-structure problem" sheds on both Waltz's theory and the approach being developed in this book.

Once the agent-structure debate is opened up, it becomes clear that Neorealism is less structurally deterministic than is often supposed. It operates from a rather more sophisticated position which is much closer than is generally realized to the one adopted by recent social theorists who have endeavored to resolve the agent-structure problem. By exploring the debate generated by this issue we hope to develop a deeper understanding of the methodology needed to comprehend the processes associated with transformation as well as continuity in the international system. We hope to show, moreover, that both Neorealism, and much more explicitly Structural Realism, are compatible with a methodology that resolves the agent-structure problem.

On the second front, we intend to assess how far Structural Realism has increased the capacity of structural theory to explore the historical record. The strengths of Structural Realism can be demonstrated most effectively by applying it to a historical case and, more specifically, one that presents Neorealist theory with intractable problems. We have chosen to focus on the rise and fall of the Roman Empire because it raises the issues of system transformation and continuity in an acute form. Unsurprisingly, critics have been dissatisfied with the way the case has to be handled within the Neorealist theoretical framework. By exploring the structural transformation associated with the rise and fall of the Roman Empire we can observe how and why our Structural Realist theory helps to overcome the weaknesses of Neorealism, and to understand these changes.

CHAPTER FIVE

Structural Realism and World History

The apparent ahistorical character of Neorealism has been a persistent source of criticism in the literature. By reconstituting and extending Neorealism into Structural Realism we hope that this criticism can be deflected. In this chapter, therefore, we wish to explore the implications of the criticism in a little more detail. It is important to recognize, in the first place, that Neorealists do not deny the relevance of history or the potential for change in international politics. But they do assert that there are important features of international politics, such as imperialism, that have occurred throughout the history of the international system and that need to be accounted for in terms of an unchanging systemic structure. It is this claim that analysts imbued with historicism wish to deny. Imperialism, they accept, is a label that has been attached to state practices throughout history. But the historicists insist that distortion will inevitably occur if it is presupposed that these practices always play an identical role in the international system or that they always carry the same subjective meaning simply because they are identified by a common label. From this perspective, then, the imperialistic practices associated with the Athenians must be distinguished sharply from those associated with the British. Pushed to the limits, this line of argument makes it impossible to engage in comparative analysis across time or cultures. But it is not intended here to engage with this extreme line of argument. Instead, attention will be focused on the work of historians who have accepted the value of comparative historical analysis but who deny that world history can be comprehended within the confines of an unchanging structural framework.

Before looking at this work, it may be helpful, first, to summarize just how extensively Waltz's theory has so far been changed. Against this backdrop we can then examine a number of competing structural frameworks that focus on the way the international system has evolved during the course of world history. Once these have been presented, it becomes easier to identify how further refinements to the Structural Realist framework will help to throw light on the relationship between system continuity and system transformation. Finally, we need to examine in more detail some of the reasons for drawing on the Roman Empire as a case study.

NEOREALISM TO STRUCTURAL REALISM

Waltz starts from the underlying premise that since international phenomena like war, alliances, and imperialism have been ever-present features of world politics, some constant factor in the international system must be identified and drawn upon to account for them. Waltz argues that the only permanent feature in international politics is the structure of the system itself. We begin by accepting that the structure of the international system must play an essential role in any general theory in the field of International Relations. The reason for paying such close attention to the agent-structure problem later in this section, therefore, is because the debate surrounding the problem focuses on the role played by the idea of structure in the theory and methodology of the social sciences.

In Neorealist theory, the structure of the international political system is characterized by only two components: (1) the anarchic ordering principle of the international system; and (2) the distribution of power capabilities among the political units in the international system. With the aid of these structural components, Neorealists go on to build a conception of the balance of power, which constitutes the core of their theory of international politics. Little reference was made to the balance of power in the previous section because attention was devoted, instead, to the structural bedrock of Neorealist theory. The reconstructions carried out on the bedrock substantially modify Waltz's conception of structure and also the way he distinguishes between the structure and constituent units of the system. The result is to produce a much richer conception of structure and a more complex relationship between the structure and units of the international system.

Attention must be drawn, first, to the illuminating metaphor of "deep structure," taken from the literature on structuralism, and which Ruggie (1986:135) has applied to the principle of anarchy. Although he does not use the idea, there is no doubt that Waltz also sees the anarchic principle as a more fundamental feature in the structure of the international system than the power component, which, extending the metaphor, can be considered to represent the "surface" or what we call the distributional structure of the system. Ruggie argues that "deeper structural levels have causal priority" with the result that "the structural levels closer to the surface of visible phenomena take effect only within a context that is already 'prestructured' by the deeper levels" (1986:150). It is for this reason that deep structures are said to be "generative," because they "generate" observable patterns of behavior in the system. Moreover, Waltz believes that the structure of the system is so powerful that it will generate common patterns of behavior among very different types of unit. He notes that "The logic of anarchy obtains whether the system is composed of tribes, nations, oligopolistic firms or street gangs" (1990:37).

The conceptual utility of deep structure becomes evident only when attention is drawn to the potential for the international system to undergo transformation. As far as Neorealists are concerned, system transformation can happen only if the ordering principle of anarchy gives way to that of hierarchy. In the international context, therefore, for system transformation to occur, independent political units must be taken over by world government or empire. At that juncture, the defining structure of international politics is eliminated. As a consequence, the shift from anarchy to hierarchy constitutes a transformation from decentralized to centralized politics. Since there has never been a global hierarchy in world history, a Neorealist transformation has never occurred. World history, therefore, can be described in terms of a continuous system that has never undergone transformation. Neorealists accept, of course, that dramatic shifts have taken place in the distribution of power among political units in the international system. But these changes at the "surface" of the structure do not constitute a transformation in the system. Indeed, the Neorealist theory of the balance of power is designed to show how the structure of the system inhibits any single political actor from achieving global dominance.

It was argued in the previous section that this position is profoundly unsatisfactory, because historically there have been momentous changes in the international system that transcend modifications in the distribution of power among the political units. The inability of Neorealists to accommodate more extensive systemic transformation represents a familiar line of criticism. In one of the most interesting and sympathetic studies of Waltz, Ruggie sets out to show how Waltz's theory contains "only a reproductive logic but no transformational logic" [1986:152]. Cox, who is more critical of Waltz, also points to the "inability of his theory to account for or to explain transformation" (1986:243). The nature of the criticism is very straightforward: while Neorealism can help to explain continuity in the international system, it lacks the capacity to account for structural transformation. Waltz is unable to describe, let alone explain, what Ruggie sees as the most important system change in the last thousand years: "the shift from the Medieval to the modern international system" (1986:141). It is seen to be essential that a structural approach to international politics should be able to describe and explain such massive transformations in the system. But it is also presupposed that in accommodating the potential for system transformation, it is vital that the important advantage derived from the idea of deep structure—that of continuity—must not be lost.

The desire to take account of both continuity and transformation within a structural framework provides the entry point for our analysis in the previous section and it represents the touchstone for Structural Realism. Like Ruggie, we reintroduce the idea of functionally differentiated units as a structural dimension of the international system. Waltz eliminated this structural component on the grounds that anarchy generates functionally similar units. Although that argument is a persuasive one, we insist that it is not a logical consequence of anarchy. It is possible, after all, to conceive of functionally differentiated units operating in an anarchic system and there are substantial historical precedents for systems with these structural features. Unlike Ruggie, however, we do not see functionally differentiated units as simply mediating the deep structural effects of anarchy (1986:135). Instead, the functional differentiation of political units is seen to dictate the character of the anarchic deep structure of the system.

By making this move, we can argue that the deep structure of the international system, defined in terms of its ordering principle of anarchy, has remained unchanged throughout world history. But by incorporating the additional structural component of functional differentiation we are also able to identify that there can be change in the deep structure of the international system, as, for example, when the complex web of competing authority relations in the Medieval world gave way to the contemporary international system made up of functionally undifferentiated sovereign states. It also allows us to distinguish between the modern international system which is made up of sovereign states and earlier systems where states were autonomous without being sovereign (Wight:1977; Wendt:1990). This line of argument seems to go some way to meeting Cox's objection that Waltz has endeavored to achieve theoretical clarity, but at the cost of relying on an "unconvincing mode of historical understanding" (1986:243).

At first sight, this solution certainly overcomes some of the criticisms directed at Neorealist structural theory. But the solution does more than deflect criticism. By consigning both functional differentiation and anarchy to the deep and most generative structure of the system, we open up the possibility that anarchy is a much more complex phenomenon than Waltz recognizes. The significance of the move becomes apparent when a comparison is made with Ruggie, who argues that the deep structure of the international system is restricted to the ordering principle of anarchy. As a consequence, according to Ruggie, the differentiation of political units can only mediate the deep structural effects of anarchy. Logically, however, if functional differentiation is considered to be part of the deep structure of the international system, it must do more than simply mediate the generative consequences of anarchy. It will be argued in this section that the notion of anarchy is more complex and problematic than is generally acknowledged. It constitutes a differentiated phenomenon and cannot simply be characterized in terms of the absence of central government. The implications of assigning functional differentiation to the deep structure of the international system and its impact on the conception of anarchy will be explored later.

A second line developed in Section I is the provision made for the analysis of different sectors of international activity. Attention is drawn to economic, societal, and strategic sectors, for example, as well as to the political sector that Waltz exclusively focuses upon. Stated baldly in this fashion, the full significance of this development is not immediately apparent. But as will be shown in more detail later, it has profound consequences for the direction theory and method should take in the discipline. The sectoral argument is made, in the first instance, because it is presupposed that the structure of the international system has an impact on a wide range of activities extending beyond international politics. But the deeper significance of this presupposition can become apparent only when the methodology underpinning the idea of structure has been more extensively spelled out. It can then be demonstrated that any attempt to understand the nature and impact of the structure of the international system will be necessarily incomplete if the focus is restricted to the political sector. It follows that a theory of international politics cannot account for the structure of the international system; only a wider theory of international relations can do that.

A third point made in the previous section is to extend the Neorealist conception of power. A distinction is drawn between relative and absolute ("attributive") power and it is demonstrated that Waltz focuses on the former rather than the latter. It is then argued that whereas relative or relational power is inextricably part of the structure of the international system, absolute or attributive power must be separated from the structure of the system, although it also has distinct and important consequences at the system level. It is argued that this attributive dimension of power cannot be pushed into the unit level of analysis. Instead, attributive capabilities are seen to be a distinct systemic level of analysis. Identified as the interaction level of analysis, attributive capabilities are seen to measure the interaction capacity of the system. By opening up this distinction, it becomes possible to differentiate between international systems characterized by system and subsystem dominance. The importance of this distinction becomes more apparent when more detailed attempts are made to describe and explain the evolution of world history.

It will be shown later that these three developments interact and so, when combined, have very important theoretical and methodological consequences for any attempt to analyze world history. An attempt is made to draw out some of these consequences in subsequent chapters in this section. Before doing so, it is worth pausing briefly to look in more detail at the implications of Neorealism for the study of world history, and to examine two alternative frameworks. It is hoped to show how Structural Realism is more effective for analyzing transformation and continuity in the international system than any of the alternatives.

90

FRAMEWORKS FOR ANALYZING WORLD HISTORY

Few theorists in the contemporary field of international relations have attempted to take account of world history. Attention has been focused instead almost exclusively on the sovereign state system which prevails today. As a consequence, when consideration has occasionally been given to world history, the temptation to think of the past in terms of the present has often proved overwhelming. When this is done, it becomes relatively easy to argue, for example, that the conflict between Athens and Sparta in the Greek city state system, or the conflict between Carthage and Rome can be taken as analogues for the Cold War struggle between the United States and the Soviet Union (Fleiss 1966). This widespread practice can also be used to illustrate the apparent dominance of Realist thinking in international relations.

But there are alternative frameworks for thinking about the past that do not rely on prevailing realist or neorealist assumptions (Alker 1987, 1990). The contrast becomes quite striking when a comparison is made of the way that the various frameworks handle familiar phenomena such as imperialism and empires. It quickly becomes apparent that the Neorealist's lack of interest in system transformation has major consequences for the way that notions of empire and imperialism are conceptualized. For example, it can be shown that frameworks which accommodate the possibility of system transformation can develop a differentiated approach to the concepts of empire and imperialism whereas the Neorealist framework encourages an undifferentiated approach to those concepts.

Empires in the Neorealist's Framework

As already indicated, Neorealists argue that imperialism is a universal phenomenon and it is presupposed, as a consequence, that it is possible to fit imperialism into a general theory of international politics. In making this presupposition, Neorealists assume that all empires take the same structural form. From this perspective, then, no structural distinction can be drawn, for example, between the British and Roman Empires. In both cases, the imperial state is seen to have extended its territory in the context of a broader anarchic system. By formulating imperialism and empire within the context of an anarchic arena, the Neorealists can contemplate a theory of imperialism that will account for the formation of empires in the ancient and modern world. Moreover, Neorealists can accommodate imperialism within their general theory of international politics, which revolves around the conception of the balance of power. It follows, moreover, that as far as the Neorealists are concerned, imperialism can precipitate system change, but it cannot be considered to be a source of system transformation. The deep structure provided by the principle of anarchy is seen to transcend the rise and fall of nonuniversal empires.

Empires in the World Systems' Framework

By contrast, at the other extreme to the Neorealists, lie the World Systems theorists, as exemplified by Wallerstein (1974). Here, a sharp distinction can be drawn between the British and Roman empires. From the World Systems perspective, Rome, unlike Britain, is seen to have effectively eliminated competing centers of power; as a consequence, it constituted a "world" empire, whereas the British empire always operated in an anarchic arena made up of competing states. Wallerstein, therefore, draws a sharp structural distinction between empires which exist within an anarchic system and those which transform the system and eliminate the anarchic structure. Wallerstein is one of the few theorists to explore this distinction and it enables him to view world history in terms of alternating patterns of world systems, with anarchic international systems, identified as world economies, being recurrently overtaken by world empires. Anarchic systems, he argues, "were always transformed into empires" (1974:16) and he gives the examples of China, Persia, and Rome. Wallerstein is quite clear that these are all examples of world empires and need to be distinguished from empires, like the British empire, that existed in the context of a broader anarchic system. A world empire is seen to be a self-contained, autonomous unit existing in a global environment. The British Empire, by contrast, was never a self-contained unit. It was always an integral part of a much larger system with which it interacted continuously.

These competing conceptions of empire raise the difficult question of what might be meant by a boundary that circumscribes a world or international system. Neorealists treat the international system as completely closed; it is not considered to have a boundary. They are unconcerned about the question of how to define the boundary of a world or international system. On the other hand, the question of boundary definition is of central importance for world systems theorists. For them, it is essential to be able to identify the grounds on which the Roman Empire, for example, can be treated as a closed system. It is on the basis of the conception of a bounded system that Wallerstein is able to argue that prior to the modern world system, a number of world systems always coexisted on the earth's surface, taking the form of either a world empire or a world economy. He argues that these world systems coexisted and should not be seen as components of a larger social system because life within each of the systems was "largely self-contained" and the dynamics of development in the system were "largely internal" (1974:347). This formulation accepts, in other words, that there was some contact between the coexisting world systems. But it also presupposes that the contact was insufficient to have any material effect.

Despite the extensive discussions of Wallerstein's work, little attention has been paid to his notion of a bounded international system or to the structural distinction he draws between a world empire and a world economy. The failure to explore the distinction says a good deal about the ethnocentric and state-centric orientation of the contemporary discipline of International Relations. The absence of discussion can be accounted for by the general lack of interest displayed by specialists in international relations in either world history or comparative method (Onuf:1982).

Empires in the World Historian's Framework

When attention is turned to the work of world historians, it becomes apparent that they do not endorse the concept of empire developed by either the Neorealists or the world systems theorists. The theoretical framework developed in world history not only poses problems for the Neorealist conception of empires operating in a closed or unbounded anarchic system but also throws up difficulties for the distinction drawn by the World Systems theorists between world empires, like the Roman Empire, formed within a closed or bounded system and the mercantile empires, like the British Empire, which constitute a type of state operating in an open anarchic system. Bozeman points out, in the first instance, that although the empires of Han China and

Rome coexisted they both pretended to hold "unique and undisputed power." Both regarded the frontiers of their respective empires as the limits of the civilized world. Nevertheless, they each knew of the other's existence and they maintained contact indirectly by means of trade. Moreover, Bozeman identifies a "steady flow of intellectually adventurous people" who managed to stimulate a "general awareness in the ancient world that no one empire is ever quite as self-sufficient as it pretends to be." It was certainly the case that "the two world states and the great area of Indian civilization touched at their peripheries" (Bozeman 1960:162–164). Bozeman goes on to assert that Han China aimed to synchronize "explorative diplomacy, economic infiltration, and military pressure, with the ultimate purpose of pressing through to the West." And she argues that Rome used similar tactics when it extended to the East. So both China and Rome must have contemplated the consequences of a direct confrontation. Bozeman goes on to argue that:

> Contrary to what one might expect under such circumstances, this prospect does not seem to have fanned fear or rivalry in either of the imperial camps. The indications are to the contrary, namely that their imperialistic policies moved each of these two powers towards an interest in direct, reciprocal, and friendly commercial relations. It is impossible to say whether this amicable attitude would have endured following the consummation of a direct meeting, however, for the Sino-Roman trade was destined to remain indirect (1960:169).

McNeill (1979), has established a general theoretical framework that builds upon this idea of indirect cultural contact. Empires can be viewed as a subordinate component of this broad scheme. According to McNeill, it is possible to explore world history on the basis of competing civilizations. He traces the evolution of four centers of civilization which, he argues, emerged in the period to 500 B.C.; the civilizations were located in Greece, India, China and the Middle East. McNeill's central organizing idea indicates that whenever a development took place in a community which was seen to make it more attractive or more powerful, then the techniques or ideas underlying the development would be borrowed and adapted by neighbors and neighbors' neighbors to suit their local conditions. By the processes of borrowing and adaption, the four civilizations managed to retain their distinctive characters while coexisting in a rough equilibrium for two thousand years from 500 B.C. to 1500 A.D.

The four civilizations, according to McNeill, occupied but did not cover the Eurasian land mass. They were separated by bands of territory inhabited by nomadic peoples. They were characterized by the Greeks and Romans as barbarians. Inevitably, as the four civilizations developed, they also expanded into the territory occupied by the barbarians, thereby reducing what McNeill refers to as the "barbarian zones," which served to insulate one civilization from another. Although contact between the civilizations increased, McNeill insists that their autonomy and the overall equilibrium between them was maintained.

There is obviously a degree of similarity here between McNeill and the Neorealists, with both pointing to the existence of a balance maintained on the basis of a process of diffusion between autonomous entities. Moreover, in each case, the balance is viewed as an unintended consequence of action taken within the entities. But there are also substantial differences between the two analyses. The entities identified by Waltz are hierarchically organized political units he refers to as states. The term is seen to embrace political actors as different as tribes, city states, and empires. By contrast, McNeill makes reference to civilizations where the identifying link is cultural. Within a civilization, he suggests, individuals conform to a "loose yet coherent life style" (McNeill 1979:v). Moreover, despite the equilibrium between the civilizations, these life-styles are seen to have diverged very substantially. The variations were certainly sufficient to ensure that the political configurations in each civilization were quite distinct. So, for example, although the Chinese civilization fragmented politically on several occasions when it came under pressure from the barbarians, political unity was always reestablished. For most of its history, China operated, in Wallerstein's terms, as a world empire. By contrast, the civilizations that evolved around Greece took a very different form. At one point, it was transformed, by the Romans, into a world empire. But the empire eventually fragmented. And in contrast to China, attempts to restore the empire failed so that the civilization remained politically fragmented.

There are other obvious differences between McNeill and Waltz. The Neorealist framework focuses on an international system that consists of interacting states. These states are considered to be mutually vulnerable, because they all represent a potential threat to each other. But in the case of McNeill, the emphasis is on civilizations that tend to coexist rather than coact. McNeill observes some interaction but identifies it as a "disturbance" or "shock" which upsets the equilibrium between the civilizations. It is possible, he argues, to identify four major disturbances in the period between 500 B.C. and 1500 A.D. These represent major "bench marks" in the course of world history (McNeill 1979:129). The first two disturbances, the Greek penetration of the Middle East and the extension of Indian influence into China and Japan, had few long-term consequences because there was a reassertion of the indigenous civilization. But other "bench marks" represented by the spread of Islam from the Middle East and the capitalist expansion of the West were both to have major and long-term consequences for other civilizations.

But these "shocks" to McNeill's cultural equilibrium are very different from the disturbances associated with Waltz's political balance of power. McNeill's framework embraces both the Roman Empire and the Han Chinese Empire which were linked by a process of cultural diffusion. But the two empires cannot both be included within the Neorealist framework, where balance of power theory presupposes that states pose each other with a direct threat and, by the same token, provide each other with the possibility of direct assistance. The Roman and Chinese empires were not linked in this way. McNeill's framework suggests that the boundary drawn by Wallerstein is too tight. It ignores the complex nonpolitical interactions that took place across the frontiers of the Roman Empire. In comparing these three approaches it quickly becomes apparent how dependent each of them is on certain assumptions about the types and levels of interaction capacity in the system. It also becomes clear how vital it is to achieving any understanding of international systems to develop a clearly specified interaction level of analysis.

World Empires in the Structural Realist Framework

The impossibility of dealing with the Roman Empire as a closed system becomes immediately apparent once it is acknowledged that the frontiers were never static. Throughout the history of the empire the boundaries were either expanding or contracting. Nor is it possible to suggest that a process of expansion gave way eventually to a process of contraction. The evolution of the Roman Empire was much more complex than such a formulation allows. But it can be suggested that during the period of major expansion Rome impinged upon and then overtook a number of independent or relatively autonomous regional subsystems.

It is not helpful, therefore, to depict the expansion of Rome in the context of a closed Neorealist system of states. It makes more sense to identify the growth of Rome taking place initially within an expanding subsystem that coexisted with and then eventually overtook other subsystems made up of political units that could be sharply differentiated from Rome. The agents of these units perceived themselves to be operating within an international subsystem that was relatively autonomous. The Greeks, for example, as Herodotus (1987) makes clear, were conscious of two international systems: the system of Greek city states and the Persian empire. According to Herodotus, these two systems naturally balanced each other and had to be kept separate but equal. Herodotus "deals with a period which constitutes a disturbance of that order by the unlimited expansionism of the Persians" (Immerwahr 1966:306). Waltz would argue, of course, that the Persians and the Greek city states were operating within a single international system. But this is not how the agents of the state saw the situation. They clearly acknowledged the need to establish boundaries between independent international systems. They were also aware when these boundaries were becoming vulnerable. World history reveals, moreover, that the Romans, in contrast to the Persians, were able to eliminate the boundaries that separated divergent subsystems of states. It is clear that the concept of *interaction capacity* can help to give some purchase on the approach developed by the world historians. One of our major aims here is to extend our framework so that it can further clarify the relationship between these subsystems and the overarching international system.

STRUCTURE, TRANSFORMATION AND THE ROMAN EMPIRE

From a Neorealist perspective, the Roman Empire is an inappropriate choice to illustrate the potential for structural transformation and continuity in the international system. For the Neorealists, the case simply provides an example of a successful unit operating in an anarchic arena of states. But as we have seen, neither Wallerstein nor

McNeill would endorse this assessment. Within the context of their frameworks, the Roman Empire poses Neorealist theory with some tricky problems. Nevertheless, most theorists in the field of International Relations have, until recently, largely ignored the enormous and controversial literature associated with its rise and fall. It could be argued that this evasion has occurred primarily because the evolution of the empire does not fit neatly into the familiar interstate framework used to analyze more recent history. As a consequence, with only a few exceptions, there has been no exchange of ideas between the study of international relations and the study of the Roman Empire. Indeed, it is the difficulties associated with any attempt to analyze the history of the Roman Empire in the state-centric framework that makes it an appropriate case study to draw upon to test the strengths of Structural Realism.

The emergence of the Roman empire provides, in the first place, an important instance when the balance of power apparently failed to function. According to Neorealism, competing political units, observing the expansion of Rome, should have been willing to collaborate in order to keep Rome in check. But this failed to happen, thereby falsifying the theory. Morrow has noted, for example, that as the Roman Empire expanded, the Diadochi Empires (Macedonia, the Seleucid Empire, and Ptolemaic Egypt) preferred to fight among themselves rather than form an alliance against the ascendant power. "Why" asks Morrow "does Waltz's argument about the stability of anarchic systems fail in this case?" (1988:87). He could have asked the same question in the context of the Italian city states at the end of the fifteenth century. Instead of consolidating their strength against the emerging nation-states, the French were encouraged by Milan in 1494 to intervene in Italy, thereby fueling an established imperial trait in France. In both these cases, Waltz's theory provides no obvious explanation as to why the necessary collaboration among the weaker powers failed to occur. Morrow is also unable to offer a solution; the best he can do is to suggest that the most effective way forward is to examine the situation on the basis of a methodology which seeks to synthesize structure and agency. The basic features of this methodology will be looked at in more detail in the next chapter.

Structural Realism provides a possible explanation for the failure of the balance of power theory. It can point, for example, to the subsystemic character of the arena within which Rome expanded, as well as to the functional differentiation of the units within the subsystem. When Rome expanded, it confronted a range of radically different political entities, including the barbarian tribes, the Greek city states, and the sprawling Diadochi empires, operating within semiautonomous subsystems. Waltz's theory assumes that the anarchic arena is made up of identical interacting units operating within a closed system. His framework is, as a consequence, ill-equipped to handle the arena within which Rome operated. By contrast, the Structural Realist framework developed in the previous section offers some possible clues that may account for evolution of the Roman Empire.

The consolidation of the Roman empire took place over a relatively long period of time. The Romans first absorbed the Italian peninsula, then they moved west, gaining control of the Western Mediterranean and eliminating the Carthaginian empire in the process. Only after their rule was secure in the West did the Romans turn to challenge the well-established and civilized empires and city states in the East. Once these areas had been engulfed by the empire, it becomes necessary to raise the question as to whether the Romans had managed to transform the structure of the international system in which they were operating. The question raises an interesting theoretical issue which the Waltzian framework must necessarily push to one side.

The competing structural assessments of the Roman Empire, therefore, have important theoretical repercussions. Waltz, for example, expresses an interest in imperialism, but his theory requires him to deny that imperialism can precipitate system transformation. Of course, Waltz can accept in principle that the movement from an international system to a world empire represents a structural transformation. But he works on the assumption that there has never been a world empire and that all empires in the past have existed in the context of a wider international system. This line of argument is certainly valid for the Diadochi Empires, but as already noted, the argument has been questioned in the context of the Roman Empire. Although it is true that the empire did not extend to the limits of the known world, a Roman goal which remained unrealized, it is possible to argue that the empire was effectively an autonomous system.

A number of recent theorists have begun to acknowledge that the Roman Empire provides a useful heuristic for breaking away from the established state-centric view of the world. The empire is now being recognized as a distinctive type of international actor. It is beginning to be argued that by understanding how the empire operated, it may be possible to come to terms with the process of system transformation in the contemporary international system. Strange has argued, for example, that to understand the role of the United States in the modern world it is essential to "escape the corset-like intellectual constraints of the conventional study of international relations"[1989:11]. These constraints are seen to be perpetuated by Neorealists. From Strange's perspective, Waltz, in keeping with other Realists, is bound by a spatial image of the international system which is seen to be neatly divided into territorial plots. Only by erasing this image, argues Strange, can we come to understand that from a contemporary perspective the nature of American power and the character of the American Empire is not territorial in character. Once the constraints of the prevailing perspective are escaped then it becomes possible to see, first, that it is necessary to draw a sharp distinction between the contemporary American Empire and the now dissolved European Empires and, second, that there are a number of interesting parallels between the American Empire and the Roman Empire that also need to be understood in nonterritorial terms. Strange calls for a careful study of the various forms empires have taken in the past and she is convinced that such a study will require scholars to transcend the structural barriers imposed by Waltz.

In making this point, she is confirming an argument made by Luttwak, who considers that the nature of security in the Roman Empire has more in common with the security problems that confronted the Western world in the aftermath of the Second World War than is generally realized. He asserts, furthermore, that scholars of the Roman Empire, like modern strategic analysts, are conditioned by a set of assumptions about the international system that reflect nineteenth-century prejudices. In attacking the judgments of contemporary scholars of the Roman Empire, he argues that they reflect "a seemingly ineradicable Clausewizian prejudice against defensive strategies and defensive construction—a prejudice as common among historians writing of Hadrian and his policies as among contemporary military analysts discussing today's ballistic missile defences" (1977:61). Luttwak believes that, paradoxically, the effect of the revolutionary changes in modern war "has been to bring the strategic predicament of the Romans much closer to our own" (1977:xii). This is an intriguing line of argument that raises important questions about the nature of structural transformation. Like Strange, therefore, Luttwak draws on the example of the Roman Empire to challenge the universality of the framework putatively advanced by the Neorealists.

There is one further point to be made about the value of using the Roman Empire as a case study to illustrate a theoretical discussion about continuity and transformation in the international system. It concerns the difficulty confronted by the Neorealist framework in dealing with the collapse of the Roman Empire. The difficulty arises because the reasons underpinning the demise of a state have not been explored by the Neorealists. Waltz argues that the "death" of a state in the international system, in contrast to the "death" of a firm in the marketplace is an unusual event. As Halliday (1989) argues, however, this is not a proposition that can be sustained when the broad sweep of history is considered. It becomes an extremely interesting theoretical question, therefore, as to why some states fail to survive. The initial success of the Roman Empire draws attention to the importance of the issue. Rome initially brought about the demise of a large number of apparently successful political actors. The question of survival under conditions of anarchy becomes even more interesting in the context of the fall of the Roman Empire because it is far from clear why the Western half of the empire, confronted by a series of weak and divided tribes, should have collapsed so completely and so rapidly while the Eastern half of the empire, confronted not only by the same tribes, but also the massive and powerful Persian empire, should have been able to survive and continue to flourish for another thousand years.

It is hoped that by using the Roman Empire as a case study, it will provide at least a crude test for some of the theoretical ideas that are discussed in this section. Attention is focused on the formation, expansion, and collapse of the Roman Empire not only because, like the Medieval period, it has been very generally ignored by theorists in International Relations, but also because it does throw up a series of difficulties for the Waltzian framework. Inevitably, it is not possible to do more than to provide a brief sketch of some of the titanic developments associated with the history of Rome. But the case study material helps to illuminate the theoretical propositions and justifies the need to think about transformation of the international system at a structural and a systemic level.

CHAPTER SIX

Structural Realism and the Agent-Structure Debate

It is necessary first to examine in more detail some of the theoretical and methodological problems associated with system transformation. At first sight, the Neorealists seem unlikely to throw any light on these problems. As already noted, Neorealists such as Waltz presuppose that there has been no transformation in the structure of the international system. Indeed, the Neorealist theory of international politics is designed to explain why the anarchic structure of the international system has persisted throughout world history. Yet paradoxically, an investigation of the Neorealist position, and Waltz's arguments in particular, proves to be surprisingly revealing. Although at first it was assumed that Waltz's views on the theoretical and methodological issues associated with system transformation were unproblematic, closer investigation shows that this is not the case.

It is possible, however, to open up the idea of system transformation to theoretical investigation by drawing on the literature of the agent-structure debate. Although this debate has always been a central feature of theoretical and methodological discussions in most social sciences, the attempt to look at its implications for International Relations has been relatively recent. Waltz, for example, makes reference to both structure and agents in *TIP*, but he does not discuss the relationship between them, nor does he conceive of their conjunction as a problem. Nevertheless, Waltz does unwittingly provide a key that can help to resolve the agent-structure debate in International Relations, and lead the way to a better understanding of system transformation.

BACKGROUND TO THE DEBATE

While the idea of structure is, of course, a familiar if problematic concept, ideas about agents and agency have received much less attention; moreover, the concept of agency, or, at any rate, the terminology, is much less familiar in the discipline of International Relations. Yet once attention is focused on the concept of agency, it quickly becomes apparent that structure and agent are inextricably linked.

Agency is defined in *Webster's New International Dictionary* as the "faculty or state of acting or exerting power." This is broadly what the term has come to mean in social theory. Although there have been attempts to restrict the use of power to human agency, these have not succeeded. As a consequence, power has been analyzed in terms of both structure and agency. The resulting conceptions of power, however, are very different. Structural explanations often turn human agents into lifeless puppets whose behavior is regulated by impersonal social forces. Explanations couched in terms of agency, by contrast, generally presuppose that it is human beings who control events in a social system. It is often suggested that an agent-based theory must embrace the intentions, the beliefs, the desires and the goals of the agents who act in the system. But Onuf (1989) has argued that a sharp distinction must be drawn between rational choice theories and hermeneutic or phenomenological theories of agents. The former type of theory presupposes that individuals are goal-oriented creatures, and that, because individuals strive to be rational, once these goals have been identified behavior becomes readily explicable and predictable. The latter type of theory, on the other hand, assumes that human beings are motivated by complex beliefs; analysts need to empathize with these beliefs before human actions can be comprehended and interpreted. Both types of theory are premised on the idea of the agent, but they are developed on the basis of very different epistemological perspectives. Onuf goes on to suggest that the study of International Relations has "no name for, or experience with" the latter type of theory (1989:56). However, the sharp distinction between these two approaches needs to be modified if the agent-structure problem is to be resolved.

The essence of the problem associated with structure and agency is quickly and easily expressed. It arises because explanations in the social sciences so frequently operate at one of two extremes. At one extreme, human beings are seen to be free agents with the power to maintain or transform the social systems in which they operate. At the other extreme, it is assumed that human beings are caught in the grip of social structures which they did not create and over which they have no control. The problem of structure and agency exists because of the failure to find any way of synthesizing these two extreme positions. Although familiar throughout the social sciences, the problem has only recently been introduced into discussions of international politics. When reference is made to the agent-structure problem in the international context, attention is almost always drawn to Waltz, who is seen to provide a perfect example of an analyst working in a purely structural mold. Critics argue that his structurally deterministic approach fails not only to leave room for human agency but also even to acknowledge the problematic nature of the relationship between structure and agent.

The accusation that Waltz has failed to accommodate the agent-structure problem does less than justice to the subtlety of his position. Indeed, there is a link between the approach adopted by Waltz and a solution to the problem of structure and agency alighted upon recently by a number of social theorists, in particular, Archer (1985, 1988), Giddens (1979), Taylor (1989), and Wendt (1987).

In one of the most extensive discussions of the agent-structure problem, Archer has suggested that it is "part and parcel of daily experience to feel both free and enchained, capable of shaping our own future and yet confronted by towering, seemingly impersonal constraints." It follows, then, that the methodological task of integrating structure and agency brings the social theorist face to face with "the most pressing social problem of the human condition" (1988:x). Yet despite the apparent universality of the problem created by the tension between structure and agency, social scientists have tended to shy away from it and have been drawn instead toward either agent-based explanations, which stress the capacity of individuals to mold the world they live in, or to structure-based explanations, which highlight the existence of unyielding social forces that shape our daily round. In the context of this bifurcation, Waltz has been neatly pigeonholed as a structuralist. Yet, with the benefit of hindsight, it can be seen that he is in the vanguard of the growing body of theorists who have reacted against both agent and structure based explanations of social behavior.

PROBLEMS WITH STRUCTURAL ACCOUNTS

It is now widely accepted that any social theory must be able to generate explanations that take account of both structure and agency.

One of the major problems with structural explanations, according to Giddens, is that they deny a role for the agent, thereby reducing human beings to "cultural dopes" of "stunning mediocrity"(1979:52). In structural explanations, human beings are moved around like pawns on a chessboard, by abstract, nonobservable forces that take no account of individual desires or beliefs. But as Grafstein asks, exactly how do "abstract entities constrain flesh-hued individuals?" (1988). In structural accounts, no answer is given to this question. It has been argued, for example, that Marxists have all too often operated on the basis of a structural theory of history which lacked any appreciation of the people who made this history. Marxists are increasingly coming to recognize that such an approach is inadequate and that it is necessary to ensure that any assessment of state behavior is "consistent with individual rationalities" (Przeworski 1985:383). The structural explanations of non-Marxists have also come under attack. Skocpol's (1979) highly regarded structural theory of revolution, for example, has been critically assessed by Taylor (1989). Skocpol argues that revolutions take place only when certain structural preconditions exist. It is then argued that these structural features of the system cannot be accounted for in agency terms. Taylor takes one of these preconditions, the solidarity of peasant communities, and endeavors to reveal how the solidarity is amenable to an agency based explanation. He argues that in prerevolutionary France and Russia, the state deliberately introduced measures designed to increase the solidarity of the peasantry. The purpose was either to undercut the influence of regional lords or to increase the revenue of the state. It follows that it is possible to show that Skocpol's structural prerequisites are, in fact, the outcome of rational and intentional actions.

PROBLEMS WITH AGENCY ACCOUNTS

But even if this argument is accepted, it remains the case, as Archer asserts so forcefully, that we are constantly aware that we are not free agents. There is, as a consequence, extreme skepticism over attempts to develop a theory of action expressed only in terms of the intentions, goals, desires, and beliefs of individual agents. Three factors negate a purely individualistic theory of action.

First, the outcome of many actions taken by one individual tends to be contingent upon action taken by another. Such situations are characterized in terms of strategic interaction. To take a simple example, if a motorist drives through a crossroad without stopping, then the outcome is determined by the intersection of this action with the behavior of the drivers on the other road. Levi has argued that one of the reasons why game theory has become so popular as a methodology in social science is because it reveals in such straightforward and remarkably clear terms "how the choice of one individual or group of individuals affects the choice of others" (1988:63). A game matrix describes how the choices of two individuals intersect, as in the case of the drivers coming to an intersection, and it illuminates how the structure of the situation they find themselves in constrains their choice of action. The matrix reveals that no rational agent operating in a structure where two decisions arrived at independently intersect can fail to take the possible actions of the other agent into account.

Second, personal experience confirms that individual action is conditioned by social institutions, some of which may even be extremely unpopular. Individuals may stand when the national anthem is being sung, for example, not out of any sense of patriotism, but simply because everyone else is standing. The example, of course, raises questions about how such institutions come into existence (Grafstein:1988). It is generally accepted that institutions are established in the first instance in an attempt to facilitate social intercourse. Institutions can help to alleviate the problems created by strategic interaction. Traffic lights can be placed at a crossroad in order to constrain the behavior of drivers, but in such a fashion as to be mutually beneficial. The traffic lights modify the existing structure. But it is also the case that social institutions can remain in place, continuing to constrain the behavior of individuals, long after they have ceased to serve their original purpose.

Third, the actions of social agents often have unintended consequences. Giddens notes that "the consequences of action chronically escape the initiators' intentions in processes of objectification" (1979:44). In a conflict situation, for example, one party may hold a parade in order to boost internal morale. An unintended consequence could be to inflame the opinions of the opposition. By the same token, a social institution established at one point in time for perfectly explicable reasons, may remain in force long after the initial reasons have disappeared. Social customs, which so often perform the unintended function of distinguishing insiders from outsiders, can frequently come about in this way.

RESOLVING THE AGENT-STRUCTURE PROBLEM

The importance attached to the idea of institutional and structural constraints has encouraged the conclusion that any social theory needs to accommodate both agency and structure. In one of the best known attempts to tackle this problem, Giddens asserts that there is a dialectical relationship between structure and agency. Very far from being cultural dopes, pushed around by impersonal social structures, Giddens depicts social agents as knowledgeable and reflexive, having not only a sophisticated view of the world and how it is structured, but also the ability to monitor their actions in the light of this knowledge. As a consequence, social agents are constantly performing actions, often intentionally, but sometimes unintentionally, which ensure that social structures are reproduced.

So, for example, there is a complex set of social institutions that shape the behavior of motorists. These structural constraints are observed, not because of the sanctions imposed on deviants, but because of the reflexive ability to see what would happen in situations of strategic interaction if the structures did not exist. It follows, as Wendt notes, that "social structures are only instantiated by the practices of agents." In other words, a structure acts as a constraint only because agents choose to be constrained; if they were not constrained, there would be no structures. By the same token, social structures are depicted as being "inseparable from the reasons and self-understandings that agents bring to their actions" [Wendt 1987:359].

It is being argued, for example, that motorists stop at red lights, not because they fear that a violation of the rule would lead to prosecution, but because they appreciate the reasoning behind the decision to locate traffic lights in a particular position. So it follows that a structure constitutes a structure only because of the behavior of the agent, which in turn is intimately bound up with knowledge of the structure. As Giddens puts it, "structure is both medium and outcome of the reproduction of practices." He refers to his method as the duality of structure or structuration which he argues is an appropriate basis for social explanations because of the essential "recursiveness" of social life (1979:93). It is because of recursiveness that it is not possible to draw a rigid distinction between rational actor and hermeneutic theories.

The term "recursiveness" is not familiar in the field of International Relations. Yet it is now making its way into the literature. Onuf defines recursion as "the propensity of knowledgeable agents to refer to their own or others" past and anticipated actions in deciding how to act" (1989:62). Giddens who has discussed the idea and implications of recursion extensively, refers to the phenomenon as "reflexive self-regulation" (1979:78). But, in fact, this graphic phrase simply provides a more vivid way of expressing Schelling's more mundane reference to "interdependent decision making" which lies at the root of his conception of strategy (Schelling 1960: ch. 4). Schelling's familiar discussion of how a husband and wife, separated in a department store, have to resort to interdependent decision-making in order to make contact again can just as easily be discussed in terms of reflexive self-regulation. Recursion, therefore, may represent a new term, but it identifies a familiar phenomenon. Indeed, it can be argued further that Schelling had a handle on the "agent-structure problem" nearly thirty years before it was self-consciously identified by social theorists and then extended into the field of international relations. And the conception is certainly not unique to Schelling.

The concept takes on a new dimension when social theorists like Giddens have extended the idea of a recursive process to describe the mutual constitution of agents and structures. Giddens insists that although the activities associated with any habitual social practice will not have been introduced by any given agent, nevertheless, by engaging in the practice, the agent will "reproduce the conditions that make these activities possible" (Giddens 1984:2). By analogy, when people walk across a field, they may unintentionally create a path. Others subsequently follow and in doing so "reproduce" the path (See Little 1985). The idea of recursion gives this process a social dimension. When Americans motor in Britain, for example, they automatically start to drive on the left-hand side of the road because they anticipate that other drivers will be doing the same thing. Contemporary social theorists interested in the agent-structure problem have extended the line of analysis pioneered by Schelling, and have now linked it to the idea of recursion, to develop a theory that explains the reproduction of the structures which underpin any social system.

The solution to the problem of structure and agency presented by Giddens has not been greeted with universal approval. It has been subjected to particular criticism by social theorists who have an interest in social change and transformation. By defining structure and agency as mutually constitutive, and a product of recursiveness, Taylor argues that Giddens has made it impossible to "unravel the causal interplay between agent and structure over time and account for social change" (1989:118). Taylor wants to argue that social action can, over time, erode the existence of a social structure and replace it with another. So, for example, if one road on an intersection with traffic lights becomes more busy than the other, because of recursion or "reflexive self-regulation," there will be an increasing tendency to "jump" the lights. At that juncture, the lights become a source of danger and either the timing of the lights will be changed or they will be replaced by an alternative structure.

Archer has also disputed the approach adopted by Giddens. She acknowledges that Giddens is aware of the potential for social change, but she insists that Giddens can only depict social change in terms of a gestalt switch. Making use of the road intersection example, again, Giddens, it is argued can depict different structural solutions to the problem created in situations of strategic interaction—say, traffic lights or an underpass—but what he cannot do is analyze the process whereby one structure gives way to an other. Archer insists that an adequate solution to the structure-agency problem must make provision for an analyst being able to identify different degrees of freedom for an agent and to specify different levels of constraint imposed by a structure. It must be possible to observe the nature of the structure and the behavior of the agent changing gradually over time. As Taylor notes "to conflate structure and action (as Giddens does) is to rule out from the start the possibility of explaining change in terms of their interaction over time" (1989,149). These analysts are clearly seeking a way to understand the relationship between continuity and transformation in a system.

To achieve this objective, Archer insists that it is essential to draw an analytical distinction between structure and agent (while recognizing that it may be correct to describe them, empirically, as mutually constitutive). By doing this, it becomes possible to examine them independently, and in this way explore how the activity of social agents can, over time, bring a transformation in social structure. Such a formulation, however, does not seem to violate the spirit of Giddens, who is unquestionably interested in how social systems develop along the dimensions of time and space. Central to his whole enterprise is the desire to identify how and why the nature of socio-political systems have changed so dramatically over time. So, for example, he focuses on the way that the distance between societies, expressed in terms of the conjunction of time and space, has been so very substantially compressed in the modern world. He has also increasingly acknowledged that the nature of society has been constantly influenced by its international setting. As a consequence, he has begun to develop a framework that allows him to explore the interaction between the structure of the state and the structure of the international system. This enterprise overlaps in some important ways with the approach of Section 1, where the compression of time and space in the international system, referred to there as interaction capacity, is seen to be a property of the systemic level of analysis.

WALTZ AND THE AGENT-STRUCTURE PROBLEM

The task of resolving the agent-structure problem is complicated at the international level because the agent is not an individual but an institution. As a consequence, attention is centered on the formulation of a deep structure based on the configuration between political units in the anarchic international system. When one examines the complex interaction between the structure of the state and the structure of the international system, one raises the agent-structure problem in an acute form.

Neorealists circumvent the problem by treating the state as a rational actor. So although Waltz accepts that human agents are engaged not only in the task of reproducing their own political unit, but also the system within which those units operate, he appears to bracket, and then ignore, the process at the unit level. Before turning to our more complex Structural Realist approach, it is useful to see what light the recent attempts to handle the agent-structure problem throws on Waltz's apparently straightforward formulation. Superficially, Waltz appears to exemplify the work of a theorist who has resolutely ignored the problem of structure and agency; it is nevertheless possible to show that Waltz has independently alighted on a solution to the problem that coincides with the position now being adopted in other areas of the social sciences.

At first sight, it may appear that there is something perverse about this line of argument because it runs so counter to the established assessment of Waltz. *TIP* has been very widely discussed and it is almost invariably held, even by its critics, to be providing an unambiguously clear exposition of a structural approach to the analysis of international politics. The critics may go on to attack structuralism but they never question that Waltz is a true and faithful exponent of this methodological stance. Waltz has also been seen to play a major role in the upsurge of interest in a structural approach to the study of international relations. The growing interest has been so rapid and extensive that it has even been argued that structuralism now represents the dominant mode of analysis in international relations (Zacher 1987:173). Such a claim is debatable, but it is unquestionably the case that structuralism has become a significant feature in the discipline and that Waltz is considered to be the chief architect.

It is not difficult to see why Waltz has been so closely associated with structuralism. The central theme of *TIP* is that there has been a persistent failure by theorists in the discipline to ascribe an independent role to the structure of the international system. It is presupposed, not always intentionally, according to Waltz, that the behavior of states (variously referred to as units, actors, and agents) can be explained only in terms of their internal properties. In other words, Waltz is primarily interested in opposing a unit-based theory of international politics. Such a theory is considered to be reductionist. But reductionism is not seen, necessarily, to be a methodological sin. Waltz accepts that the systems examined by physical scientists are amenable to a reductionist form of analysis. But he insists that the complex systems examined by social scientists do not fall into this category. In social systems, he argues, agents are constrained by the structure of the systems in which they operate and explanations need to take account of these structures. It is for this reason that Waltz has been designated as a structuralist.

The inaccuracy of this description quickly becomes apparent when Waltz's methodology is explored from the perspective of an analyst attempting to overcome the problem of structure and agency. Wendt, for example, has drawn on the idea of structuration. His line of analysis points him in the direction of the argument developed by Archer and Taylor, with the result that Wendt also asserts that both the structure of the international system and the agents operating within it must be given an independent ontological status. He adopts the epistemological posture that invisible structures have just as tangible an existence as the individual agents constrained by them. This line of argument is related to the philosophical posture identified as scientific realism. The link between structuration theory and scientific realism is now coming under close scrutiny. (Layder:1990). It will not be examined here. The whole debate about structure and agency takes on an additional complexity in the international context because states are generally identified as the principal agents. But this equation is simply a form of shorthand. Reference is actually being made to the human agents who represent the state. The state, like the international system, needs to be conceived of as a set of structures. In the international context, therefore, agents are constrained by the structure of the state as well as the structure of the international system. The state, as a consequence, is no more visible than the international system. Wendt insists that both must be accorded equal ontological status and he asserts that it is not possible to develop a coherent and effective theory of international politics without treating both the system and the state as problematic. A theory of international politics must be able to explain the emergence and development of both the state and the system. Wendt argues that this is not "mindless synthesis" because it "forces us to rethink fundamental properties of (state) agents and system structures" (1987:339).

Working from this perspective, Wendt is able to see quite clearly that Waltz cannot be classified as a structuralist. On the contrary, he argues that Waltz and other Neorealists have managed to develop a "conception of the agent-structure relationship in international relations which recognizes the causal role of both state agents and system structures" (1987:341). But he goes on to argue that the Neorealists develop an "individualist definition of the structure of the international system as reducible to the properties of states" and that, as a consequence, the approach must be considered "decidedly state-or agent-centric" (1987:341–42). Ironically, from this perspective Waltz certainly cannot be considered to be a wholehearted structuralist; and while Wendt accepts that Waltz does provide a solution to the structure-agency problem, he also makes clear that the solution is deeply flawed, not because of its emphasis on structure but because of its bias toward agency. Wendt contrasts Waltz unfavorably with the world systems approach adopted by Wallerstein, although Wallerstein is also seen to provide an inadequate solution. Wendt's assessment of Waltz runs directly counter to the one developed by Hollis and Smith (1990), who depict Waltz as an unreformed structuralist. In a subsequent debate between Wendt (1991) and Hollis and Smith (1991), neither side is willing to accept that their divergent interpretations could be reconciled by accepting that Waltz's position is compatible with the idea of structuration. To justify this interpretation, it is necessary to demonstrate that Waltz has a theory of the state as well as a theory of the international system and that, in accordance with the structurationalist methodology, the one instantiates the other. Waltz's theory of the state is examined in the next chapter.

CHAPTER SEVEN

Agency and Competing Theories
of the State

A major criticism leveled at Waltz relates to his conception of the units in the international system. As already noted, Waltz has been attacked for being unconcerned about the ontology of the units. He is seen to argue that the rigid structure of the international system will have an unchanging impact on the behavior of states irrespective of their internal characteristics. Critics argue that this reputed lack of interest in the state has fatal consequences for his theory of international politics because it means that he is unable to account for the origins of either the state or the system. According to Wendt, the problem arises because in Neorealist analysis, the state is treated as an ontological given—a primitive concept which does not require further explanation. Wendt, however, also asserts that the state is a concept that requires the sort of substantial explanation that can be provided only by a full-blown theory of the state.

This line of argument then leads Wendt to attack Waltz's conception of the structure of the international system. He argues that Waltz defines the structure in terms of the distribution of power among states in the system. As a consequence, the international system can only be thought of in terms of states, because the structure of the system has been defined by the characteristics of the constituent agents. It follows that it is not possible to think of the system pre-existing the state and helping the state to emerge. So no generative element exists within the system to account for the formation of the state, or, indeed, any new kind of structure for the system. Wendt accepts Ruggie's argument that the theory can account only for how states once in existence endlessly reproduce themselves and the system in which they operate. There is no provision for system transformation.

WALLERSTEIN'S THEORY OF THE STATE

Wendt contrasts this approach to the international system with the one established by Wallerstein. He argues that Wallerstein's framework represents an improvement because the structure of the international system is not defined in terms of the attributes of the agents under investigation. It is therefore possible to develop a theory to explain how the state emerged in the first instance. In contrast to the Neorealists, therefore, the world systems theorists have access to a theory of the state rather than to pre-theoretical intuition. The world systems theory of the state is embedded in the theory of the world economy. According to world systems theory, at the end of the Middle Ages an economic surplus began to be produced. As a consequence, trade began to increase and an economic division began to take place, with some regions becoming responsible for the production of primary products and other regions concentrating on more advanced activities—processing primary products, ship-building, and banking. Each economic activity, it is argued, produced a particular type of labor and a specific type of class structure and there was a movement away from the simple feudal relations that had prevailed during the Middle Ages. Complexity required a stronger state to mediate among the conflicting classes and to assert collective interests in the international arena. The strong states could then use their power to establish increasingly beneficial terms of trade, thereby reinforcing their power. It follows that the strong states operated at the core of the international system, while the weak states operated at the periphery.

Wallerstein argues, therefore, that "the world economy develops a pattern where state structures are relatively strong in the core areas and relatively weak in the periphery"(1974:355). The center then pursues policies that have the effect of reproducing the structure of the system, although the world systems theorists also acknowledge that the world economy operates on the basis of its own logic and that states do not stay in the same position. Change is possible and is identified when states move from the center to the periphery of the world economy. The basic structure of the system, however, remains unaltered, although Wallerstein does assume that at some point in the future there will be system transformation and the existing exploitative world economy will give way to a more just socialist world system.

Gourevitch (1978) has identified some very serious weaknesses in the approach. In the first place he points to a certain circularity in the argument. It is unclear if states are powerful because they are at the center of the world economy or if they are at the center of the world economy because they are powerful. The issue becomes more problematic when attention is turned to the empirical correlation between strong states and core economies. Gourevitch analyzed conditions in 1550, when the situation was as follows:

> *Core economies*: Netherlands, northern Italy, southeastern England, parts of Spain, parts of France, parts of Southern Germany and Portugal;
> *Strong states*: Spain, England, France and Portugal.

It follows that some of the most advanced areas had weak states. Conditions had changed by 1700, but from the standpoint of Wallerstein they remain problematic:

> *Core economies*: Britain, France and Netherlands;
> *Strong states*: Britain, France, Prussia, Austria and Sweden.

Here we see that there are more strong states than core economies.

At the very least, this exercise suggests that it is not possible to derive anything like a complete theory of the state on the basis of a theory of the world economy. Nevertheless, it can be suggested that the world systems theorists have a much more advanced theory than the Neorealists.

WALTZ'S THEORY OF THE STATE

Wendt's claim that the Neorealists are devoid of a theory of the state is false. It is possible to extract at least a rudimentary theory from Waltz's *TIP*. In the first instance, Waltz insists that states represent the "primary political units of an era be they city states, empires, or nations." Waltz, therefore, has an undifferentiated theory of the state. His theory also presupposes that the emergence and initial evolution of these institutions is unrelated to the existence of the international system because they precede the existence of such a system. Although he does not elaborate on this point, it can be inferred that he would concur with the view of Thucydides (Pouncey 1980:51) that, in the first instance, states are purely inward looking institutions that lack the necessary power to bring them into contact with each other. It follows that the structure of an international system can only "emerge from the coexistence of states" and is then consolidated by the "coaction" of these units. The international political system, therefore, is deemed to be "individualist in origin," generated "spontaneously and unintentionally" because, as Waltz observes, "No state intends to participate in the formation of a structure by which it and others will be constrained." Because states precede the emergence of an international system Waltz argues that they are "formed and maintained on the basis of self-help." The relevance of self-help may become more important when states start to "coact" but, both before and after that point, the fact remains that whether states "live, prosper or die depends on their own efforts"(1979:91).

Once states are coacting, however, Waltz is quite clear that the structure of the international system does have an important bearing on the development of the state. This is because he believes or theorizes that the ordering principle of anarchy generates a competitive environment. States, it is argued, have no alternative but to compete with each other. This is because the anarchic international arena requires them to formulate self-help solutions to problems. In the absence of a central institution to police cooperative solutions, states have no alternative but to assume that they are operating in an antagonistic or at any rate a competitive system. Their own actions then help to reproduce the system's competitive character.

Waltz therefore acknowledges this competitive logic of anarchy and develops his theory of the state on the assumption that the international system is a "competitive realm" (1979:127). He goes on to argue, as a consequence, that however different states may be when they come into existence, there will be a tendency for certain basic features to converge once they begin to coact in an international system. The reason used to justify this position is very straightforward. In a competitive system, states have no alternative but to try to match any progressive development that occurs in another state. A state that fails to match such developments in other states will inexorably find itself falling behind and becoming vulnerable. As a consequence, any advance in one state will be quickly copied in the others. Waltz observes how states "imitate each other" so that it becomes possible to predict that "states will display characteristics common to competitors"(1979,128). For example, "the weapons of major contenders and even their strategies, begin to look much the same all over the world"

(1979:127). The argument need not be restricted to the military dimension. It operates equally well in the economic domain. Failure to adopt successful commercial practices will give rise to uncompetitive and unsuccessful states.

Waltz's theory of the state, therefore represents the internal dimension of his balance of power theory and thus plays an integral part in the process that maintains the balance of power and, in turn, sustains the anarchic system. Waltz admits, however, that there are limits to his theory of the state. He acknowledges that the theory does not lead one to expect that "emulation will proceed to the point where competitors become identical" nor does it give any clear indication about what will be imitated or "how quickly and closely the imitations will occur"(1979:124). The external dimension of the balance of power—alliance formation—compensates for the deficiencies of the internal dimension.

It is apparent from this discussion that Wendt is incorrect when he argues that Waltz's approach is ontologically reductionist because he has no theory to account for the emergence or generation of the state. As Waltz himself admits, the theory is individualist in origin, but this is not from his point of view a methodological weakness. It is a necessary consequence of his theory of the state. States were ontologically prior to the international system. Once states start to coact, however, Waltz's theory presupposes that there will be a growing homogenization because they exist within an anarchic system.

Because of this homogenization of the state Waltz believes it unnecessary to distinguish between empires, city states or nation states. He assumes the logic associated with strategic interaction will apply to any kind of political unit provided the system is made up of like units, that is, functionally undifferentiated units that emerge as a product of the internal dimension of the balance of power. But Waltz accepts that there will still be differentiation of power between the units in the system. This represents an important feature of the international system. As Waltz sees it, the move from a multipolar to a bipolar system, for example, represents a major change in the system, although not enough to constitute a system transformation. This is because the basic logic of the system remains the same no matter how many units there are in the system or how power is distributed between them. His theory presupposes first that there will no functional differentiation between states because of the internal dimension of the balance

of power, and second that power differentiation between the functionally undifferentiated units will not affect their capacity to reproduce
themselves because of the external dimension of the balance of power.
Waltz's theory of the balance of power thus conceals a theory of the
state in which states are differentiated in terms of power but not
function.

Waltz's theory of international politics does embrace an embryonic
theory of the state, but the theory cannot be incorporated into Structural Realism without considerable development. As it stands, Waltz's
theory is unable to account for why functional differentiation can
become a feature of the international system. We shall now reconstruct
Waltz's theory of the state to account for divergent patterns of adap-
tation, which generates functional differentiation between states.

THEORY OF THE STATE AND THE DOUBLE
SECURITY DILEMMA

While in Section I we opened the way to a consideration of type 4
anarchic systems where political units are functionally differentiated,
we did not explore the nature of this functional differentiation in
detail. As the result of the modifications made in so far in this section
it is also not clear whether or how the idea of functional differentiation
impinges on Waltz's theory of the state and his theory of the balance
of power. Although multinational corporations and colonies are obviously functionally differentiated from states, Waltz insists that they
have relatively little impact on the structure of the international system. As a consequence, although Waltz accepts that many international actors "flourish" in the international system, he insists that only
states, the "major" actors, play any role in defining the structure of the
system (1979:93). But this still leaves open the question of whether
tribes, city states, and empires, all of which Waltz treats as states, are
nevertheless functionally differentiated units. Waltz fails to explore
this issue because his theory of the state commits him to the conclusion that any significant functional differences between political units
will disappear once they start to coact. In other words, the anarchic
structure of the international system generates functional, and therefore structural, uniformity among states.

Waltz's theory predicts that the anarchic structure will over time eliminate the differences between tribes, empires and city-states, because structural pressures push them in the direction of functional uniformity. States are treated as like units; any residual structural or functional differences can then be ignored. Waltz does not deny, of course, that there will be residual functional differences. But he insists that these can be treated as unit-based characteristics, and therefore irrelevant as far as his structural theory is concerned.

One of the obvious dividends of introducing functional differentiation into Waltz's theory is that it forces us to look more closely and take more seriously the presumption that states can be functionally differentiated across time and space. Unlike Waltz, our analysis is not constrained by a homogenized state-centric model. As a consequence, our approach can accommodate, for example, Strange's idea of imperial political units that are not territorially based.

This line of argument runs counter to Waltz's circumscribed theory of the state. Waltz, of course, is unperturbed by the limitations of his theory. From his perspective, before coaction takes place, the structure of the isolated states in the incipient international system may take many different forms. He does not need to explain why these different forms emerge because he is committed to the theory that the functional variations will disappear when states begin to coact. The absence of functional differentiation between states once coaction occurs is considered, as a consequence, to be purely a product of the logic of anarchy that prevails in the international system. Waltz's assumptions about the impact of anarchy and thus the balance of power on the structure of the state allows him to circumvent the need to develop a more sophisticated theory of the state. This escape route is blocked off in our reformulation, which makes explicit provision for functional differentiation between states. As a consequence, it is necessary to develop a more extensive theory—one that needs to take into account that the agents of the state are constrained not only by the international structure associated with the balance of power, but also by the domestic political structure.

The agents of the state, like Janus, are required to look in two directions simultaneously. They are confronted by two sets of structures: one internal and the other external. Waltz is able to override this argument by assuming that the agents of the state are infinitely malleable and operate under no domestic structural constraints. Here this assumption is relaxed and it is accepted, as a consequence, that the two sets of structures generate a double security dilemma. Waltz argues forcefully that the external security dilemma requires the agents of the state to take actions that reproduce the state. But the internal structures of the state also precipitate a security dilemma that constrains the decisionmakers to reproduce the state in a particular fashion. Agents of the state are aware that the fabric of the state can be destroyed not only by external forces, but also by internal forces. To remain in power, they have to respond to the constraints imposed by both external and internal structures. Once it is accepted that agents of the state are constrained by two sets of structures, it becomes possible to understand why the anarchic structure of the international system does not always generate homogeneous units. Structural Realism thus requires us to look more closely at the reasons why domestic structures sometimes prevail over international structures, with the result that, despite coaction, homogenization does not occur and radically different types of political units may coexist within the same system. This line of argument can be illustrated by looking at the very different modes of reproduction adopted by the Greek city states, the Diadochi empires, and the Roman state—all of which eventually coacted within the same subsystem. Once these empirical examples have been explored, it is possible to return to the theoretical implications.

REPRODUCING THE GREEK CITY STATES

The Greek city states were highly successful political communities and continue to elicit respect and admiration. During the course of their history, these small political units managed to survive in an international system that included massive and sometimes hostile empires. Although the internal political structure of the city states changed over time, attempts to transform the states into a single empire, emulating the powerful neighbors of the Greeks, were not successful. Yet despite the ability of the city states to preserve their independence for several centuries, they failed to retain their autonomy when confronted by the power of Rome. As the Roman Empire spread eastwards, it successfully absorbed the independent Greek states as well as the Diadochi empires with which the Greeks had interacted. The capacity of the Greek city states and the Diadochi Empires to interact and the reasons for their demise will be examined later. The aim here is to reveal how the internal structure of the Greek city states as well as the external structure of the international system constrained the agents of the state in their task of reproducing the city state.

By the sixth century B.C. there were 1,500 Greek cities, most of which had begun life as commercial centers, so that none was more than 25 miles from the sea (Anderson 1974:29). The cities, however, were established not by traders, but by tribal aristocracies and there was intense competition and rivalry among them. From an early stage in Hellenic history, the city states established colonies outside of Greece in Italy and Asia minor. But after the colonialization process came to an end in the late sixth century, Anderson notes that the typical path of expansion was "military conquest and tribute"(1974:37). As Waltz predicts, as the cities began to coact, the military (i.e., the strategic sector), quickly became an essential element of the capacity of states to reproduce themselves.

When the city states were first established, the aristocracy possessed a monopoly on the right to fight and conflicts between states took place on the basis of individual combat. In a highly competitive system, however, it was impossible to maintain this restricted mode of fighting for any length of time. Although it is not known how or when the change came about, the Greek city states began to acknowledge the advantages of fighting in organized groups. These developments made it necessary to extend the number of citizens who could fight for the state. The resulting developments precipitated a military and political revolution in Greece, because as Aristotle argued "the class that does the fighting wields supreme political power" (cited in Cartledge 1977:24). By the seventh century, conflicts between the Greek city states were fought by heavily armored hoplites—infantrymen who carried among other things a round shield called a hoplon—who were organized to fight in a phalanx formation. Although it has been argued that alternative strategies could have developed (Cartledge 1977), when one of the city states developed this strategy, it would have been suicide for the others not to follow (Halladay 1982). Cartledge argues that by the middle of the seventh century nearly all the major Greek city states had adopted phalanx tactics, although he suggests that the Asiatic Greeks and the Western colonists did not follow suit until a little later (1977:21).

From the perspective of the ruling aristocrats, this new mode of fighting had two advantages. In the first place, the expensive equipment required by the hoplite could be afforded, of course, only by wealthy citizens. As Cartledge notes, "the devolution of military responsibility did not obviously imperil the aristocratic structure of society" (1977:24). Functional differentiation within the state was preserved intact. In the second place, it was an extremely efficient mode of warfare. Adcock asserts that it is "hard to conceive of a method of warfare that, in peace, made a more limited call on the time and effort of most citizens of most communities"(1957:4).

Over time, however, the emergence of the hoplite mode of fighting inevitably changed the social and political composition of the Greek city states. The hoplite troops were drawn from the farmers and the craftsmen class of the cities. In fifth-century Athens, for example, about a third of the citizens (ten to twelve thousand) were hoplites; the rest, the thete class, were poor peasants, unable to afford the cost of equipping themselves for heavy duty. As Anderson has noted, the precondition for movement away from the aristocratic mode of government was the "self-armed citizen infantry"(1974:33). This development first became apparent in Sparta where eight or nine thousand citizens formed a professional army. They were both economically self-sufficient, relying on the helots to relieve them of any direct involvement in economic production, and politically enfranchised. Sparta as a consequence, was the most egalitarian of the aristocratic city states. The hoplites, moreover, proved their worth when the city states allied in 478 in order to resist and eventually eliminate the threat posed to Greece by the Persian Empire.

The Persian menace proved to be particularly acute for Athens. Doyle notes that "As a commercial society, Athens depended for its prosperity and for its survival (its food supplies) on keeping the sea lanes of the Aegean open and free from an equal naval power" (1986:62). Athenian agriculture was highly specialized. Grain was imported from the Black Sea granaries, while Athenian prosperity was achieved by the export of high value-added goods derived from the olive and the vine and the manufacture of pottery and weapons (Doyle 1986:621). Athens as a consequence became the main focal point for trade in the Aegean. Athens also had access to a major source of wealth in the form of the silver mines in Attica. Silver financed the Athenian navy, which was to defeat the Persian navy at Salamis. The creation of the navy gave the Athenians a very distinctive role in the alliance of the Greek city states and also had a major impact on functional differentiation within Athens itself. The sailors were recruited from the poorer class of thetes who were paid a wage and were required to serve for eight months of the year. They almost equaled the number of hoplites and eventually the thetes were also enfranchised—turning Athens into a democracy (Anderson 1974:401). The agents of the state recognized, in other words, that if the state was to be successfully reproduced, the distribution of power within it had to be extended.

The evolution of the Greek city state demonstrates that the agents of the state are constrained by both internal and external forces. The example therefore does give qualified support to Waltz's theory of the state while providing an inkling as to how political units become and remain differentiated. In the first place, in line with Waltz, the case of Athens demonstrates that once the idea of an organized fighting force crystallized, each state found its only alternative was to make appropriate adjustments to the internal structure of the state. But it would appear that the aristocrats believed that these adjustments could be safely made without threatening their position of power. Although the necessary historical detail is not available to reveal the precise process, it is apparent that, over time, this initial development had the long-term consequence of eroding the power of the aristocrats. But in most states they managed to hang on to the vestiges of power. As a consequence, there was a continuous struggle for power within the state. So, despite the need to accommodate to external structural constraints, the internal structure of power continued to exert a powerful influence on the nature of the state.

The case also demonstrates that because of the Athenian dependence on trade, functional differentiation developed between Athens and Sparta. Athens had no alternative but to develop as a naval power, although this required substantial internal structural readjustment, turning Athens into an unequivocally democratic state. The oligarchs in Sparta failed to follow suit because they had no wish to divest themselves of power. Once this differentiation occurred, it had the effect of rendering all the other states vulnerable to intervention because of the existence of their chronic power struggles. The initial differentiation between Athens and Sparta, moreover, generated further differentiation, because as a democratic, naval state, Athens was ideally suited to develop an informal empire. Ironically, the capacity to consolidate the empire was constrained not by external structural forces, but by internal ones. As we shall see later, the democratic distribution of power within the state, which facilitated the creation of the empire, had the further effect of making its consolidation impossible. The agents of the Greek polis were constrained by its very structure from developing an effective empire. It becomes of interest, therefore, to turn to the reproduction of the Diadochi and Roman empires to see how easily this structural constraint could be circumvented.

REPRODUCING THE DIADOCHI EMPIRES

Diadochi is Greek for successor and the Diadochi empires emerged after the failed attempts to hold together Alexander's massive empire. Alexander was the son of Philip, the King of Macedonia (359–336 B.C.). McNeill portrays Macedonia as a "border state"—a tribal monarchy—which benefited from its position on the "margins" of the Greek civilization (1979:149). So the noblemen from Macedonia were educated in the Greek manner (Alexander, for example, was tutored by Aristotle) with the result that feuding among the noblemen gave way to loyalty to the king. Citizenship was extended to inhabitants of the newly conquered regions who were then required to give their loyalty to the King of Macedonia. According to Anderson, moreover, because Macedonia was "morphologically much more primitive" than the Greek city states, it was able to "overleap" their structural limits (1974:45). The Macedonians, unlike the Greeks, were not constrained by beliefs about the democratic polis. In particular, there were no constraints to limit the size of the state or prevent the formation of a state bureaucracy, which was essential for the administration of a large geographical area.

At the same time, the Macedonians were also able to graft their cavalry skills onto the Greek military innovations. Macedonian peasants began to be trained as hoplites; but they were also armed with a long lance and were given lighter armor to make them more mobile. The Macedonian phalanx was then flanked by the cavalry. As a result of these changes, all linked to the process of Hellenization, Macedonia—a Hellenistic rather than a Hellenic state—was soon in a position to pose a considerable threat to its neighbors. Under Philip, the

Macedonians proved capable of overwhelming local barbarians and then the Greeks themselves. Under Alexander, Macedonia subdued the Persian Empire and his rule extended as far as India.

Alexander died in 323 and conflict among his successors persisted until 311, when there was an agreement about how to divide up the empire. It was only after thirty more years of warfare that three stable great powers were established in the Hellenistic world. They were ruled by descendants of a Macedonian general: the Ptolemies in Egypt, the Seleucids in Asia, and the Antigonids in Macedonia. These Hellenistic kingdoms were hybrid political creations that combined in a complex fashion Hellenic and Oriental features. In the first place, there was a proliferation of cities throughout the Near East, making it the most densely urbanized area of the ancient world. But although modeled on the Greek cities, the new Hellenistic cities were much larger (Anderson 1974:47) and developed in a very different political setting. In the Hellenic world, strong walls were impregnable and the city could survive as a defensible political unit. With the development of the torsion catapult and the siege tower, however, Philip and his successors established a means of overpowering the city. Walls were strengthened, but this merely led to improvements in the catapults, so that the security of the city was always in jeopardy. As Price notes this "crucial fact underlies the dominance of kings over cities"(Price 1986:330).

The scale of conflict increased dramatically as a consequence. In Greece, conflict was restricted to fights over disputed territory between city states. But in the Hellenistic kingdoms there were vast tracts of land at stake and the kings could muster 60,000 to 80,000 men against each other. The size of armies would never be larger until the end of the eighteenth century. There was a concomitant increase in destruction and whole cities could be razed to the ground. Nevertheless, the Hellenistic kings established only a hegemonial status over the cities, with their power often being exercised informally or indirectly. The kings used a range of diplomatic devices to ensure "harmony between and within cities without involving invidious direct interventions"(Price 1986:332). Yet the threat of force always persisted because whereas in Greece legitimacy came from tradition, the Hellenistic kings derived their legitimacy from military prestige (Price 1986:326).

The Hellenic influence, however, was pervasive. It was reflected in the monetary standard, which was generalized throughout the Hellenistic Kingdoms, and the banking system. These developments encouraged commerce and trade (Anderson 1974, 47–48). But slave labor, although of great importance in Greece, failed to develop in the Hellenistic East because of the strength of established social and political traditions. These traditions also encouraged a veneration of the Hellenistic kings unknown in Greece (Anderson 1974:48–50). As we shall see, these factors were to prove very significant when an attempt is made to account for the survival of the Eastern half of the Roman Empire.

What this case study demonstrates, therefore, is that the process of emulation does not necessarily lead to the increasing homogenization of political units, as Waltz's theory predicts. On the contrary, when the Macedonians copied Hellenic techniques and grafted them onto the structure of their state, a new and very much more powerful political entity emerged, which looked nothing like the Greek city states. The Greeks, moreover, with their fixed belief in the virtues of the polis, were structurally constrained from emulating the Macedonians. It is important to note, moreover, that the Macedonians did not emulate the Greek city states out of strategic necessity. The Macedonian state underwent its transformation as the result of cultural transfusion rather than as a consequence of the pressure of operating in an anarchic arena. Waltz's theory, therefore, performs much more effectively in the context of the Greek city states than it does in the context of the Macedonian Empire. We shall examine the reasons for this, but first let us look at the way the Roman Empire managed to sustain itself for so long, when compared to the almost instant "death" of Alexander's empire.

REPRODUCING THE ROMAN EMPIRE

Like the Greek city states, Rome emerged in an intensely competitive international environment. But its horizons were initially local. What is perhaps most remarkable about Rome is that its agents eventually should have come to think in such universal terms, and that they could have contemplated ruling the entire orbis terrarum (Brunt 1978:168). While they failed to achieve this goal they did successfully unify into a larger subsystem what had previously been a number of independent international subsystems. To be able to do this, the agents of Rome had to overcome or circumvent the structural restraints experienced by the agents of the Greek city states and the Hellenistic empires.

The methodology of structuration suggests that to understand how the expansion of the Roman state came about, it is necessary to look more closely at the process of reproduction implemented by the agents of the state. Although very little is known about the early history of Rome, it is clear that from the very start its evolution must be considered in the context of a broader system. Rome began as a village on the Tiber at a time when the peninsula of Italy was fragmented by competing tribes. To the North of Rome were the Etruscans, who operated within a loose confederation of twelve cities. They represented the dominant power in central Italy in the middle of the first millennium B.C. From an early stage, the Romans must have recognized that they had no alternative but to develop a military capacity in order to maintain their independence against armed neighbors and thereby reproduce their city state. During the early phase of Rome's development, the main rival was the Etruscan city of Veii, which lay ten miles north of Rome. Although Veii and Rome were both were much bigger than other cities in this region of Italy, Keppie insists that the wars between Rome and her neighbors "were little more than scuffles between armed raiding bands of a few hundred men at the most"(1984:14).

As Fox has observed, in primitive combat superior numbers are likely to prevail, so there was always an "inherent logic that led inexorably to larger and larger political units" (1971:21). The competition between the Romans and Etruscans, according to this logic, encouraged them to extend their borders. But as Mann has argued, in line with Waltz, the competition also meant that both the Romans and the Etruscans were constantly looking for new strategic ways of achieving military superiority. In the seventh century, for example, the Etruscans began to copy the military tactics associated with the Greek hoplites. However, once the Romans had copied the Etruscan tactics, to ensure the reproduction of the state, then the independence of their neighbors to the North was simultaneously threatened. Moreover, while Rome was consolidating its strength, the Etruscans' power was being steadily eroded as new actors entered the system. The Etruscans had to face the Celtic tribes, in particular the Gauls, who migrated across the Alps during the fifth century. Keppie notes that with hindsight it can be seen that the Etruscans unintentionally provided "a buffer" for Rome and in doing so whittled away much of their own strength (1984:18). Ironically, therefore, when Rome eventually captured Veii in 396 they were almost immediately confronted by the Gauls, who defeated the Roman forces and looted Rome in 390 before being repelled. The experience was salutary and the Roman army underwent major changes over the next fifty years as they endeavored to adapt the tactics of the phalanx to the more mobile tactics used by the Gauls (Keppie 1984:19).

Because of the double security dilemma, the agents of the state seek to reproduce the state in such a way as to preserve both the internal and the external power structures. As already observed, the Greek aristocracy introduced the hoplites only to find, in the long term, that this method of fighting eroded their own power base. By contrast, the aristocratic agents of Rome managed to develop an effective fighting force without democratizing the state. Anderson (1974:57) notes, for example, how "a hereditary nobility kept unbroken power" despite substantial constitutional changes for two centuries after the emergence of the Roman Republic. It has been argued that continuous expansion proved to be a vital feature in the reproduction of the aristocratic state (Harris 1979). Closely associated with this development was the decision to promote a conception of citizenship. Such a conception did not initially exist. During the early history of Rome, for example, there was "no rigid conception of citizenship to tie a man to a community of his birth" (Crawford 1986:393). As Rome expanded its area of control the importance of possessing citizenship increased dramatically. Land acquired in the course of expansion was given to peasants who in turn were used as soldiers in the process of acquiring more territory. New communities absorbed by the Romans were granted citizenship, given land, and they too became liable to serve in the military operations that saw the further expansion of Rome's area of control. Land, however, was never equally shared. There was always a segment of the community more generously treated, providing the basis for a social elite and a governing class.

Rome did not rely simply on military superiority and territorial conquest to extend its influence. It also developed an elaborate system of alliances designed not only to aid expansion, but also to underpin the aristocratic mode of government in the territories on the border of Rome. The alliances, therefore, were very different from those postulated in Waltz's balance of power theory. The Roman alliances involved "horizontal penetration." When Rome offered to form an alliance with a neighbor, it extended privileges to the upper classes in the communities they allied with, and there were frequent intermarriages. Rome invariably supported this class whenever there were internal or external threats. These allies were therefore soon tied by very tight bonds to Rome. These bonds ensured, moreover, that Rome's major demand on its allies—the supply of troops—was invariably fulfilled. Allies tolerated this exercise of power because these troops did not return empty handed. Although not as generously treated as the citizens of Rome, they did share in the fruits of victory, at the expense of the newly conquered territory. Crawford (1986:399) argues that most ancient empires demanded tribute from the areas they subjugated. The demand for troops represents the distinctive and very effective feature of Roman imperialism permitting not only the reproduction but also the expansion of the system. This form of client relationship was to play a crucial role in the future running of the Roman Empire.

As the Roman Republic extended across the peninsula, the aristocracy acquired huge tracts of land from defeated tribes. These tribes also initially provided the slaves who worked the land. As the empire extended overseas, the slaves were brought from further afield. Anderson (1974:62) argues that the development of a slave economy released the necessary personnel to fight further wars and precipitated a "gigantic social upheaval" in Italy. According to estimates made by Brunt (1971:121–25), in 225 B.C. there were about 4,400,000 free persons in Italy to 600,000 slaves. By 43 B.C. he suggests that there were 4,500,000 free persons and 3,000,000 slaves. Anderson also observes that although the Greeks had slaves, they were used only on small plots of land. The Romans, by contrast, were the first people to introduce large-scale slave latifundia. The consequences of this development proved to be very important, because when the Roman Empire moved West "for the first time, classical Antiquity was confronted with great interior land-masses, devoid of previous urban civilization. It was the Roman city-state, that had developed the rural slave-latifundium, that proved capable of mastering them. . . . The successful organization of large-scale agrarian production by slave labor was the precondition of the permanent conquest and colonization of the great Western and Northern hinterlands" (Anderson 1974:63).

The capacity of the Roman state to expand, in contrast to the Greek city state, can therefore be partially explained by reference to a structurationist theory of the state. According to this theory, agents of the state are constrained not only by external structures of the international system, but also by internal structures of the state itself. The agents of the Athenian state were encouraged to engage in imperialism because of the need to combat the oriental threat posed by the Persian Empire, which possessed a quite different structure from that of the Greek city states. But because of internal constraints the Greek city states were never able to consolidate their imperial possessions. By contrast, although external threats also encouraged the Roman city state to engage in imperialistic ventures, because of its distinctive mode of reproduction it was able to expand successfully. The expansion, of course, was not world wide and this raises questions about the factors that constrained the continuous development of Rome.

What we have demonstrated in this chapter is that because of the constraints generated by the internal structure of the state, it does not always follow that the units in a system eliminate any signs of functional differentiation, which can persist because of the external dimension of the balance of power. Although the Diadochi empires were functionally differentiated from the Greek city states, they nevertheless pursued policies under balance of power constraints which secured the independence of the Greek city states. Whereas Waltz presupposes that the balance of power will generate like units in the first instance, and generate alliances to deal with the residual problem of power differentiation only in the second instance, the case studies looked at here indicate that this logic needs to be reversed. Anarchy does not necessarily eliminate functional differentiation. Instead, the external workings of the balance of power can ensure that states continue to be reproduced in very different ways. The logic developed here suggests that functional differentiation will be eliminated only if it cannot be accommodated by the workings of the external balance of power. Reformulating Neorealism in this way makes it possible to account for both the differentiation and the nondifferentiation of units in an anarchic arena.

CHAPTER EIGHT

The Structure and Logic of Anarchy

Waltz's assessment of the logic of anarchy is very simple and yet absolutely central to Neorealism. He asserts that an anarchic system emerges as soon as independent political units begin to coact. Once this happens, the logic of anarchy requires that the agents of these units pursue actions that will ensure not only that the political units can survive and reproduce themselves in the anarchic system but also that the anarchic structure of the international system is simultaneously albeit unintentionally reproduced. Unintended actions, however, are not necessarily unanticipated actions. It is important to recognize that while agents may not intend to reproduce an anarchic arena, this does not mean that they are unaware that in consolidating the state they are simultaneously helping to reproduce an international anarchy.

This assessment of the logic of anarchy has been strongly criticized by poststructuralists on the grounds that it obscures some very important features of the contemporary structure of the international system. According to their line of argument, anarchy is a multifaceted phenomenon that can be explored from contradictory perspectives. This assessment strikes a common chord with our argument here: that anarchy itself is a differentiated phenomenon. In other words, we shall challenge Waltz's argument that the logic of anarchy is unaffected by the nature of the units that make up the anarchy. Because we have incorporated functional differentiation into the deep structure of the system, it becomes necessary to take account of the way states reproduce themselves. Because states reproduce themselves in different ways, it will be argued that this can affect the logic of anarchy. Despite the echoes of poststructuralism, the similarity is deceptive. The poststructuralists wish to argue that reality is inherently contradictory and they wish to expose that the international system embraces competing modes of anarchy. We wish to identify how different modes of anarchy are reproduced and transformed. After looking at the poststructural position, therefore, it is necessary to explore in more detail how the reproduction of political units interacts with the logic of the anarchic system.

ASHLEY'S DECONSTRUCTION OF WALTZ

Using poststructuralist techniques, Ashley (1989) sets about "deconstructing" *TIP* to show how Waltz presents a one-dimensional and inadequate conception of anarchy, arguing that poststructuralists adhere to two fundamental but contradictory truths: that human beings are not free agents, because their lives are controlled by undetected, invisible structures; and that human beings are free agents and can organize their lives in whatever way they like. The purpose of "deconstructing" *TIP* is to reveal that in promoting the first truth Waltz has no alternative but to "silence" or "conceal" the second. Deconstruction requires the analyst to read the text for its overt meaning and then reread the text to show how the case being made is undermined by the text itself.

Ashley argues that Waltz is intending to suggest that statesmen are in the grip of structural forces over which they have no control. The structure of the international system requires them to take certain actions in order to hold at bay the international anarchy posing a constant threat to the domestic order it is their duty to protect. A poststructural reading of the text reveals that, in developing this argument, Waltz is closing off from the "passive" reader certain essential areas of discussion. In particular, Ashley argues that Waltz "silences" questions about the source of the islands of domestic order that exist in the international arena. The poststructural approach is said to provide a voice which can open up these silences. It reveals (1) that without the identification of a dangerous international anarchy, there could be no notion of a well-bounded domestic society; (2) that the expansion of the modern state's role in domestic society involves hardening the boundary distinguishing domestic and international society; (3) that in order to maintain the conception of domestic space it becomes necessary to constitute ever more encompassing international threats; and (4) that by casting the international society in this negative light, an ambiguous space is created where further problems can be projected.

It follows from this line of analysis that to free the analyst from the restrictions of structuralism it is necessary, first, to displace the state from its central position in discourse about international relations; second, to accept that the distinction between domestic and international politics can no longer provide the starting point for discussing international politics; and, third, to acknowledge that the distinction between domestic and international politics is indeterminate. When this is done, it becomes possible to see, as Ashley (1988) argues elsewhere, that there are two competing conceptions of international anarchy. One view of international anarchy, that of Waltz, identifies a world of competing states, another view, that of the early Keohane and Nye (1972), depicts international anarchy in terms of a transnational or pluralistic world of competing interest groups. Ashley argues that both of these views of international anarchy are valid. But because we have no alternative but to use language to describe reality, there is never any possibility of capturing this ambiguity, except by poststructural analysis, which self-consciously acknowledges that any description of reality necessarily closes off or silences alternative and equally valid descriptions. Ashley's line is unduly pessimistic, as we will try to demonstrate in Section III. Language is well able to express incompatible views and readers can get used to treating texts, like the world of their daily lives, as indeterminate.

The argument being made by Ashley is obviously very different from the one made earlier by Luttwak and Strange. From their perspective, there is a real world out there which is amenable to empirical analysis and description. It is, as a consequence, possible to argue not only that Waltz is representing just one possible view of international anarchy, but also that it is an outdated and unhelpful image, distorting what is actually happening. As Strange sees it, we are living in a period of dramatic change, and to understand what is happening it is necessary to appreciate that "like a chrysalis in the metamorphosis from caterpillar to butterfly, the American Empire today combines features of a national-exclusive past with features of a transnational-extensive future"(1989:11). Failure to appreciate this fact has led analysts, locked in an anachronistic framework, perpetrated by Waltzian type analysis, to argue about whether or not the American empire is losing its hegemonic position. As a consequence, they have overlooked fundamental questions about the nature of power and the basis on which hegemony is established.

WALTZ'S LOGIC OF ANARCHY

Waltz has been remarkably unperturbed by the criticisms leveled at him about structural transformation. Although he has not responded to the most recent arguments developed by Ashley in his poststructural mood, it is likely that he would indicate that in so far as the argument is intelligible, Ashley is simply drawing attention to different levels of analysis. Waltz would insist that he has not "silenced" the analysis of transnational activity in the international system. He explicitly argues that such activity can be understood only at a different level of analysis.

In the same way, Waltz is perfectly happy to acknowledge that his theory cannot account for system change or transformation. But he does question whether any such transformation has ever taken place. For example, in commenting on Ruggie's "fine and rich account of the historical transition from the medieval to modern state" he remains convinced that the account tells us "nothing about the structure of international politics"(1986:328). What happened at the point of transition, according to Waltz, was that the nature of the units changed; the structure of the system was unaffected. Waltz can make this argument because as far as he is concerned, it is immaterial for his theory whether the units of the system are city states, medieval states, nation states, or empires. What his theory explains is why political units will be constrained to take the same form by the anarchic structure of the system. As a consequence, the theory predicts that once one state moved away from the highly decentralized medieval state toward the highly centralized and more powerful nation state, the other political units had quickly to follow suit.

While Waltz's position does not mean that he denies that the structure of the system can change (although he does find it difficult to envisage what form this structure would take) the argument that "the international system is not fully generative" is central to his position. In other words, he does not believe that a theory established at the level of the international structure can explain how changes in that structure can take place. He insists that, like Durkheim, he sees unit level processes "as a source both of changes in systems and of possible changes of systems, hard though it is to imagine the latter." He concludes, therefore, that "Neither structure nor units determine outcomes. Each affects the other"(1986:328). Waltz therefore clearly recognizes that there is an interaction between structure and agency. But he insists that it is necessary to separate out the two levels of analysis. When this is done, it can be seen that system maintenance can be accounted for at the level of structure, while system transformation can be understood only at the level of agency. This line of argument accords exactly with the position adopted by Archer and Taylor but differs from the position adopted by Wendt.

The argument developed so far suggests that it is invalid to criticize Waltz for failing to develop a theory of the state. It is worthwhile looking a little more closely at Wendt's related argument that the international system as well as the state must not be treated as an ontologically primitive concept. Again, Wendt fails to follow through the logic of Waltz's position when he suggests that Waltz has nothing to say about the origins and emergence of the international system. Waltz argues very clearly that the international system comes into existence only when states begin to coact. Before states come into contact with each other they operate in the absence of a political environment.

Wendt makes a further error when he suggests that Wallerstein also fails to examine this issue. Wallerstein, according to Wendt, treats the international system as a primitive or unproblematic concept and is consequently unable to account for the emergence of the international system. The international system is thereby reified and there is a failure to show that the existence of the system is historically contingent and a "problematic creation and recreation of state and class agents"(Wendt 1987:348). But Wendt's assessment fails to take into account that Wallerstein views the international system as the product of a fragmented empire. His theory of the international system is part of his broader cyclical theory of world systems. Built into Wallerstein's theory, therefore, is the notion of system transformation. By contrast Waltz, who assumes that the anarchic international system has been a permanent feature of world history, excludes this possibility.

ANARCHY AND COMPETING MODES OF REPRODUCTION

This ontological assessment of the international system leads Waltz to presuppose that the logic of anarchy is unaffected by the nature of the units operating in the anarchic arena. In other words, although his theory of the state acknowledges that the units themselves may be constantly evolving, for example, from the medieval state to the modern state, he presupposes that the way these different states seek to reproduce themselves will have no effect on the deep structure of the anarchic arena in which they operate. It is possible to challenge this argument by drawing attention to the well-known and long-standing criticisms of the comparison that has been made between the logic operating in Hobbes's state of nature and the logic operating in the international system. It is often asserted that the two systems share a similar logic. But critics of the comparison argue that the logic is different in the two cases because the nature of the units in the two systems is different. In the state of nature, the logic of the system is seen by Hobbes to generate a situation of absolute and unbearable insecurity. Each member of the system is seen to live in a constant fear of being killed by another member. The critical point about Hobbes's state of nature is that even limited cooperation is ruled out of court.

By contrast, Hobbes considers the condition of war to be tolerable. There exists what Warriner (1957) refers to as "relative security." In the world of states, as has often been pointed out, the potential for instant death does not exist. At least when Hobbes was writing, states could be subdued only over time and they could always inflict wounds on an adversary. In conditions where survival is possible, there is an incentive to cooperate. It becomes possible to conceive of forming alliances and thereby deterring potential aggressors. Hobbes also argues in favor of being heavily armed; to be lightly armed is to become very vulnerable to attack and begin to resemble individuals in a state of nature. The nature of the logic begins to change at that point. The distinction between the state of nature and the state of war suggests that the logic of anarchy is tied in a rather fundamental way to the nature of the units operating within the anarchic structure. As a consequence, to understand the character of anarchy it is necessary to take account of the nature of the constituent units. By incorporating the functional differentiation of political units into the deep structure of the international system, we have made provision for this line of argument, but its implications need to be further examined.

The idea of the state of nature is, of course, a fiction. But it draws attention to the possibility that the activity required to reproduce an anarchic arena is dependent upon the nature of the constituent units in the arena. It is possible to postulate that as the nature of the units change, so too do the methods used to reproduce them. This line of argument has rarely been explored because it has so widely been accepted that anarchy generates a competitive environment. Although this assumption would be challenged by theorists of political anarchy, there have been virtually no attempts by theorists in the field of International Relations, apart from essays by Falk (1978) and Alker (forthcoming), to examine the work of the theorists of political anarchy. This hiatus is not, in fact, surprising, because theorists of anarchy are interested in situations where the existence of the state has been dissolved, while international theorists have traditionally been concerned almost exclusively with the activities of the state, albeit in an anarchic arena. It has been left to theorists like Bull (1977) to emphasize that anarchy and society are not incompatible concepts.

It can be argued, however, that anarchists, like the analysts of Hobbes's state of nature, are dealing with hypothetical systems. And, according to most political theorists, they are unrealizable systems as well. But it is possible to reinforce the argument that there is a complex interaction between the deep structure of an anarchic arena and the units operating in the system by exploring an empirical example provided by anthropology. Generally speaking, anthropologists are drawn upon to support the idea that conflict between independent political units is ubiquitous. It is not possible, in other words, to identify primitive social systems that live in complete harmony with their neighbors. Indeed, many anthropologists have concluded that conflict is endemic between primitive tribes. This finding would surprise neither Hobbes nor Waltz, both of whom would expect conflict to be endemic in an anarchic arena made up of weak and vulnerable tribes.

THE KULA AND THE LOGIC OF ANARCHY

There is an interesting exception to the pervasiveness of international conflict which poses a real problem for the Neorealist framework and raises important questions about the relationship between the structure of an anarchic system and the structure of the units within the system. The exception is provided by the tribes who lived on the Trobriand Islands in the Western Pacific. These tribes constituted "stateless" societies because they lacked any form of central government. Although it has become conventional to refer to such societies as "stateless," they do not lack political organization. They constitute independent political units. But because of the absence of a central government, political organization takes an anarchic form. As a consequence, the islanders operate within anarchic units set in an anarchic system. This is, of course, an extreme and unusual case. Although Waltz asserts that the internal constituents of a state will not affect its reaction to the structural constraints imposed by anarchy, he is assuming that the states themselves are hierarchical in structure. It is perhaps not surprising to find, therefore, that the external behavior of the Trobriand islanders does not fit Waltz's theory. What anthropologists have observed is that when these tribes interact, their activities serve to reproduce the essential characteristics of a stateless society and at the same time sustain the anarchic international system.

The tribes were observed by anthropologists to come into contact with each other on a regular basis in order to engage in trade. But the trade was also accompanied by an elaborate ceremony called the kula. It involves an exchange of valuables—Malinowski compared them to the crown jewels—which circulated continuously from one political community to another. There are two types of valuables: long necklaces made of red shell, which travel in a clockwise direction around the islands, and arm bracelets made of white shell, which move in an anticlockwise direction. Every other year, the members of a tribe who participate in the kula travel in a clockwise direction in their canoes to an adjacent island. There, each member of the expedition has a life-long partner from whom he receives a number of shells in the course of the kula. On a return expedition, the partner will receive some necklaces in exchange. There is a high degree of reciprocity in these exchanges. In return for a valuable necklace a donor will expect an equally valuable bracelet. Each political unit conducts the kula with two adjacent units and, because the islands form a ring, the valuables travel continuously in opposite directions.

The kula was first investigated by Malinowski (1922). But the evidence was later reassessed by Uberoi (1962) who has argued that the kula is not simply a peace ceremony but also represents a form of political organization that plays an important role in the power relationships within each society, as well as stabilizing relations between the societies. So, for example, in addition to the formally paired partners, ad hoc exchanges also take place and these give scope for cheating. For example, an individual with a very famous bracelet may use it as collateral on an expedition to a neighboring island, and receive in return several valuable necklaces from partners who each believe they are to receive the bracelet. When the sharp practice is revealed on the return visit, however, animosity is not directed against the member of the neighboring tribe who perpetrated the trick but against the member of the home tribe who is lucky enough to receive the famous bracelet. The acquisition of the bracelet enhances his prestige within the tribe and therefore becomes a source of jealousy. This complex interaction between internal and external transactions indicates that "conflicts within the smaller social group contribute to the cohesion of a wider society" (Uberoi 1962:74). The main source of prestige for all the tribes is, therefore, located in the international system and is obtainable only through the kula. As a consequence, transactions enacted through the kula, serve to reproduce not only the international system but also the decentralized system within each of the tribes. Although it can be argued that the kula is an exceptional mode of international transaction, it does provide a very clear illustration of the close interconnections between the domestic and the international system.

Other examples of isolated regional systems have displayed a distinctive logic. Before Rome unified the Mediterranean region, for example, the Carthaginian empire and the Greek city states were essentially autonomous systems of independent political units. Agents within these systems were, of course, aware that there were other political systems, but their aim was to preserve their independence by minimizing ties with them. Warmington (1960) describes how the Carthaginians endeavored to establish the Western Mediterranean as their special preserve and eliminate the influence of the Greek city states. He argues that a "deliberate attempt to cut a state off from the broad current of Mediterranean advance was not unique nor wholly impractical" (Warmington 1964:61). Because of the relative albeit temporary isolation of Carthage, and its distinctive mode of reproduction, it is possible to argue that relations with its trading partners in the West reflected a distinctive logic. It can then be shown that the logic underlying the relations amongst the Greek city states was quite different.

CARTHAGE AND THE LOGIC OF ANARCHY

Carthage, originally established as a Phoenician colony in the eighth century B.C., was, unlike most of the other colonies, restricted to a narrow strip of land by a treaty with Libya. When the colony began to grow, it therefore became necessary to establish extensive trading links to provide staple products to support the population. This pattern persisted even after Carthage began to extend into its hinterland. Whittaker has argued that until the third century the extensive connections Carthage established in the Western part of the Mediterranean cannot be really identified as imperialism. Evidence of the structures usually associated with imperialism is almost completely absent and there is no evidence of tribute being paid to Carthage. It is true that Carthaginians emigrated, but there is no evidence that they did so to establish positions of dominance in their new community. Whittaker (1978) accepts that Carthaginian troops were posted abroad on the territory of allies but insists that they were there to ensure uninterrupted trade. It is stressed that recent research also reveals the polycentric character of trade in the Mediterranean at this time. There was no centralized trade empire directed by either Tyre or Carthage, although Whittaker does accept that Carthage may have had extraterritorial jurisdiction over its citizens within the boundaries of a foreign port. But Carthage was not interested in using this jurisdiction to promote domination. From its origins, therefore, Carthage was locked into a system where wealth and privilege was associated with trade rather than the possession of land. Its main aim was to promote conditions that would facilitate trade.

It can be suggested, therefore, that Carthage established an international system that involved interaction among what Fox has referred to as "commercial" societies engaged in "long-distance commerce in luxuries or the water-borne exchange of staples that had persisted in the Mediterranean for centuries" (1971:34). Water travel involves a considerable initial investment, but once made, it becomes a relatively inexpensive and easy way of moving goods in bulk. Fox goes on to argue that there is then established "a virtually unlimited potential for linear extension of water-borne communications" and with this ability came correspondingly "increased opportunities for agricultural specialisation" (1971:35). Rational actors recognizing the economic benefits that can accrue from specialization would take advantage of the system and thereby help to reproduce it. These rational actors will thereby find themselves committed to "the interdependence of a large linear (circular) economic system capable of indefinite rationalisation and expansion" (1971:37). Because of this interdependence, more-over, Fox argues that a "consultative approach to action proved more practical than constraint and compulsion." He also observes that be-cause these commercial or linear societies did not have extensive areas to administer, they "normally had no need for government of the sort we usually take for granted in the state" (1971:38).

Herodotus provides an interesting description of Carthaginian trad-ing practices that illustrates the informal and noncoercive basis on which trade was conducted.

> The Carthaginians also tell us about a part of Libya and its inhabitants beyond the Straits of Gibraltar. When they reach this country, they unload their goods and arrange them on the beach; they then return to their ships and send up a smoke signal. When the natives see the smoke, they come down to the sea and place on the shore a quantity of gold in exchange for the goods and then retire. The Carthaginians then come ashore again and examine the gold that has been left; if they think it represents the value of the goods, they collect it and sail away, if not they go back to the ships and wait until the natives have added sufficient gold to satisfy them. Neither side tricks the other; the Carthaginians never touch the gold until it equals in value what they have brought for sale, and the natives do not touch the goods until the gold has been taken away. (Herodotus 1987 IV:196)

Although Rome and Carthage were eventually to engage in bitter conflict, for several centuries they coexisted without serious problems arising between them. There was some contact, but it was primarily to remove areas of friction. It is in this light that Whittaker assesses the treaty established between Carthage and Rome in 509 B.C. which gave Carthage control of the ports of trade in Eastern Libya and Sardinia and the treaty of 348 B.C. which prohibited Rome from trading or settling in these regions. Whittaker insists that these treaties arose "out of friendship" and were not "truces dictated from hostility." They are seen to be characteristic of agreements associated with Phoenician or Levantine trading history and were "designed to assist traders and strangers, not to keep them out" (Whittaker 1978:87–88). But the agreements do indicate that Carthage regarded this region as its sphere of influence. This meant that city states in the area were prepared to permit Carthage to define their foreign relations by guaranteeing to protect their shipping.

This relationship represented the defining characteristic of the Carthaginian empire. It can be suggested then that for a time the Roman and Carthaginian Empires coexisted but operated in international subsystems that were independent and subsystem dominant. Indeed, it can be suggested that the agreements established between the two empires were designed to institutionalize the separation, so that there was coexistence without coaction. This example of a regional system that managed to sustain its own distinctive subsystemic form of anarchy immediately raises questions about the factors that brought the subsystem within a broader system where the logic of anarchy described by Waltz dominated.

Whittaker notes that by the end of the fourth century the nature of Carthage's relations within its informal empire and regional subsystem began to undergo a shift. The growing power of Syracuse and Sicily made it more difficult to maintain a stable system, so the level of insecurity in the system increased; and the problem was exacerbated because of the development of central state institutions in both Syracuse and Carthage. Whittaker argues that there was a "shift in the balance in inter-state relations from the personal bonds of friendship between great houses to the more impersonal, collective interests in the ruling elite" (1978:9). Although the more informal bonds never disappeared completely, the shift created a need for formal definitions of alliances and intercity relations, as well as a clarification of spheres of influence and boundaries.

At the same time, Carthage began to move into the hinterland, with a concomitant growth in landed property ownership. Inevitably, this brought about greater inequality, and a greater potential for internal unrest in the event of any foreign invasion. As the internal structures changed, so also did the perception of the international system. Sicily, for example, was seen to be posing a security risk rather than as a source of trading opportunities because it was seen to be a potential base from which an attack on Carthage could take place. It was not long, moreover, before the Romans began to appear as the most likely perpetrator of such an attack. The increase first of Greek, and then of Roman power in the Western Mediterranean raised the interaction capacity of the wider international system, thereby threatening the integrity of the older subsystems. The distinctive logic that characterized the Carthaginian subsystem then quickly changed. The Carthaginian state became more centralized and the capacity to resist attack was enhanced.

The important role initially played by transnational forces in the Carthaginian system was possible because the agents of Carthage saw no need to develop the state in order to preserve their internal or external position. As the potential for internal and external threats increased, so did the desire to strengthen the state. The system became more centralized and in doing so it lost its regional or subsystemic character as the agents of Carthage began to respond to the anarchic structural force of the broader international system. This case can be contrasted with that of the Greek city states which coexisted with Carthage. The city states operated within a wider system, but can initially be characterized as an international subsystem. As will be seen, however, the structural constraints operating within the subsystem continued to influence the city states even after their behavior began to be constrained by the larger system.

GREECE AND THE LOGIC OF ANARCHY

Subsystem dominance among the Greek city states began to be challenged when they were confronted by the threat of Persia. The Greek city states, in line with Waltz's balance of power theory, collaborated in order to maintain their independence. In the aftermath of the conflict, subsystemic forces continued to be profoundly affected by the wider international system. At the same time, changes in the internal structure of the city states began to affect the underlying logic of the subsystem. In the first place, agents of the Athenian state began to recognize that their commercial status in a highly competitive international system rendered the city state extremely vulnerable to external threats from the wider international system. When the war with Persia was over, therefore, the Athenians used the possibility of future oriental threats to consolidate their dominating position within the Greek alliance—the Delian League. Athens refused to allow the dissolution of the alliance and it was, as Anderson notes, "converted into a de facto Empire" with about 150 states—at its height—paying tribute to Athens (1974:41).

Athens was able to maintain support in its colonies because it established democratic institutions, which were favored by the poorer sections of the community. The wealthier class, on the other hand, which favored the displaced oligarchic system, looked to Sparta for support where that system continued to flourish.

The internal class division permeated every city state according to Thucydides and created the potential for ubiquitous intervention. Thucydides argues that during the Peloponnesian War between Athens and Sparta, when instability prevailed throughout the Hellenic world, there were

> rival parties in every state—democratic leaders trying to bring in the Athenians and oligarchs trying to bring in the Spartans. In peace-time there would have been no excuse and no desire for calling them in but in time of war, when each party could always count upon on alliances which would do harm to its opponents and at the same time strengthen its own position, it became a natural thing for anyone who wanted a change of government to call in help from outside (Thucydides [1954]:208).

Because of these deep rifts in the Greek city states, Ferguson comes to the conclusion that "Dependence on Sparta or Athens was, in fact, regarded by none of their allies except as the lesser of two evils, the greater was dependence on domestic foes" (1913:24).

These powerful transnational ties obviously helped to sustain the Athenian informal empire. But practices that reproduced the democratic state in Athens could not be extended to its allies and it was impossible to weld them into a unified political system. In particular, as Anderson notes, "the direct residential democracy of the mass Assembly" was possible only "within a small geographical compass" (1974:42). In the same vein, he observes that the democratic nature of the system prevented the emergence of any separate or professional apparatus of the state. As a consequence, the Athenian democracy "precluded the creation of a bureaucratic machinery that could have held down an extended territorial empire by administrative coercion" (1974:43). The Athenian empire, therefore, was unsurprisingly short-lived. But the transnational links between states persisted, providing the anarchic system of city states in Greece with a very distinctive character that, as will become apparent later, substantially affected the expansion of Rome into the area.

The Carthaginian and Greek cases open up an obvious weakness in the Neorealist framework, which excludes the possibility of exploring the relationship between the structure of the state and the structure of the system. The two are irrevocably fused in Neorealist theory. Waltz, confident that the structural principle of anarchy will generate a competitive system of units that share a common internal political structure, fails to identify that weakness. It is important to recognize that Waltz's theory of the state does not deny the possibility of an anarchic unit operating within an anarchic system. His theory predicts, in fact, that before coaction takes place, political units can develop in innumerable ways. A state without a central government is certainly a logical possibility. But Waltz's theory also predicts that once coaction is initiated, then states structured in a way that renders them uncompetitive will either have to change their internal structure or accept external domination. Although Waltz does not explore the issue, it is likely that he would agree that states without a central government will be unable to compete successfully with states possessing centralized governments.

But this still leaves open the question of what happens when all the "states" in a system lack a central government. Waltz's framework can predict only that the relationship will be competitive; but the kula case study does not support this conclusion. It follows that there is a need to look more closely at the relationship between political units and the international system within which they interact. In Section I, where we accepted that the basic thrust of Waltz's argument about anarchy is correct, we give causal priority to the anarchic structure of the system, acknowledging Waltz's argument that "anarchy tends to generate like units." Functional differentiation is then characterized as a "deviant" structure in the international system because the existence of functional differentiation demonstrates that the generative effects of anarchy have been unsuccessful. This line of argument identifies a contradiction or tension in our analysis, but the contradiction has been resolved in this section. By defusing the structure of the state and the structure of the system, it has been shown that the external dimension of the balance of power can actually help to sustain functional differentiation.

The implications of this resolution have been extended here. In Waltz's theory of international politics, the logic of anarchy necessarily generates a competitive balance of power. But the cases we examined suggest that this assessment is oversimplified. In the Kula and Carthaginian examples, the logic of anarchy militates against the formation of a balance of power. In both cases, power remains highly decentralized within the political units as well as within the system. Because of the decentralization of power within the political units, neither the internal nor the external balance of power mechanisms come into play. Waltz, of course, can negate these examples by arguing that he is concerned only with the relations among political units where power is centralized. He can then argue that the examples on the whole tend to support his theory. The establishment of a more centralized state in Carthage as the power of Rome began to extend confirms the Waltzian argument that political units become undifferentiated over time. By the same token, the ability of the Greek city states to collaborate when confronted by Persia is also clearly in line with Waltz's balance of power theory. But the advantage of our Structural Realist approach is that it can accommodate for the possibility of differentiated anarchic systems.

The gap in Waltz's theory created by a "transitional" phase is particularly disturbing in the case of the Greek city states, where the political units were structurally differentiated—with power being centralized in some states (Athens and Sparta) and decentralized in others. As Thucydides reveals, in such a system, the logic of anarchy institutionalizes intervention. Since intervention is a good example of the kind of phenomenon which Waltz wishes to explain, the shortcoming is significant.

But there are still gaps in our theoretical formulation and they exist in what we have identified as "transitional phases." The failure of the balance of power to protect Carthage, the Greek states, and the Diadochi Empires, which all succumbed to the Roman Empire, for example, is anomalous. We shall return to this gap in our theoretical framework, but first, it may be useful to take an empirical look at why the balance of power apparently failed to restrain Rome.

ROME AND THE DEMISE OF THE HELLENISTIC SYSTEM

As already indicated, the Hellenistic system embraced the enormous Diadochi Empires, as well as the small and much more vulnerable Greek city states. At first sight, historical assessments of how the Hellenistic system operated tend to confirm Waltz's theory that the unintended outcome of states seeking to reproduce themselves is the formation of a balance of power that ensures the reproduction of the system. But a closer examination of the system reveals that the balance of power in this system is more complex than Waltz allows because the political units reproduce in a way that functionally differentiates the Greek city states from the Diadochi Empires.

Superficially, the application of Waltz's theory is unproblematic. It has been argued that although there is no evidence that the Diadochi Empires "formally or informally, recognized the principle of the balance of power, in fact such a balance had existed because no great state was in a position to destroy any of the other great states" (Walbank 1981:240). It has also been observed that the third century "saw the creation of an uneasy balance of power between the great kingdoms, with conflict confined to disputed areas: the Ptolemies and the Seleucids fought over Syria and Palestine, while the Greek cities of the Aegean area sought to manipulate the great powers in order to achieve independence" (Boardman, Griffen, and Murray 1986:845). But the independence of Greece was tenuous, because of the proximity of Macedonia. Nevertheless, the leaders of Macedon had to take account of the "equilibrium" as much as did the Ptolemies and Seleucids because to have "aimed at complete domination of Greece would certainly have been regarded by them as a threat to it" (Briscoe 1978:147).

According to this account, therefore, the behavior that generated the balance of power ensured the survival of small as well as large states. But a closer examination of the system reveals the need to incorporate functional differentiation within the deep structure of the system. As indicated earlier, when the internal divisions between the democrats and the oligarchs opened up in the Greek city states, a persistent potential for transnational links was created. Competing parties in the Greek city states displayed a willingness to call in partisan actors from other city states to resolve either internal or external conflicts in their favor. Once the Greek city states were coopted into the larger Hellenistic system, the dynamic that had precipitated this behavior in the Hellenic subsystem was extended to the Hellenistic subsystemic level. Inevitably the dynamic affected the balance of power, giving it a transnational twist. Macedon, the nearest great power, often received requests to support a particular party within one of the Greek city states. As Briscoe notes, if Macedon had turned down all the invitations, they would have been redirected to one of the other great powers, thereby posing Macedon itself with a security problem. But when Macedon did intervene, the hostility of the Greeks on the opposing side was inevitably aroused (Briscoe 1978:148). In the third century Macedonian intervention grew more dictatorial and the level of anti-Macedon sentiment within Greece increased. Then, when Macedonia decided to join forces with Carthage during the Second Punic War, the boundary separating the two subsystems centered on the Eastern and Western Mediterranean was effectively eliminated. With this development, the Greek opposition to the Macedonians began to be expressed in terms of regular calls to Rome for support.

It is important to recognize that the agents of the nascent Roman Empire, after taking control of the Italian peninsula, were still a long way from viewing the world in terms of Waltz's closed anarchic system. They did not see themselves as part of a system of independent states. To the West lay uncivilized, and disorganized, barbarian tribes. To the East and South, on the other hand, lay civilized and long-established communities believed by the agents of Rome to pose a serious and long-term threat to the survival of their state. The Romans were particularly concerned about the power of the Seleucid Empire. As a consequence, the Romans displayed no urgent desire to breach the boundary separating them from the Hellenistic system. Carthage, by contrast, posed a more immediate threat and the outcome of the conflict with Rome was not seen to be self-evident to contemporaries. During the second war between Rome and Carthage, for example, the Greek states were also engaged in a major conflict with each other. At a conference called at Naupactus to seek a resolution, one of the members argued that "it is self-evident even to those of us who have given but scanty attention to affairs of state that whether the Carthaginians beat the Romans or the Romans beat the Carthaginians, it is not the least likely that the victors will be content with the sovereignty of Italy and Sicily, but they are sure to come here and extend their ambitions and their forces beyond the bounds of justice" (Walbank 1981:231).

The association of the Eastern Mediterranean with the subsystem in the Western Mediterranean containing two dynamic and expanding states seemed to create an extraordinary degree of insecurity. The speech reveals not only that the outcome of the struggle was uncertain, but also a lack of faith in the balance of power. As far as this Greek is concerned, whatever the outcome of the struggle between Rome and Carthage, the security of the Greeks was likely to deteriorate. It could, however, also be argued that the Greek was merely making a rhetorical statement, designed to persuade the Greeks to make peace without outside intervention.

Taking a wider perspective, it appears that the response of the actors in the Hellenistic system accords very closely with the balance of power expectations in Waltz's theory. The alliances between Macedon and Carthage and between Rome and the Greeks can certainly be accounted for in terms of balance of power prescriptions. The success of the Roman Empire cannot be attributed to the failure of the external adjustments in the balance of power. The inability of the Hellenistic system to resist the Romans flowed in part from internal structural constraints that made it impossible for the political units in the Hellenistic system to copy the structural features of Rome, discussed earlier, which facilitated Rome's acquisition of power. But in addition to these balance of power considerations, Rome was able to take advantage of the fact that the Hellenistic system was rule governed. To understand the nature of this advantage, however, it is necessary to look in more detail at how the existence of rules can affect the logic of anarchy.

RULES AND THE LOGIC OF ANARCHY

Because Waltz establishes a conception of deep structure that militates against cooperation in the international system, his theoretical framework precludes the possibility of explaining the complex body of rules governing the relations between states (Ward 1991). As theorists have become increasingly interested in the process whereby cooperation takes place and rules get formed, they have become increasingly frustrated with the restrictive framework imposed by Waltz where rules and cooperation appear as anomalies (Kratochwil 1989; Onuf 1989). In Waltz's formulation, the anarchic system poses a structural obstacle to cooperation which has to be overcome. Cooperation and rules, as a result, are seen to be extremely tenuous and fragile, in constant danger of being overthrown because they exist in fundamental tension with the structure of the system. Yet this is a rather odd conclusion, because rules and cooperation are, like war and alliances, universal features of the international system. Why should they not be explained in terms of the structure of the international system? As Kratochwil and Ruggie have pointed out, one of the insights derived from game theory is that both "conflict and cooperation can be explained by a single logical apparatus" (1986:762).

Frustration with the self-imposed restrictions on analysis imposed by Waltz has led to the erroneous conclusion that he presupposes that states operate on the basis of a nonstrategic form of rationality (Snidal 1985). In other words, according to Snidal, Waltz works on the assumption that states do not take each other's preferences into account when they arrive at decisions. But this is quite wrong. Waltz's analysis can easily be accommodated within a game theoretic matrix. Waltz depicts states as rational actors seeking to survive in an anarchic arena. As Grieco (1988a, 1988b) has shown, Waltz's analysis suggests two structural factors that inhibit cooperation. Both require the state to take the preferences of other states into consideration. The first is the potential for cheating in an anarchic arena; all states are thereby encouraged to compete rather than cooperate. The second obstacle arises because the benefits of cooperation are rarely symmetrical, and in an anarchic arena which breeds competition, states would rather forgo the benefits of cooperation in preference to seeing a competitor improve its relative power position.

But despite the force of these arguments, the fact remains that states do cooperate and develop rules among themselves. Analysts working within the rational choice model have suggested that cooperation can take place in the anarchic arena when the potential for mutual benefits exists and when what has come to be called "the shadow of the future" prevails. (Oye 1985) Because states know that they are in a relationship, the threat of cheating is diminished because a potential cheat knows that other states will reciprocate and any benefit gained by cheating will be short-run. Under these circumstances, cooperation can enhance the chances of a state surviving in the anarchic arena. It is denied, in other words, that cooperation and rules exist in opposition to the deep structure of the international system.

The potential for cooperation and rule formation in the anarchic international system has also been reexamined from the perspective of literature which has endeavored to overcome the problem of structure and agency. This reexamination has led Dessler (1989), for example, to question the ontological assumptions underpinning Waltz's theory. In particular, he attacks Waltz's assumption that structure can emerge only as a byproduct of the interaction between states. (1989:450)

Waltz, in other words, assumes that structures can be formed only as the result of the actions of rational agents who are not intending by their actions to reproduce the structure of the international system. Dessler rejects this ontological posture in favor of another, associated with analysts such as Giddens and Bhaskar, which, he argues, provides a richer and therefore more effective theory of social action. In essence, the new model not only embraces the interactions between states that unintentionally preserve the anarchic arena, but also makes room for intentional interactions that perform the same function.

This line of argument does not deny, of course, that actions taken to preserve the state have the unintentional consequence of reproducing the deep structure of an anarchic system. But such actions are not incompatible with the actions performed by states when they self-consciously set out to reach agreements with each other. In making such agreements, states explicitly confirm each other's sovereignty and therefore actively help to reproduce the deep structure of the system. Treaties and acts of cooperation all intentionally serve to reconfirm and reproduce the anarchic system of independent states.

So we are brought back to our starting point which asserted the importance of recursiveness in accounting for the relationship between structure and agent. Onuf has argued that "If recursiveness is the key conceptually, then rules are the key operationally" (1989:62). Waltz reveals the flaw in this line of argument, because he demonstrates that it is possible to conceive of an anarchic structure being reproduced unintentionally. But what the recent literature on anarchy and regimes has revealed is that the logic of anarchy does not preclude cooperation and that anarchy, therefore, is not incompatible with the formation of rules. Once these rules are formulated, they constitute in our terms a process formation, constraining the behavior of the member states. It then becomes possible to distinguish between anarchy operating in the absence of rules and anarchy operating in accordance with them. This corresponds to the distinction between an international system and an international society. As Bull and Watson put it:

> By an international society we mean a group of states (or, more generally, a group of independent political communities) which not merely form a system, in the sense that the behavior of each is a necessary factor in the calculations of the others, but also have established by dialogue and consent common rules and institutions for the conduct of their relations, and recognize their common interest in maintaining these arrangements (1984:1).

Bull and Watson use this distinction to discuss the evolution of the modern international system, but it applies equally well to the Hellenistic subsystem into which Rome expanded (Wight 1977:chs. 2,3).

RULES AND THE EXPANSION OF ROME

Having located the role of rules in an anarchic arena, it is possible to distinguish between the way Rome expanded to the West and to the East. In essence, in the West, the Romans used military force to expand the empire while in the East they were able to rely much more extensively on the rules associated with diplomacy to regulate or contain any potential threats. The Romans did send troops East, but never initially for the purpose of conquest.

To a very large extent, this divergence was dictated by the very different anarchic structures in the two sectors. In the West, expansion could be achieved only by military conquest. The conquest also proved to be a long drawn out affair, and the Romans were not anxious to see troops permanently tied down in the East before the West was secure. The Romans found, however, that in the areas influenced by Hellenic culture in the East they were able to establish diplomatic links similar to those which existed in Roman municipal life. These links established a system where the dominant party provided rewards in return for services rendered. In the context of the international system, Rome offered security guarantees in return for services rendered by the client states.

The Romans implemented this strategy when Macedon decided to join forces with Carthage during the Second War with Rome. Once this alliance was forged between Carthage and Macedon, Rome quickly moved to establish an alliance with one of the major power groupings in Greece, the Aeotolian League. The Greeks agreed to the link because of the disaffection with Macedon. As a result, the influence of Macedon was replaced by that of Rome. Instead of annexing Greece, Rome developed a stable system of alliances. These alliances were based on treaties which in turn were built on the bedrock of diplomatic rules and practices that represented an important feature of the Hellenic and later the Hellenistic subsystems. As a consequence, the alliances with client states in the Hellenistic system were always more effective than the client states which the Romans endeavored to establish in the barbaric kingdoms of continental Europe. Nevertheless, the

Romans tried to promote the German tribes into clients by educating their rulers. By channeling money and favors to certain key chiefs, they helped them to increase control over their own subjects, thereby tightening the hold which the Romans had over the chiefs. (Luttwak 1976:36)

When Macedon tried to renew its influence in Greece in 174 B.C., however, the Romans chose to see the move as threat to the Greek allies, and in place of diplomacy they resorted to force. The Macedonians were decisively defeated at Pydia in 168 B.C. The Macedonian monarchy was brought to an end and the territory was divided up into four republics. Twenty years later, when this solution failed and Rome was once again confronted by resistance in Greece and Macedonia, both were annexed and Greece was placed under the control of the Governor of Macedonia.

As Crawford observes, whenever one solution failed, the Romans were always sufficiently flexible to try another (1978:94). The move East was slow and cautious and the Romans displayed a constant reluctance to annex territory, preferring always to rely on diplomatic methods that presupposed the existence of established rules and a mutual willingness to abide by agreements. Roman expansion to the East eventually came to a halt when the Parthian Empire was confronted. Once the Romans discovered that they were unable to use either force or diplomacy to dominate the Parthians they recognized that it would be beneficial to establish a diplomatic settlement with them. Roman security depended primarily on the agreements struck with the Parthians on the Eastern border of their empire.

The agreements between the Romans and the Parthians open up a number of theoretical questions about the nature of the relationship between the two empires. It is necessary, in particular, to pose the question as to whether the agreements enabled the two empires to coexist rather than coact. This distinction plays an important role in both Waltz's theory and in ours. In Waltz's framework the distinction is used to identify when a system comes into existence; in our framework, the distinction helps to identify the movement from subsystem dominance to system dominance. This issue needs to be located in the context of a wider discussion about the relationship between continuity and transformation in the international system.

CHAPTER NINE

Continuity and Transformation in the International System

We shall now relate the previous discussion about the intimate relationship between agent and structure to the issue of continuity and transformation in the international system. As we observed in the opening chapter to this Section, the competing theoretical perspectives adopted by Wallerstein and McNeill throw very different light on the meaning of continuity and transformation provided by the Neorealists. The simplest framework is Waltz's, who argues that an international system comes into existence only when states start to coact. From his perspective, it is possible to envisage an international system steadily expanding as an increasing number of states come into contact with each other. But it is also possible on the basis of this perspective to conceive of independent international systems coexisting simultaneously. In either event, as far as the Neorealists are concerned, transformation can be said to have taken place only if the ordering principle of anarchy is replaced by hierarchy. It follows that if the Roman Empire is conceived to be an independent system that did not coact with other political entities, then in terms of the Neorealist framework, the emergence of the empire can be discussed in transformational terms.

This is indeed how Wallerstein describes the formation and the collapse of the Roman Empire; but clearly Waltz does not picture the Roman Empire in this way. As far as he is concerned, the Roman Empire was constantly interacting with other political entities. Waltz's position is partially endorsed by McNeill, who postulates that there were, from a very early stage, links between the political communities right across the Eurasian land mass. The Romans, for example, are seen to have coacted directly with the Parthians and the barbarian tribes on the periphery of the empire's borders and indirectly with the Chinese. But McNeill's framework is also very different from the

155

Neorealist one because he conceives of the Eurasian landmass as being occupied by four competing cultural areas separated by the tribes of barbarians. Structural Realism aims to take advantage of the insights offered by McNeill while acknowledging the importance of parsimony in the Neorealist position.

DISTINGUISHING SYSTEM AND STRUCTURE

Central to our theoretical framework is the conception of an international system. Waltz argues that a system consists of a set of interacting units and a system-wide component—its structure—that makes it possible to think of the system as a whole (1979:79). This definition is more elaborate than most; a system is usually defined simply as "a set of interacting parts" (Reynolds 1980:185). It could be argued that Waltz's notion of a structure does no more than spell out the criteria that identify the interacting parts as a set. But as we have seen, this is not the case. By looking in detail at Waltz's conception of structure we have shown that it is inextricably tied to the conception of agency. Rational agents, according to Waltz, are constrained by the structure of the system to act in a way that reproduces the structure of the system. His conception of structure, therefore, points in the direction of structuration theory rather than system theory. Systems theorists argue that a system can be identified by the fact that "change in any of the components, or in the interactions among them, produces changes throughout the system, or its breakdown" (Reynolds:1980:186). Such a formulation does not require the existence of rational agents and it can apply to natural as well as social systems.

It is important to recognize, however, that in the first instance our initial conception of system coincides with system theory rather than structuration theory. Consequently, in a primitive international system, it is not necessary for all the political units to be directly linked with or even aware of each other. So, to take an extreme example, a chain of states, where each state has contact with, and knowledge of, only its immediate neighbors, nevertheless constitutes an international system. The point about such a system is that goods and knowledge can potentially pass from one end of the chain to the other, bringing about change in each state in the process. Provided that all the information or goods do move along the chain in this way, then all the states are, albeit indirectly, linked and thus constitute an international system. Waltz, of course, would deny that such an arrangement constitutes an international system. From his perspective, the component states are not responding to or reproducing an international structure. They are simply interacting with their neighbors and Waltz is quite clear that interaction of this kind does not generate a systemic structure.

It is evident, for example, that a balance of power could not be developed in this system. Although there could be a process of internal balancing, it would take place on a sequential basis, as one neighbor emulated another along the chain. Even this possibility presupposes that the states in the chain are all identically structured and are equally receptive to new developments. If one state hiccupped and distorted the change carried out by its neighbor, then it would be the distortion that would be emulated further along the chain. As in the game of Chinese whispers, in such a system it is likely that any beneficial change introduced by a component state would be rapidly modified or distorted as it was passed along the chain. There could, moreover, be no effective provision for external balancing. It follows that if, in line with the analogy of Chinese whispers, the absolute power of states was steadily magnified as one neighbor endeavored to emulate another, the state at the end of the chain would be stronger than every other neighboring state and it could, slowly but surely, and with increasing ease, absorb each successive and weaker neighboring state.

It can, of course, be argued that this chain model is unhelpful because social systems always do possess a structure. But such an assessment can be challenged on the grounds that units do interact in the absence of a systemic structure. The chain model, as a consequence, does not have to be treated as counterfactual. If the chain is turned into a circle, for example, it has more than a passing resemblance to the Kula Ring discussed in chapter 8. It can also be suggested that missing from the initial discussion was the recognition that the Kula Ring represents an anarchic system which lacks an anarchic structure. In contrast to the Neorealist model of an international system, therefore, it can be suggested that the tribal agents were not rationally endeavoring to ensure the survival of their political units; their rational interest was in trade. The survival of the anarchic tribal units can thus be seen as an unintended consequence of the complex transnational trading links associated with the kula. The resulting international anarchy, therefore, is a second-order and contingent consequence of the kula. As a result, it cannot be seen as a structure, unintended or otherwise, constraining the participants in the kula. On the other hand, if the units became centralized and generated a security dilemma with associated balance of power behavior, then it would be appropriate to suggest that the anarchy had developed structural properties which would necessarily constrain the behavior of the tribal units. (See Section III for a discussion of necessary and contingent anarchy). It would also be appropriate to suggest that the system has undergone a transformation.

Very far from being counterfactual, it could be argued that the chain model outlined above sheds considerable light on the early evolution of the international system, when levels of interaction capacity were low. It suggests that, in the first instance, it is appropriate to think of the early international system as one without a political structure. To help in the analysis of such a system, it is useful to draw upon the notion of sectoral analysis. The system can be seen to lack any political or strategic dimension. But it does contain a societal and economic dimension because it is the circulation of knowledge and goods that makes it appropriate to identify the political entities as forming an international system. But it can now be argued that such a system is necessarily subsystem dominant, as indicated in Section I, because the system itself lacks any overarching structure.

It is an anarchic system in which the component units interact in the absence of an anarchic structure. Waltz is unable to incorporate this idea in his theory because he assumes in the first place that the state is inevitably a repository of power. As the Kula and Carthaginian examples suggest, however, this is not necessarily the case. Waltz also fails to distinguish between different types of coaction. By focusing exclusively on coaction of a strategic and political nature, he inevitably postulates a structured anarchy.

Of course, states can develop as repositories of power, and when they do so, they will start to coact on a political and strategic basis. Under these circumstances, Neorealist theory can be seen to come into play. But in terms of the evolution of the international system, it must be recognized that coaction of this kind emerged initially on an isolated or local basis. In other words, within the unstructured international system there emerged regional or local subsystems with an identifiable structure. This structure constrained the behavior of the rational agents and the structure of the system was thereby reproduced. Neorealist theory applies to these subsystems whenever this structural condition can be seen to be in operation. Because these structured subsystems were part of the unstructured international system, however, unit behavior was necessarily affected by environmental interaction with the international system as well as by the structure of the subsystem. Inevitably, there would be occasions when structural constraints conflicted with environmental interaction. Under these circumstances, rational agents could endeavor either to minimize the effect of environmental interaction and maintain the structure of the subsystem, or respond to the environment and accept that the subsystem would lose its identity. The expansion of the Roman Empire at the expense of the Carthaginian and Hellenistic subsystems helps to throw light on these possible responses.

THE REPRODUCTION AND DECLINE
OF THE ROMAN EMPIRE

It has already been suggested that it is unhelpful to think of the rise of Rome taking place in what Waltz identifies as a closed and structured international system. Roman agents were aware of a wider system, but their actions were systematically constrained only by the structure of the local subsystem within which they operated. As the interaction capacity in the Western Mediterranean subsystem rose, however, coaction with the neighboring Hellenistic subsystem increased. This eventually had the effect of dissolving the boundary that separated the two subsystems. As discussed earlier, the Macedonian Empire, conscious of the growth in power of Rome, allied with Carthage, while the Greek city states, disturbed by the intrusive power of Macedon, were more than ready to take up the offer of an alliance with Rome. With the development of these balance of power maneuvers, the two subsystems merged under a common anarchic structure.

It is important to note that the merger of subsystems can bring about structural transformation. The Romans quickly discovered the desirability of taking advantage of the existing international society in the Hellenistic subsystem. In the West, where the behavior of the barbarian tribes was unconstrained by any established diplomatic or political structures, the Romans had no alternative but to use brute force to establish control. In the East, by contrast, the Romans quickly saw the benefits to be derived from the existing diplomatic rules that helped to sustain the patron-client relationships which prevailed in the area. In the Hellenistic subsystem it was possible for the Romans to use power rather than force to establish a hierarchical structure in the subsystem. As Luttwak notes, "The rulers of Eastern client states and their subjects did not have to see Roman legions marching towards their cities in order to respond to Rome's commands, for they could imagine what the consequences would be" (1976:32).

Although the system of client states in Asia may have come into existence for essentially pragmatic reasons, Roman agents, realizing the effectiveness of the system, came to use it as the basis of their strategy for organizing and defending the empire as a whole. As a consequence, there was no demarcated and defended frontier at this time. Instead, defense against external enemies was left to client states and beyond them to client tribes on the very periphery of the empire. Roman troops were retained within a core region where the possibility of internal threats to the empire still persisted. But these troops also served as a vehicle of power and force. They could be sent to the periphery of the empire to bring new territory within its ambit. They could also be used to give assistance to the troops of client states unable to cope with internal or external threats.

The concentration of troops at the center of the empire provided a source of power. Fear of Rome's troops served to keep client states and tribes compliant. The clients recognized that Rome could not only provide assistance if they were in danger of being overwhelmed but also annex the territory if a client stepped out of line. During the era of expansion, therefore, the Roman troops operated as mobile striking forces and were concentrated along the major routes that led outward to the unconquered territory and inward to the areas of potential unrest. The routes outward were referred to as limes and they ran perpendicular to the secured territory. Underlying this strategy there was the assumption that the empire would continue to expand until it embraced the world. Mann asserts that Tacitus believed that any Roman leader who did not actively promote the expansion of the empire "was guilty of criminal irresponsibility" (1986:177). The Romans, therefore, very effectively managed to incorporate units from the unstructured anarchy as well as units in anarchically structured subsystems into their hierarchically structured subsystem. The empire provides a clear example of subsystemic transformation taking place in the context of the unstructured anarchic international system.

While the Roman Empire was expanding there was a constant interaction between the empire and political communities on its periphery. Civil conflict and determined external opposition, however, were to pose major threats to the hierarchical structure of the system. These two threats played a major role in bringing about a shift in the strategy designed to ensure the survival of the empire. As the opportunities for expansion dwindled, a strategy capable of defending a delimited empire evolved. Symptomatic of the change was the redefinition of established terminology. Instead of denoting a route to an as yet unconquered land, the term "limes" now came to identify the defense barrier enclosing the established territory of the empire. Client states were absorbed and the empire came to be demarcated by defended borders, by deserts and rivers and seas.

Luttwak insists, however, that it is a mistake to see the Romans suffering at this time from some kind of irrational Maginot mentality. He argues that the defense tactics adopted by the Romans at that time can be understood in terms of a rational response by agents confronted by a new security situation which generated new security goals. In the earlier phase, it was intended that the Romans could, ultimately, maintain the security of the Empire, although the unguarded borders meant that in the frontier zones insecurity was endemic. Areas could readily be attacked before assistance could be given. In the second phase, however, there was a demand for what Luttwak calls "continuous security" for life and property (1976:78). The aim now was not to rely on non-Romanized clients. It was intended instead that there should be a sharp divide between those who lived within the empire and barbarians who lived outside. Within the boundaries of the empire there was economic development, urbanization, and political integration. These activities could not go on in the absence of guaranteed security.

In the second phase, therefore, Roman strategy embraced two potentially contradictory requirements. On the one hand, as in the earlier period, there was a need for large striking forces that could deal with major attacks on the empire. It was still essential that the Romans could ensure the ultimate survival of the empire against any form of external attack. On the other hand, it was now necessary to reinforce this requirement with a capacity to prevent isolated raids across the frontiers, disrupting day-to-day security of the population living in the frontier zones. To deal with this kind of threat it was necessary to disperse the troops around the frontier zones. Luttwak argues that the Romans developed a frontier strategy designed to overcome potential conflict between these two very different requirements (1975:75). In the first place he infers from the record that the population living within the empire was fully integrated and that there was no attempt to extend the frontier if in doing so it would embrace a population that would be difficult to Romanize (1976:96).

The Romans then developed a multifaceted approach to defending the frontier that allowed them to deal with low level threats in an economical fashion: in the areas where there were natural barriers, for example, the emphasis was on surveillance, by means of watch towers and signal stations; in desert areas, where the population was concentrated into oases, defense was concentrated instead on the areas of habitation; in more populated regions the Romans relied on the fortified frontier. The fortification did not simply consist of a physical barrier. It also embraced the means for effective surveillance and good communication routes on either side of the barrier to permit rapid movement and concentration of forces. The essential aim of this strategy was to curb environmental interaction. It was being dictated not by the structure of the international system, because there was no structure, but by the desire to eliminate contact with the system. The agents of the state devised a strategy, in other words, designed to reproduce a hierarchical structure in the context of an unstructured anarchic system.

The ultimate collapse of the empire in the West and its survival in the East reveals very clearly the dangers of restricting the analysis of how the state reproduces itself to the idea of a grand strategy. When attention is focused on the division between East and West, it becomes apparent that there were major differences in the way that the two sectors were reproduced in the international system. A comparison can help to explain why the Western sector collapsed while the Eastern sector survived for another thousand years.

Once the comparison is made, it becomes apparent that the familiar explanation, which links the collapse of the empire to the waves of barbarians who swept into the empire, is inadequate. The barbarians had always existed on the other side of the frontier; they were not a new phenomenon. Moreover, the Eastern Empire was also confronted by enemies, among whom were not only the barbarians but also the Persian Empire—a much greater military threat. Indeed, Goffart has gone so far as to question the whole idea of a barbarian invasion. He argues that "Hardly anything has done more to obscure the barbarian question than the talk and images of wandering peoples tirelessly battering down the Roman frontiers and flooding into the empire" (1989:10). He denies, moreover, that the idea of the barbarian invasions represent "a direct reflection of the experience and thinking of those immediately involved in the events" (1989:113). Our image of the decline of the Western Empire is seen to have been largely dictated by Medieval historians. By contrasting the fragmentation of the Western Empire with the persistence of the East, it becomes possible to give a clearer picture of what happened in both sectors.

From the onset of the Empire, the East was more urbanized than the West, with its wealth coming from trade and industry. The agricultural base was also different in the two sectors. In the East, land was owned by independent peasants; in the West it was controlled by the wealthy aristocracy who relied primarily on slave labor. Once the empire stopped expanding, however, slaves became an increasingly expensive commodity. The population decline, which had begun in the third century, also had a bigger impact on the less populated West. Wealth, derived from agriculture, decreased during this period; at the same time, the taxes to pay for an enlarged army increased. By 350 A.D., the land tax had increased three times within the memories of the oldest taxpayers. While the peasant farmers in the East were able to raise enough money from the sale of corn to pay these taxes, the peasant farmers in the West were unable to do so (Brown 1971:36). Anderson notes how the free tenants in the West "fell under the 'patronage' of great agrarian magnates in their search for protection against fiscal exactions and conscription by the State, and came to occupy economic positions very similar to those of ex-slaves" (Anderson 1974:94). The effect of taxation in the West, therefore, was to concentrate wealth even further into the hands of the rich. In the East, by contrast, wealth was more widely distributed and the peasants were able to preserve their independence.

The attitude to the empire in the East and West also increasingly diverged. In the East, where there had always been a tendency to deify the rulers, the provincials became committed "Romans" in late Antiquity. Brown argues that the provincials felt this loyalty "not through the brittle protocol of senatorial or civic institutions, but directly—by falling on their knees before statues and icons of the emperor himself" (1971:42). Christianity reinforced this strong sense of identity in the East where Brown argues there could be observed "violent waves of xenophobia and religious intolerance." (1971:111) In the West, on the other hand, Rome was still a semi-pagan city in the year 400 and the aristocracy subscribed to pagan rather than Christian beliefs.

While it is thus unsurprising to find that the Western Empire was much less united than the East, it should be noted that the West had always been much less stable. The difficulties can be traced back to the Republican period when the Western aristocracy had been unwilling to pay the legionnaires adequate compensation for the victories they won for Rome. As a consequence, the soldiers gave greater loyalty to their generals than to the state. As Anderson notes, "soldiers looked to their generals for economic rehabilitation, and the generals used their soldiers for political advancement" (1974:68). Although the reforms of Diocletian and Constantine improved the situation, the West, "with its strong armies guarding Britain and the Rhine frontier, remained a point of instability, a springboard for generals with the ambition to make a grab for power" (Goffart 1989:19).

Goffart goes on to argue that a very different attitude to the question of security began to develop in the two halves of the empire. He suggests that the dangers posed by the barbarians had to be measured against the instability threatened by a strong army in the West. What began to happen was a conscious decision to transfer military control to Gothic, Frankish, and Vandal chieftains in preference to strengthening the army in the West. In earlier centuries, the Romans had always endeavored to drive the barbarians beyond the frontiers of the empire. But beginning in 382, when the Romans first negotiated a settlement of this kind, the main instrument for ending barbarian aggression was to "grant the offending tribe an area of settlement within imperial territory" (Goffart 1989:14). By 450 a set of autonomous Gothic, Vandal, and Burgundian districts had been established in the Western Empire.

Like Goffart, Brown insists that the barbarians did not engage in perpetual or destructive "organized campaigns of conquest." He views them instead as "gold rush" immigrants from underdeveloped regions who were attracted by the wealth of the empire. But Brown goes on to argue that in the East there was a greater sense of the empire's vulnerability. The "East Romans came to learn that their empire was one state among many, in a world that had to be scanned anxiously and manipulated by adroit diplomacy" (1971:139). When confronted by the Visigoths the East responded with a "combination of force, adaptability and hard cash" (Brown 1971:124). By contrast, the aristocrats in the West preferred to work in cooperation with the barbarians. As Brown notes, "The idea of a united western empire was increasingly ignored by men who genuinely loved the smaller world of their province" (1971:129). The notion that the Western Empire was engulfed by a barbarian invasion is, from this perspective, a historical invention of a later age.

Having explored the rise and fall of the Roman Empire, it is now possible to conclude this Section by spelling out the relationship which exists in Structural Realism between transformation, continuity and deep structure in the international system.

TRANSFORMATION, CONTINUITY, AND DEEP STRUCTURE

The aim of this Section has been to demonstrate that our definition of deep structure as incorporating both the organizational principle of anarchy and the differentiation of units is compatible with the theory of structuration that has been advanced as a way of resolving the problem of structure and agency. But it has also become apparent that the consequences of introducing structuration theory into the study of international relations are both complex and profound.

Three main points about deep structure can be drawn out from our discussion. The first relates to the importance of recognizing that there is an indissoluble link between actions that reproduce the deep structure of the state and those that reproduce the deep structure of the international system. Our emphasis on structure and agency forces this conjunction to the surface. Human agents mediate between the state and the international system. The structures defining the state and the system are constituted or reproduced by the practices established and implemented by these agents. For Neorealists, the link between state and system is indissoluble because the same set of practices are involved. The central task of any political leader is to ensure that the state will survive against internal and external threats. But the leader's actions, argues Waltz, unintentionally reproduce the deep structure of the international system. This line of argument can be consistently maintained because Neorealists identify an invariant relationship between the structure of the state and that of the international system. In reproducing hierarchy within the state, its agents will always be simultaneously and unintentionally reproducing anarchy within the international system.

Structural Realism breaks the extraordinary coherence of this position by introducing the idea of differentiation into the deep structure of the international system. The effect is to open up the idea of divergent political units within it. As Ruggie notes, in the Medieval period the major units in the international system "were known as civitates, principes, regni, gentes, and republicae, the common element among them, the idea of statehood, not yet having taken hold. To these must be added cities, associations of trades, commercial leagues, and even universities, not to mention the papacy and the empire—all of which, for some purposes, were considered to be legitimate political actors" (1986:155). The important consequence which follows the decision to locate both the principle of anarchy and functional differentiation in the deep structure is that the actions reproducing different kinds of political actor must, according to Neorealist logic, necessarily affect the nature of the international arena which is simultaneously generated by these actions. It follows that if the actions required to reproduce the United States in the contemporary international system involve the penetration of other political units, as Strange suggests, then this must affect the way the international system is being reproduced.

The second point directly follows from the first. It relates to the idea that cooperation and rules between states intentionally reproduce the deep structure of the international system. It can be suggested that an international system in which the deep structure is reproduced intentionally will take a very different form from the Neorealist one which is reproduced unintentionally. The difference corresponds to the distinction drawn by Bull and others between an international system and an international society. It is unlikely that there has ever been a structured international system which has operated at either extreme but it can be asserted that the modern international system is increasingly being reproduced on an intentional basis. Our sectoral analysis has an important bearing on this issue. The potential for rule formation extends across all the sectors. It may, in fact, be possible to

		STATE A	
		compete	cooperate
STATE B	compete	international system	hegemony by B
	cooperate	hegemony by A	international society

Figure 9.1. Differentiating the Logic of Anarchy

discuss the reproduction of an international system by focusing on the political and strategic sectors. But to understand the reproduction of an international society, it is necessary to embrace every sector. Rules have been established between states to regulate activity in all the sectors and they cover everything from coffee prices to narcotics trafficking. In the process of performing specific functions in all these sectors, however, these rules also simultaneously help to reproduce the state and the international system/society.

Attention has been drawn to game theory to illustrate this point because of the suggestion that a common logic explains both conflict and cooperation. It is apparent that this argument does not neatly square with the Neorealist claim that the logic of anarchy drives states to pursue competitive policies. A simple matrix (figure 9.1), representing a two state system, reveals the inadequacies of the Neorealist line of argument.

The Neorealists assume the dominance of a strategy where interdependent actors seek to avoid their worst option: the hegemonic outcome where a subordinate state adopts a cooperative strategy, while the dominant state pursues a competitive one. If such a situation persists, the logic of anarchy would give way to that of hierarchy. To avoid this possibility, Neorealists insist that states have no alternative but to pursue mutually competitive strategies, and thereby generate a competitive anarchic system. But the matrix makes clear that there is an alternative outcome, whereby states cooperate and generate a cooperative anarchic society. It is now being recognized that the structure of an anarchic society has a very different form and logic to that of an anarchic system. In an anarchic *system* competition drives states to reproduce their autonomy, and in the process, reproduce the structure of the anarchic system. But in an anarchic *society*, the states are sovereign units and they are reproduced by the process of mutual recognition and common practice. The practices associated with sovereignty simultaneously and intentionally reproduce the anarchic society. Although it is often assumed that anarchy is incompatible with cooperation and interdependence (Milner 1991), it is now beginning to be acknowledged that the logic associated with competitive, autonomous states operating in an anarchic system needs to be distinguished from the logic associated with cooperative sovereign states operating in an anarchic society (Wendt, forthcoming).

The third and final point concerns the relationship between continuity and transformation in the international system. For Neorealists the question scarcely arises. As far as they are concerned, the international system has persisted throughout world history. It follows that their theory does not need to make provision for the emergence or the fragmentation of a world empire. A transformation of this kind can be depicted within the Neorealist framework in terms of a gestalt switch between hierarchy and anarchy, but such a switch is not considered to have taken place and is, as a consequence, left unexamined. Structural Realism introduces the idea of international subsystems that exist within the context of the international system and we have attempted to work out the implications of such a distinction. We can draw on the idea of structure to distinguish between system and subsystem dominance.

In cases of subsystem dominance, the international system lacks a political structure and thus cannot influence the behavior of the units in the system. The subsystems, by contrast, are defined by a political structure that can take the form of either a hierarchy or an anarchy. Transformation can occur within the subsystems but not in the international system itself. Transformation, therefore, can be seen to occur within the context of continuity. This situation changes only when a globally structured international system emerges. Identifying exactly when a fully global international system did come into existence is an important but as yet unfulfilled task. Establishing the answer would require both theoretical work (on the criteria distinguishing subsystem from system dominance), and empirical investigation (into levels and types of interaction, and responses to them). It could be suggested that such a system did not emerge until as recently as the end of the nineteenth century.

III

———

Rethinking the Methodology of Realism

C H A R L E S J O N E S

One reaction to the project undertaken in this book might easily be to protest that the era of structuralist theory in the social sciences has gone, never to return, and ask why we continue busily fitting a copper sheath to our man o' war while the submarines slink by, just as though nothing had happened.

Details of exposition would naturally vary from one critic to another, but it is easy to imagine a pincer movement: historical and philosophical. The historical strand of the argument would point to the Cold War functionality of structuralist theories, claiming that while Karl Popper attacked totalitarian thought directly in *The Open Society and its Enemies* and *The Poverty of Historicism*, he mounted a more subtle but equally necessary defense of reason through work on scientific methodology which yielded in the doctrine of falsification a keystone for mid-twentieth-century positivist methodology, binding together law, conjecture, experiment, and theory. His work, in turn, the argument might go, underpinned neoclassical economics during the crucial decades of Western economic growth following the Second World War. Structuralism in the social sciences, it might be said, was inextricably linked with the statist project which dominated the twentieth century, only to founder in the 1980s.

A second, more philosophical, line of argument would be that the conjunction of individualist and anthropocentric ontology, positivist methodology, and empiricist epistemology associated with structuralist social theories of recent decades was the only possible support of structuralism, and a faulty one at that. Take away these supports, it might be said, and structuralism cannot stand. But this is wrong, and the argument of this final section is an attempt to persuade readers that many supposed foundations of structuralist theory and of modern conceptions of reason itself may be discarded without jeopardizing the disciplined or theoretically informed exercise of practical judgment in the world. More strongly, it will be claimed that the rotten founda-

170

tions need to be hacked away and the prudential nature of statesman-ship again made apparent if we are to have any hope of navigating rather than merely drifting in the seas of post-Cold War international politics.

Such a view runs the risk of alienating more or less everybody. The project will be dismissed from the outset by post-structuralists as hopelessly conservative. But neither can it be accomplished without employing familiar arguments from the sociology of knowledge, and slightly less familiar ones concerning the relation of language to the world, which will immediately provoke howls of rage from philosoph-ical conservatives directed against the reflexive and relativist nature of all such critiques of traditional epistology.

Some readers are bound to feel that truth is reduced here to the status of a privileged metaphor and that an attempt is being made to deprive them of criteria for judging between competing theories, including those contained in the earlier sections of this book. But to say that truths and theories—assuredly two very different classes—are socially constructed and provisional does not amount to an abandon-ment of reason any more than to admit that cookbooks have authors amounts to a denial that there are right ways of cooking and recipes that work, given suitable ingredients, equipment, and conditions. The aim here is simply to switch emphasis and responsibility away from law, theory, recipe, or truth as timeless, certain, or objective sites of authority, vesting it instead in statesmen, scientists, cooks, or philoso-phers acting reasonably in circumstances not of their own choosing. Right recipes do not guarantee good meals; well-conceived theories do not guarantee understanding. But saying so does not inhibit rea-sonable, informed deliberation and discrimination from playing their part in good cooking or effective action. Put another way, the strength of structuralist abstraction lies not in the simplicity and elegance of the structures themselves but in the quality of their articulation with the complex and contingent world in which they serve as guides to action.

The question of why Kenneth Waltz, though clearly much more aware than many of his contemporaries of this articulation of theory and contingency, should have allowed himself in *TIP* to draw back and vest excessive authority in theory *per se*, provides a valuable oppor-tunity to open up these issues. It will be argued that, when carefully examined, the methodological assumptions of Waltz's *TIP* turn out to be mutually inconsistent. ("Methodology," frequently used to refer to the study of practical research procedures, is understood throughout Section III in its broader sense, as the general study of forms of scientific inquiry and explanation.) Is methodological incoherence an inescapable defect of structuralist theory? No, because a viable methodological basis for a systemic theory of international relations can be devised which happens to be consistent with part of Waltz's work but will serve also to bind Structural Realism much more effectively into the broader Realist tradition. This is because the methodological incoherence of Neorealism, which will first be traced to confusions in epistemology, or theory of knowledge, turns out to stem from assumptions about the relation between language and the world. And once this is made clear, and this relation restated in a way that eschews any idea of language as mirror or representation of the world, the way is open for the effective deployment of a Structural Realist approach on the lines set out in the first two Sections of this book.

Any reconciliation of this sort has implications which are bound to be viewed as costs by some and gains by others. Some of these are spelled out in what follows. Perhaps the most important is a more open awareness and acceptance of the role of rhetoric—the persuasive use of language—in what may nevertheless still claim to be a social *science*. The clearest expression of this rhetorical turn here will be the provision of a fresh characterization of the analogous relationship between balance of power theory and microeconomics which pervades *TIP*. Waltz construed this within a broadly Popperian discourse about theory, hypothesis, and confirmation; here it is reformulated as a particular instance of the use of metaphor, and none the worse for that. A neo-romantic theory of language-as-metaphor will be employed to account for the genesis of scientific explanations, to explore what has earlier been referred to as the "idealism of Realism," and to develop discussion, begun in chapter 3, of the disaggregation of state power and the vertical sectoring of the international system.

This approach will involve a critical development of Waltz's structuralist approach of a far-reaching but not wholly unsympathetic kind. It is consistent with the accounts he provides of language and of the genesis of theory, and with the developments and elaborations of Structural Realism provided in earlier chapters of this book. It has the additional advantage of offering methodological support for the positions taken on the disaggregation of power and the mutually constitutive character of structures and agents (and interacting structures) in earlier sections of our book. It also tries to provide further justification, on methodological grounds, for a less sparse theory than Waltz offered, while pointing to the practical advantages of a richer theory as a basis for empirical research and policy prescription.

It might be argued, though the task is not undertaken in this volume, that the rhetorical turn of Section III could prove compatible with a form of scientific realism, rather than with the pragmatism that lies at the heart of the Neorealist position ιand is retained here. The reason for hesitancy is that attempts to spell out this compatibility too easily run into philosophical quicksands. While scientific realism (a philosophical position quite unrelated in its origins to political Realism) is basically an ontological position—a view of what sorts of things there are—it inevitably throws up old epistemological questions of what is involved in identifying such things as there are through concept and language, let alone knowing anything about them. Roger Spegele, for example, with whose work we have sympathy, seems rather too trusting when he bases his "quasi-naturalistic" scientific realist theory of reference on the perceptions of a community of experts, who are able to dodge dogma, ideology, and the unconscious to find agreement on the reference of basic terms employed in discussion of international relations (Spegele 1987:203). Yet a transcendental path in the manner of Roy Bhaskar, important though it may be, seems to require a complementary empirical track to help guide and construct research. It is not at all clear what this should look like in practice.

CHAPTER TEN

Analogy, Theory, and Testing

A majority of social scientists might accept that within the frontiers of the nation state there is a great variety of sources and expressions of social power. Yet many, even of those who hold this position with regard to domestic politics, still accept a Realist view of international relations, regarding coercive force exerted by functionally homogeneous states as ultimately decisive within an anarchic system.

REALISM: DISCOURSE AND POLICY

The breathtakingly audacious appropriation by the modern state of processes of enforcement and of concepts of law, regulation, and order to which this general consensus bears witness has made out of International Relations possibly the last redoubt of unregenerate structuralism in the social sciences. This appropriation has been overwhelmingly successful in modern history. Resistance to it has generally taken the form of attempts, *within* the territory of particular states, to salvage some distinctiveness for the concepts—and realities—of civil society and personal emancipation in the face of the omnipresent totalizing state. This is probably why relations *between* states have often been marginalized, their study too frequently deferred, so that they have been able even at this late date to seem simple, and therefore ideally susceptible to heroic abstraction.

Moreover this state-centricity has identified the Realist approach especially closely in recent years with a politically conservative strand of structuralism and with the positivistic methodology thought bound to accompany it. Realism is ideology to the extent that its employment of the mental trick of abstraction "obscures the real condition of society . . . and thereby stabilizes it" (Mannheim 1936:36). But Realism need not be ideology. It may even, if those familiar with the terminology of International Relations will forgive what must at first seem a paradox, be utopian; better, since utopianism is too often little more than ideology wearing a smile, it may instead be emancipatory.

One reason that Kenneth Waltz's *TIP* led to such prolonged and often tetchy debate during the 1980s was that he inadvertently opened up a battle front between those within the coercive-state consensus, who thought a severe structuralist approach, once clearly enunciated, to be so obvious as to require no defense, and those, often from elsewhere in the social sciences, who had believed structuralism to be already brain-dead, only waiting for its Cold War life-support machine to be turned off.

One intention of this book has been to move beyond the blank mutual incomprehension and evident distaste which were present in some of the early exchanges. In Sections I and II an attempt has already been made to entertain the flux and uncertainty of events, to avoid privileging social structures over the actors who constitute, reproduce, and transform them, and to differentiate, even within the international anarchy, between various forms of power based in a multiplicity of social formations, including the sectoral divisions of the international system offered in Section I. We have contended that all this sums to a reintegration of serious concern with social structure—albeit now in a more subtle and guarded form than Mark-1 structuralism—into a Realist tradition that has always had at its core the unity of deliberation about society and social action: theory and practice.

Because of this essentially conciliatory purpose, and the gentle tone to which it gives rise, the disagreements about many facets of a Neorealist theory of international politics which will so clearly distinguish the authors of this volume from many of their recent Realist predecessors in the eyes of those familiar with the literature may easily appear to the more casual reader as mere family disagreements or scholarly nuances. Yet any such interpretation would miss a most fundamental difference of emphasis concerning the logical status claimed here for any Structural Realist analysis or theory. That is why this Section of the book tries, starting from an examination of the epistemological and methodological assumptions underlying the analogy with microeconomics employed in Waltz's *TIP,* to argue that any theory of international politics is much less a passive representation of unalterable conditions of the social world it treats than a means to the active shaping of that world.

In E. H. Carr's terms, power was divisible into political power, economic power, and power over opinion. In our terms power, which cannot always be reduced to state power, is manifested in several discrete though related sectors of the international system, including the cultural or ideological sector. Though it will often be ineffectual, discourse about international relations amounts to endogenous action within the policy-making process; it is part of the game, never the innocent exposure by disinterested Martians of exogenous constraints upon human policy. In short, what is proposed here is a reaffirmation of the pragmatism and of the unity of purpose and analysis which, even more than its emphasis on the state, constitute the core of political Realism (Carr 1939:6).

All this needs spelling out a little. Carr long ago made clear that the price of exposing the socially constituted character of other people's perceptions of international politics was an admission that one's own views, too, arose within a prior context of culture and interest. Knowledge of society was always relative to one's position in society. Great powers produced ingenious and self-serving arguments to justify the status quo; revisionist powers produced equally ingenious and self-serving critiques of the dominant ideology. Reasoning along these lines had led Karl Mannheim, on whom Carr was to rely so heavily, to exclaim that "political discussion is, from the very first . . . the tearing off of disguises" (Mannheim 1936:35).

Empiricists might be inclined to make light of this. If there is an independent way of testing knowledge claims against the world then it makes sense to reply to Carr that why people hold the views they do is a quite different and perhaps a less important question than whether or not those views are true. But the statesman who, perhaps unconsciously, adopts a rationalist or pragmatist view of knowledge will not escape so easily. Driven, like Carr, to the conclusion that Realism is "just as much conditioned as any other mode of thought," he may feel unable to make universal claims and pursue clear policies based upon them, and so fall prey to less sophisticated opponents who lack such scruples, remaining fully and uncritically convinced of the justice and enduring truth of their claims (Carr 1939:113). It is precisely this sort of moral funk, widely but wrongly believed to follow remorselessly from acceptance of a social constructivist approach to knowledge, which has led many to regard any move along that path as an assault on reason itself.

Alternatively, however, one may take the much more positive view of the relativist dilemma outlined by Mannheim in a work Carr knew well, finding empowerment in the recognition of constraint (Mannheim 1936:42–43). His argument is that discovering the manner and extent of the social determination of one's thought and behavior is a liberating experience—almost a secular revelation—because it brings within reach the explicit choice of struggling to surmount that determination by transforming the social structures through which it operates. Think of knowledge as a social structure and the individual knower as agent, and it will be apparent that this is very much the picture we have been trying to develop in the treatment of structure and agency offered in Section II. All this sounds grand (or vacuous) until one realizes that it is the kind of thing people do all the time, walking across grass, and so creating a new path, because they realize that the old one, however convenient for their predecessors, is taking them out of their way. And calling them "deep" or "generative" renders the major continuities of international politics by which Waltz is almost bewitched no less specifically historical, no less optional, and no less dependent on our behavior for their continued reproduction.

It is impossible to describe the process of political deliberation without at the same time contributing to it in some measure. The idea that there is some more objective meta-discussion of political discourse which is itself removed from the struggle is precisely the illusion that Carr and Mannheim strove to expose. Yet often the political effectiveness of such descriptions appears to depend precisely on their being perceived as something quite apart from the policy-making process, with an authority distinct from and higher than that of world leaders and diplomats smirched by close engagement in political action: an authority deriving from their status as History or Theory or Science.

This argument may be flawed; after all, understanding how the advertisement manipulates need not necessarily stop one from choosing freely to buy the product all the same. But, flawed or clear, it has been widely accepted in practice. Thus Carr conceals his plea for the admission of the Soviet Union to the Great Power club behind what was, to his target audience of British Conservative politicians, a more acceptable, though precisely parallel, argument for appeasing Hitler's Germany. He then grounds both in an overarching historicism. In the meantime, Carr's explicit treatment of propaganda is, to say the least, ingenuous and underdeveloped when judged by his own employment of rhetorical technique.

177

Waltz, for his part, cast his topical appeal for continuity and responsibility in United States foreign policy in a mold of enduring and supposedly universal truths. In each case, history or theory seems to be politically effective precisely because and to the extent that its instrumentality is concealed beneath a wash of science. There is a persistent tension between the requirements and standards of analysis and prescription, science and policy, understanding and action, the academic and the politician.

The argument that follows will therefore be that the Realist tradition of analysis of international relations consists, and is bound to consist, not simply in radical *un*-masking of the kind suggested by Mannheim, nor in "the conservative ideology of the exercise of state power" with which it was recently identified by Justin Rosenberg, but in the taking off *and* putting on of masks by an alternation of creation and criticism, exposure and concealment, conjecture and formalism, utopianism and ideology (Rosenberg 1990:296). Kenneth Waltz's Neorealist theory of international politics, like Carr's *Twenty Years' Crisis,* came at a moment when circumstances were judged by the author to require criticism, concealment, and formalism. This seemed during the brief months between the fall of the Berlin Wall and the invasion of Kuwait to be less the case than at any time since 1914. Nevertheless, even the most masked and statist of Realists, Carr and Waltz included, have always provided possibly unintended clues to escape routes by the use of metaphors that put the state in question by identifying it as person, as actor, or as firm; and it is through an examination of these metaphors, the last most of all, that an attempt will be made to complete and ground our liberalizing move from Neorealism to Structural Realism.

THE ANALOGY WITH ECONOMICS

Throughout *TIP* Waltz makes extensive use of an analogy or formal comparison between balance of power theory and microeconomics (Waltz 1979, 54–55, 72–74, 89–94 and passim). Microeconomics is the study of interactions between economic agents in markets. It is generally contrasted with macroeconomics, the study of the performance of the whole (national!) economy. Economists still start their students off in microeconomics with the model of a free and perfect market as a frame of reference: "free" because there is no bar to entry, "perfect" because no single agent can have a perceptible influence on prices and all must therefore respond to the sovereign market as price-takers. No one pretends that such a market exists, and the student is accordingly led step by step into the more complex and realistic world of imperfect competition. Here—where the number of firms in the market may be a few (oligopoly), just two (duopoly), or one alone (monopoly)—possibilities of manipulation, collusion, and strategy abound. Each actor must be constantly aware of others' actions. Each must calculate the variety of responses to be anticipated in reaction to its own moves. The game has seemed to many observers, Waltz included, to bear an uncanny resemblance to the maneuverings of the balance of power. Oligopoly, with a handful of firms accounting for sixty or seventy percent of the market or more, is seen to resemble the pre-1939 balance; duopoly, with just two firms dominating the market, is readily compared with bipolarity.

Argument by analogy has long held a prominent place in writings about international relations; this, in addition to its centrality in Waltz's *TIP*, is why it has been selected for close examination here. Most familiar is the domestic analogy, where states in an international anarchy are compared to individual persons in a state of nature. More recently, historical analogies have been popular, and students have been invited to examine alliance systems or to compare the *pax Britannica* and the *pax Americana,* asking whether each depended upon the provision of international public goods by a hegemonic power (Kindleberger 1973; Olson and Zeckhauser 1966). Yet one seldom reads a clear account in the International Relations literature of why it is that structural similarity in one sphere of human activity should offer insights into other activities which are similarly structured, or of how one is to decide just which features of a structure are to be transposed in the analogy and which are trivial or irrelevant. Equally, when arguments by analogy are attacked, the attack is usually piecemeal rather than systematic.

Waltz is distinctive, therefore, not so much in his use of analogy as in his justification of it. He provides an explicit account of the methodological basis for argument by analogy, and our next task is to examine that account. It will be argued that Waltz's attempt to use analogy as a method of confirmation within a positivist understanding of scientific theory is incoherent, and indeed that his whole treatment of the testing of theory, both by analogy and by hypothesis, is inconsistent with the greater and better part of his own methodological recipe. There is a ground-clearing job to be done.

SOME TRADITIONAL CATEGORIES

"Reasoning by analogy is helpful," Waltz writes, "where one can move from a domain for which theory is well developed to one where it is not. Reasoning by analogy is permissible where different domains are structurally similar" (Waltz, 1979:89). By his own rules, then, the analogy between balance of power theory and microeconomics that pervades his work requires Waltz to satisfy the reader on several criteria. What is a well-developed theory and how is it recognized? How is one domain distinguished from another? What is it for two domains to be structurally similar? Does the analogy between balance of power systems and markets satisfy these criteria of similarity? And just what kind of help does a legitimate analogy provide? Is its function that of theory? Does it explain? Does it suggest hypotheses? Does it confirm? Or what? Again, how important anyway is this argument to Waltz's theory? Are his central contentions threatened if this bastion falls?

The first of these questions plunges us straight away into something of a mire. The best way to begin would appear to be to establish what would count for Waltz as a well-developed theory, and to see what his views on this subject commit him to. The epistemological question is fundamental here, because methodology, best defined as procedures of investigation and standards of explanation, generally follows from epistemology. How you set about establishing truths is a function of what you think knowledge consists in. But the account both of knowledge and theory which Waltz provides is a hybrid, uneasily combining at least two incompatible epistemological traditions. Because of this, and because his positivist attitudes toward testing (methodology) might automatically though wrongly brand him for many readers as an empiricist (epistemology), a few paragraphs must first be devoted to clarification of the terms in which the analysis of these questions has customarily been couched. Three are used here—"empiricist," "rationalist," and "pragmatist"—to refer to broad attitudes toward the nature of human knowledge, or to use the philosophers' neater term, epistemologies. To avoid confusion it should at once be said that for much of the modern period the problem of knowledge and the quest for secure foundations of knowledge—for certainty—has been central to Western philosophy and that each of these positions stems from this core epistemological project. Yet now it no longer holds the center of the stage. Indeed, it will be argued below that ontological, rather than epistemological, distinctions provide the ground of social inquiry and account for its peculiar richness and difficulty. More of this later.

Empiricists take the view that knowledge derives from experience. We receive information through our senses, and whatever we know of the world is ultimately derived from these sense data. The central function of language is simply to represent experience, and it is possible, in principle, for language to function as a transparent medium facilitating a near-complete and wholly literal description of the world. Our knowledge is regarded as a representation—doubtless sometimes erroneous or incomplete—but a representation none the less, corresponding to the external world.

(Notice already how shot through with metaphor is this description. We use the phrase "external world" without thinking about it. Is the perceiving self material? [a series of brain-states, perhaps?] If so, it, too, is part of the world that can only be known about by experience: that is, the "external" world. Outside what? Is it instead something incorporeal? Then it has no location, and the spatial metaphor of internal/external must be taken as figurative. There are not two things here, each of the same kind, one of which is inside and one outside. The figure [internal/external] is a way of covering up or smoothing over an incoherence in a great deal of our talk about perception and knowledge. Exposing this is not equivalent to peeling off a rotten layer of the onion to reveal clean white growth beneath, nor need it make any difference to our beliefs, behavior, or talk, for there is no obvious literal clarity beneath the metaphor [Beneath?!].)

The rationalist, while still intent on the quarry of certainty, gives a much more prominent role in the creation of knowledge to the knower. Rationalists very often set out from the question: "How can anyone make sense of the constant stream of sense data?" The argument is that there are certain categories—space, time, number, and the like—which must logically be prior to knowledge, since without them we could make no sense of our experience. One way of putting this is to say that though there may well be a world "out there," our knowledge of it is constrained by the kind of beings we are, the kinds of senses our bodies are equipped with, the way our minds work, or the kinds of social practices, language above all, which we have developed in order to interpret the world and to act and survive in it. Human knowledge, this is to say, is not direct, universal, or absolute, but is constrained by human nature and needs or, at the very least, by the constitution of human reason.

Before turning to pragmatism—the third and, it must be said, the favored position—it may be worth recalling why this brief excursus into epistemology was necessary in the first place. For empiricists, no truth about the world can be established other than on the basis of experience. Rationalists, on the other hand, take the view that we may have a priori knowledge of the world. This means, literally, knowledge *before* experience; but the sense of "before" is not temporal. Rather, the rationalist claim is that there are things we know independently of experience, so that, for example, we might confidently dismiss the evidence of our senses as illusory if it appeared to be supporting a proposition we knew, a priori, to be false. Sometimes we cannot believe our eyes; rationalism helps to justify such disbelief. There is also a stronger implication to be drawn from a rationalist position: there may be a class of a priori truths which are not true simply by virtue of the meanings of their constituent terms, but inasmuch as the world is as they claim it to be. Statements expressing such truths are "synthetic" in the sense that their predicates are not just restatements of their subjects but add something new; they are also a priori, known independently of experience. Synthetic a priori knowledge, if it makes any sense at all, would seem to consist in all those things we know about the world because they must be true of any possible world which, being as we are, we could know about.

It will shortly become clear that Waltz commits himself to positions in the first chapter of *TIP* which make it quite impossible to regard him an empiricist. At the same time he is at pains to avoid an outright rationalist position, and for good reason. His theory therefore purports to identify and explain an orderly reality beneath the flux of events without making entirely clear either the ontological status of this reality or how we may have knowledge of it. This, coupled with a positivist methodology with empiricist implications, has led some critics to brand him, confusingly, as an empiricist. Spegele, for example, accuses Waltz of espousing an empiricist theory of meaning

182

while in the same paper quoting methodological declarations from his work that are more consistent with a pragmatist, or even a rationalist epistemology (Spegele 1987: 196, 201).

All this might seem mere nit-picking. Yet how these questions are decided makes a tremendous practical difference to the manner in which one may properly set about the study of international relations, to the status and implications of truth claims, and to views of the relation between investigation and policy. Accepting the empiricist position, one may set out to hypothesize and to test one's beliefs against the observed world; accepting a rationalist viewpoint one is more likely to place emphasis on social order as the working out of rule-governed behavior in a world of happenstance and contingency. The first position aspires to greater objectivity, and hence to a different relationship with policymakers, than the second.

The distinction is comparable to that between the two routes leading to knowledge of natural law as outlined by Aquinas. The first lay through observation of the extent to which different peoples shared common behavior and institutions; the second, through a quasi-deductive process of deliberation from allegedly self-evident fundamental principles (Aquinas [1973]). The results of the first process may effectively be delivered by advisers as an intermediate intellectual good to statesmen who have not themselves done the work. The second requires that statesmen themselves participate in the deliberative process rather than simply act as its executants. This is because in the Thomist scheme of things the contingency of human affairs means that arguments from first principles of natural law, unlike theoretical deductions, are indeterminate in outcome. It matters just who does the deliberating, and good statesmen are those whose deliberations are most prudent. Waltz shows great reluctance to decide between the two paths, his world leaders seem much more molded by than molders of the structures in which they operate, and the methodological compromises stemming from this epistemological fudge pervade the whole of the *TIP*. But they are perhaps more than commonly evident and most easily exposed in the analogy between the balance of power and microeconomics, shortly to be considered.

This digression has delayed consideration of the third epistemological viewpoint, pragmatism, which, alongside empiricism and rationalism, has dominated philosophical debate. It is time to get back on course. Pragmatism is in some respects a compromise position, in others a rejection—some would say an evasion—of the traditional question concerning the grounding of knowledge. It is less concerned with the source of knowledge, whether in experience or in human rationality, than with the consistency of one knowledge claim with another. Rationality is founded on certain basic logical rules, so the argument runs. One such is noncontradiction. We cannot simultaneously hold it to be the case that both "a" and "not-a," where "a" is some claim about the world. The dialogue between experience and reason continually poses questions about which of our beliefs may be preserved and which must be rejected, but it does not absolutely determine the answers. We are left with choices; and our criteria for choice always include the question: "If we drop this or that cherished belief—if, for example, we drop the claim that the earth is the center of the solar system and replace it with a Copernican claim placing the sun at the center—just what do we gain and what do we lose? Which of our old beliefs will have to go because they are incompatible with the new claims? What previously anomalous observations from experience can now be made sense of systematically?"

Why should there be anomalies? Why should it ever be the case that one knowledge claim is incompatible with another? If empiricism were correct, incompatibility could arise only from error. It should therefore be resolved, not by arbitrary choice, but by scientific investigation, which might consist in procedures of hypothesis and testing of theory or else the cleaning up of the language of investigation so as to yield a pure descriptive language in which the whole set of truths about the world could, in principle, be rendered in a set of mutually consistent propositions.

It was precisely this logical positivist project of developing a logically perfect language, perfect, that is, in its correspondence to and total representation of the world, that foundered between Ludwig Wittgenstein's *Tractatus Logico-Philosophicus* of 1921 and his later *Philosophical Investigations* (though it must be said that the worm was already in the bud in the earlier work, as Bertrand Russell observed in his prefatory comments on Wittgenstein's distinction between meaningful propositions and the inexpressible expressiveness of language) (Wittgenstein 1961:xxi). By his later years, Wittgenstein had come to the view that certainty did not stem from the faithful execution of a sequence of logical steps or from careful observation but from a belief's being "anchored in all my questions and answers, so anchored that I cannot touch it" (Wittgenstein 1969:16).

If clear and transparent expression of knowledge about the world is not to be had, whether because of the fallibility of our senses, the nature of our rationality, or the shortcomings of language, then epistemological emphasis shifts from correspondence to coherence, the methodological emphasis from testing to action. The pragmatist question emerges: are our beliefs consistent one with another, at least to the extent that we may have mutual understanding and some degree of social order? Empiricism and rationalism survive in the background, one may say, so long as pragmatism strives for a bundle of propositions which is to be considered maximally consistent with experience, or rationality, or both. This consistency might seem to let empiricism or rationalism back in, but perhaps this is only so if consistency is read in terms of some strictly spatial or geometric metaphor involving the point-to-point projection or mapping of propositions constituting a belief system on to the world around us or out of our minds. If consistency is modeled instead on the image of game playing, defined by the ability to make successive, never pre-determined steps within a set of rules, then this problem may seem less important.

Later it will be argued that pragmatists are no better off in any attempt to use hypothesis or analogy to test a theory than are empiricists, precisely because they cannot justify the projection of theory on to the world through hypothesis any better than empiricists can. But this is not nearly such bad news for pragmatists as for empiricists, since the former group can still fall back on the consistency of belief with action, thereby dodging ontological and epistemological wrangling. "Children do not learn that books exist, that armchairs exist, etc., etc.,—they learn to fetch books, sit in armchairs, etc. etc." (Wittgenstein 1969:62). Waltz's epistemological error, in a nutshell, is not to have disentangled his pragmatism from remnants of rival positions; his consequent methodological error, not to have realized the flexibility conferred on political discussion by a thoroughgoing pragmatism and the impediment, by contrast, presented by a positivist approach to theory and testing.

Going further, there are advantages in moving from a traditional pragmatist position, still within the traditional epistemologically oriented philosophical debate, to a more ontologically oriented view which locates the interaction of material and conceptual entities in a broadly defined sphere labeled "action," which subsumes language. This removes stress from epistemology and places it instead on ontology: are the material instruments and constraints encountered by any human design the same kinds of things as social institutions, language and personality included? If not, then how do they interact? It may have to be conceded that the dualism we hoped to bury alongside the epistemological project (the search for certain knowledge) crops up again when attention is moved to ontology. Provisionally, the changed emphasis might nevertheless be defended because it facilitates treatment of language as a medium both of reflection and deliberation, theory and practice, knowledge and action.

WALTZ ON THEORY

The reason for these philosophical preliminaries will now be spelled out through an examination of Waltz's views about the nature of theory, which, in turn, will help explain his use of and expectations from the device of analogy. The strategy adopted against Waltz might, in the terms of the preceding section of this chapter, almost be characterized as pragmatist; its central thrust is not that Waltz was wrong, but that he tried to construct a single picture using the pieces of not one but two jigsaws, and that this led to needless confusion.

An important way of expressing what is more immediately at stake in all this is to speak of the degree of privilege accorded to different classes of cause. The extremely sparse structural theory of international politics Waltz developed does not suggest that structural forces are the only causes influencing world politics. That would be absurd. Instead, an order of causation is established. The structure of international politics is said to set up constraints within national political systems which influence the choice of leader in great powers and govern the behavior of each leader while in office. The reader is asked to take comfort in the thought that "those who direct the activities of great states are by no means free agents. . . . The pressures of a bipolar world strongly encourage them to act internationally in ways better than their characters may lead one to expect" (Waltz 1979:176). And Waltz very appositely cites Richard Nixon as an example. But this is dangerously close to saying that the security of the structure gives states and world leaders leeway for error and frailty, which cannot be the case if the task of continually reproducing social structures falls upon individuals, as we have contended in Section II. The idea of privilege—of certain classes of cause, of the literal over the metaphorical, of economics over international politics—runs throughout these deliberations and is a principal target of this chapter because in methodology, as in life, privilege exists essentially to resist change and is for this reason in the end not so much wrong as futile.

Returning, now, to Waltz on theory, notice the privilege given to structure over unit, continuity over detail, theory over fact. Notice, too, the privilege given not simply to structural or system-level cause over unit level or individual causes, but also to efficient cause over any notion of final cause or intention. In privileging structure over agent one is necessarily also privileging efficient cause over intention. Structures—whether markets or the balance of power—transform the intentional behavior of uncoordinated actors into orderly but unintended outcomes. Furthermore, structuralist accounts provided by modern economics or by post-Darwinian biology provide powerful reasons for regarding the apparatus of final cause and teleology as redundant when explaining this unintended order.

It is very hard to see how any such privileging could emerge from a radically empiricist account of causation as mere constant conjunction; and indeed, Waltz takes a strongly anti-empiricist line on the nature of theory in the early pages of his book. He goes out of his way to reject naive positions which would represent theory as the mere cumulation of observations of law-like regularities in the world (Waltz 1979:6). Facts do not speak for themselves. In the manner of Kant, whose work he knows well, Waltz outlines two paradoxes before proceeding to a slightly shaky solution (Waltz 1962). Thus Waltz recognizes that "Knowledge . . . must precede theory, and yet knowledge can proceed only from theory" (Waltz 1979:8). He goes on to admit that "facts do not determine theories; more than one theory may fit any set of facts." Conversely, "theories do not explain facts conclusively; we can never be sure that a good theory will not be replaced by a better one" (Waltz, 1979:9).

At this point, all the preliminary moves have been made for Waltz to embark on a discussion of the status of the assumptions of any theory that would place him firmly in one or other of the traditional epistemological camps. Are they analytic or synthetic; are they known a priori or a posteriori; are they necessarily or contingently true (if indeed they can be *true* at all)?

But this discussion does not take place. Faced with deciding whether the origins of scientific theory lie in representation of the world or in some projection of rationality on to the world, Waltz turns instead to a consideration of scientific creativity. "The longest process of painful trial and error will not lead to the construction of a theory unless at some point a brilliant intuition flashes, a creative idea emerges," Waltz claims. This is the end of the line. He continues: "One cannot say how the intuition comes and how the idea is born" (Waltz 1979:9). But however difficult it may be to deal with the question of the logical and epistemological status of theory it is not a problem to be neglected with impunity, and Waltz's failure to pursue it is unfortunate.

Confusion arises in the following manner. While firmly avoiding the empiricist horn of the Kantean dilemma, Waltz is no more anxious to impale himself on the dogmatist or idealist horn directly. But he makes commitments in his first chapter that lead him well down this second road before seeming to double back in a final subsection dealing with the testing of theories. Here he embraces a positivist methodology which seems to presuppose the empiricism he has just rejected.

Let us examine these commitments. Theories, for Waltz, are made up of two sorts of statements, descriptive and theoretical. Theoretical statements are those which include theoretical terms or notions. These have, Waltz insists, no meaning outside the theory (Waltz 1979:6). Their meaning, it seems, arises from differences within the discourse of the theory rather than from reference to a world outside of the theory. The truth of the statements containing them would appear to be a matter of internal coherence rather than external correspondence. Surely this means that such statements—the axioms of a theory—must either be analytic or, just possibly, synthetic a priori judgments (which is to say truths known independently of experience which must nevertheless necessarily be true of any possible world in which entities of the kinds to which they refer are to be found); but there is nothing in the text to indicate that Waltz intends to take this latter, and difficult, route, while there is much that points in the alternative direction.

For example, Waltz maintains that theories are not the kinds of entities that can be judged true or false. Rather, they are successful or unsuccessful, to be judged by "the number of previously disparate empirical generalizations and laws that could be subsumed in one explanatory system" and "the number and range of new hypotheses generated" (Waltz 1979:6). This begins to sound very much like a form of Quinean pragmatism in which truth figures first and foremost as coherence, constrained by experience and by some notion of the marginal cost of holding the very last view that can be tacked on to the hem of a theory before it starts to drag in the mud.

Any reference which theoretical statements make to a possible world is, then, not a matter of one-to-one reference of proposition to fact or mirror-like reflection of reality in theory, in which truth arises unproblematically out of being, but rather an active, shaping, interpretative, or, in Waltz's terminology, an explanatory relation between human reason and the world. "The reason why the use of the expression 'true or false' has something misleading about it—Wittgenstein once remarked—is that it is like saying 'it tallies with the facts or it doesn't,' and the very thing that is in question is what 'tallying' is here" (Wittgenstein 1969:27).

(Note how much more active a part in scientific activity this account of theory gives to scientists, as compared with their rather passive role in empiricist accounts. Scientists are the judges of what is explanatory. Scientists are, it seems, above the game. Scientists—and not the world—give meaning to terms; but in Waltz's account this is done, to his evident disappointment, on the basis of "brilliant intuition" defying further explanation [Waltz 1979:9].)

Where is Waltz's grounding of theoretical discourse in the subjectivity of the scientist to lead us? Perhaps to a sociological account, in the manner of E. H. Carr, of the origins in history and group interest of some of these "brilliant intuitions," plunging scientists back into the objective social world in which they act and from which they derive their intuitions? (Carr 1939). Perhaps to some variety of scientific realism in which the reference of scientific terms is rooted in the continually evolving research community? (Hollis and Nell 1975; Bhaskar 1979). Perhaps into an argument for a broadly dialectical social science construed as conversation, edifying philosophy, or deliberation? (Collingwood 1939; Rorty 1980; Aquinas 1973).

But it turns out to lead to none of these things. Waltz takes cover behind one of the least attractive stratagems of pragmatism, intuitionism. Creativity is to be regarded as beyond explanation. There follows an abrupt U-turn, as theory is welded back to the external world through a positivist characterization of the testing of hypotheses (Waltz 1979:13–16).

WALTZ ON TESTING

Since no theory can be directly tested, so the argument runs, it is necessary to test hypotheses derived from the theory. Successful hypotheses strengthen or confirm a theory, though they can never render it invulnerable. Failures may lead to modifications—dare one say improvements?—but may, on the other hand, accumulate to the point where an alternative paradigm suggests itself.

But Waltz is evasive about the relation of theory to hypothesis. If hypotheses are to be testable against experience, then at a minimum they must be synthetic. This is to say the truth or falsehood of the claims they make must be such as cannot be determined wholly by conceptual analysis. The claim that all bachelors are unmarried is simply not worth testing. If Waltz were the positivist that he has sometimes been taken to be, then he would face the problem of how to derive synthetic hypotheses from the analytical (and therefore empirically vacuous) axioms of his theory.

An obvious stratagem to adopt here would be to suggest that this could be achieved through the reference of terms defined within the axiom system to phenomena in the world. But any such reference would appear to require criterial statements to help identify states, wars, alliances, and other entities central to the theory unambiguously, and these in their turn would have to be either synthetic or analytic. And if such statements are analytic, Hollis and Nell insist, "they do not serve to anchor terms to the world; if synthetic, they do not state the sort of criteria required" (Hollis and Nell 1975:96). Making a closely related point, Wittgenstein once remarked that "the same proposition may get treated at one time as something to test by experience, and at another as a rule of testing" (Wittgenstein 1969:15).

There are two routes out of this predicament. The first requires acceptance of the radical contingency of language. Naming is exposed as arbitrary. There may well be given divisions and patterns in both the natural and the social worlds, but the job of language is not simply to approximate to these, nor can approximation to them ever be simple, because they may not all be captured at one and the same time and, to some extent, they are changed by the manner in which they are named. The mere naming of things is already an exercise of will.

The second view is a form of scientific realism in which science, including social science, can be grounded through real definitions and axioms that amount to truth claims about possible worlds. The gist of this second position may be summarized here as the suggestion that the potential manipulative power of axiomatic systems is such that it is generally worth trying to discover whether the world we find ourselves in is one of the possible worlds for which a given theory happens to yield plausible interpretations or a reliable guide to action. In practice, of course, one never goes out cold to try out a theory and its attendant descriptive language on the world. There is instead a gradual exploration of fit in which behavior, including linguistic behavior, and the world of efficient cause and physical systems accommodate to one another. The great difficulty with such a position, signaled earlier in this chapter, is that it nicely skirts old epistemological wrangles only to land fair and square in analogous and equally intractable problems of ontology and reference: what kinds of things (material? conventional?) are real, and are they all similarly real? However purposeful our language may be, and however infused with metaphor, dead and alive, do some at least of its descriptive terms mark natural kinds of real entity—the chemical elements, perhaps? Finally, must that seemingly privileged reference of descriptive terms to reality be limited to material reality, or might it extend to the kinds of real-though-immaterial entities (states, persons, and the like) that could provide the foundations of social theory?

The positivist project of testing theories against the world poses the question of the status of descriptive language and the way language refers to or latches on to the world in an especially stark way by placing the whole of this burden of accommodation on language, which is expected faithfully to reflect the reality of the external world, and claiming language as being primarily or basically concerned to carry out this charge. Waltz appreciates this and makes it quite clear that he does not wish to travel the empiricist route. He accepts that we experience the world only through language which is already theoretical. "Even descriptive terms acquire different meanings as theories change," he suggests, and "changes of theory produce changes in the meaning of terms, both theoretical and factual ones" (Waltz 1979:12). Neorealist theory, it seems, is happily adrift from the world.

In his methodology, as in his epistemology, Waltz turns out to be a transitional figure, caught like Milton Friedman or Karl Popper, taking shelter under the umbrella of American pragmatism (McCloskey 1986:10; Cottingham 1984:141–43). This has been, in part, the specific predicament of a long generation for whom the experience of totalitarianism had made rationalism uninhabitable. The same generation produced, not by coincidence, classical Realism and structuralist social science.

ECONOMICS AS "MORE DEVELOPED THEORY"

The reason for this detailed examination of Waltz on theory and testing has principally been to expose the inconsistency of his positivist approach to testing with the loosely pragmatist account of knowledge and of the nature of theory which he provides and with which we sympathize. It is no good looking to Waltz himself to provide clear criteria for "more developed theory" which can then be applied to modern microeconomics in order to see whether it is, as he hopes, up to the job of acting as senior partner in the analogy. Waltz manages to make pragmatism seem a compromise between empiricism and rationalism stumbled across in the dark, whereas it is a far more viable and autonomous position than this description suggests.

But it is worse than this. First of all, the incoherence of his own position makes it difficult for one to identify some significant group of economists of a methodological disposition to which Waltz could clearly assent. Secondly, there is in any case no general agreement about the status of theory among economists. Moreover, such agreement as there is turns out to suffer from much the same schizophrenic oscillations between empiricism, rationalism, and pragmatism as does the position adopted by Waltz. It is under attack. The interesting thing—at this point one hardly knows whether it is encouraging or discouraging—is that most economists (and a good few political scientists) still seem quite unperturbed by the rising tide of methodological uncertainty, even though global ideological warming suggests that intellectual defenses everywhere are in for prolonged battering from the waves of inquiry. "It will not do to say about the methodological rules of economists, as a professional philosopher might, 'No one believes that stuff anymore.'" (McCloskey 1986:11). Does this indi-

cate that they are simply obtuse, getting on with the job, made secure
by their privileged status as advisers to powerful organizations? Does
it indicate rather that the profession is shifting gradually to the adoption of a new methodological paradigm, a new way of accounting for
and justifying the procedures customarily adopted in the course of
practical work?

To most outsiders, economics appears much more self-confident
and unconcerned with methodological wrangling than other social
sciences. They have often been dismissively characterized *en bloc* as
empiricists. "Economists," as Michael Nicholson so charmingly puts
it, "tend to be more cheerfully empiricist than political scientists"
(Nicholson 1985). Hollis and Nell, the latter no outsider, cast the
whole Neoclassical tradition into what they regard as the pit of empiricist epistemology and consequential positivist methodology (Hollis
and Nell 1975).

Yet this is gross oversimplification. Economists differ widely on the
importance and logical status they attach to empirical testing of theory. Many are out and out rationalists with no more than a passing
interest in whether this world happens to be one in which their
theories apply. Yet those in the profession most closely concerned
with advising firms and governments have on the whole have been
inclined to be more pragmatic than the rhetoric of their textbooks and
methodological debates would indicate. Models, even where they are
not open to falsification in principle through the testing of hypotheses,
tend to be heavily protected against the cold, just in case. There is an
abiding rationalist concern with the internal consistency and elegance
of models. The position is a curious one, summarized from one perspective by Marc Blaug, who has claimed that "for the most part, the
battle for falsificationism has been won in modern economics [so that
the] problem now is to persuade economists to take falsificationism
seriously," and from a quite opposed perspective by Donald Mc-
Closkey, who notes with approval that "falsification, near enough, has
been falsified" and goes on to remark upon the pragmatist tendencies
indicative of an attempt to escape the bounds of positivism in Milton
Friedman's celebrated 1953 essay, "suggesting that modernism cannot
survive intelligent discussion even by its best advocates" (Blaug
1980:260; McCloskey 1986:10, 15).

How can Waltz seriously appeal to, as "well developed," an inquiry
which is just as riven by methodological dispute, and of the very same

kind, as his own field? Any claim that one area of inquiry is more developed than another clearly requires criteria for judging scientific progress, some sort of meta-methodology; but Waltz does not provide this and one wonders if it is to be had.

STATES AND FIRMS

It now remains only to expose two more problems involved in Waltz's use of the analogy with microeconomics before moving on in the next chapter to consider an alternative way of regarding the relationship and sketch the kinds of microeconomics this might admit.

The first of the two methodological problems concerns the supposed similarity of form between balance of power theory and microeconomics. "It is likeness of form—Waltz claims—that permits applying theories and concepts across disciplines" (Waltz 1979:55). But one cannot at one and the same time hold on to the notion that states are the major units in the international system and the claim that the balance of power and the market are similarly structured. If the first of these claims is true then economics is in a very important sense subordinate to politics because states set the terms on which markets operate. Politics, insofar as it consists in the behavior of states, may be held constant, temporarily frozen, to facilitate economic analysis, but because they are in this sense dependent institutions, markets must be regarded as only *contingently* anarchic. The balance of power by contrast is *necessarily* anarchic. While states may impose their authority upon firms, no institution has equivalent authority over states.

If, on the other hand, the market is to be regarded—like the balance of power—as necessarily anarchic, then it can only be because property rights, and from them the whole pattern of production and exchange, are to be seen as pre- or extra-political social institutions, able to function, in principle, in a world without states. At this point, theories of the need for a hegemonic power to underpin the liberal world economy are threatened, and it is open to thoroughgoing economic liberals to argue that the state system is merely one, and perhaps not the best, possible way of organizing authority relations globally. They might easily argue that the sovereign state is a quite distinctive and recent invention, certainly a sight more recent than systematic exchange of goods between otherwise autonomous societies.

It may be helpful at this point to run through two arguments in a little more detail, the first of which, called "Hobbes," regards markets as contingently anarchic, while the second, called "Rousseau," regards them as necessarily anarchic. In distinguishing these two positions I shall hope to unpack the seeming paradox with which Douglass North opens his chapter on the neoclassical theory of the state. He writes: "The existence of a state is essential for economic growth [Hobbes]; the state, however, is the source of man-made economic decline [Rousseau] (North 1981:20). The interpolations in square brackets are mine; they are, of course, no more than nick-names.

Both views start from the question of what makes it possible for markets to function. One reply is that without the state to allocate and protect property rights, guarantee the enforcement of contracts, and provide standardized weights, measures, and money, markets simply cannot work. It is hard to imagine voluntary exchange in a Hobbesian state of nature where life and property are radically insecure. It is on this basis that Frederick Lane and, later, Douglass North, developed the idea of the state as a special kind of firm, the essential functions of which were to deploy coercion in such a way as to create zones of security and set the permitted levels of monopoly in a whole variety of subordinate economic sectors within such zones (Lane 1966; North 1981:20–32). Waltz appears to share this view. "When the crunch comes," he writes, "states remake the conditions by which other actors operate" (Waltz, 1979:94).

These might seem perverse examples. Are not Lane and North to be regarded as imperialist economists, arch-enemies of political Realism, for their attempt to cast states as firms and, implicitly, to explain political phenomena by applying economic rationality? Are they not reductionists by the useful criteria set up by Waltz? Perhaps so. Yet the key feature of political Realism which is retained, even in their economistic vision of world history, is the privilege given to the state. The state, albeit an economized state, is still required as the actor without which the market system could not operate. Good structuralists that they are (in a general way, if not by the specific criteria set by Waltz), Lane and North respond to the apparent incompleteness of the world normally analyzed by economists by bringing the state and coercion within economics and subjecting them to the kind of analysis paradigmatically applied to the production and exchange of private goods. The market for protection from violence (or the market for public goods such as deterrence or equity) may be a funny sort of market, but that is surely better than no market at all. This strategy promises to restore the autonomy of economics and extend its scope at one and the same time by releasing it from dependence on an exogenous initiating force. It is Realist by its state-centricity and structuralist by its reliance on and privileging of microeconomic analysis.

A second possibility, referred to here as "Rousseau," but available in paperback as "Paine," is to argue for the possible emergence of voluntary exchange on the basis of mutual interest or custom in a pre-political civil society. This argument has a very lengthy pedigree. Unlike "Hobbes," it offers an economic system that, however much it may interact in practice with the political, is every inch as anarchic in essence and origin as is the world of states. But it does so at a price. It requires the consistent Realist to take a step back from customary assertions of the privileged position of the state in international relations and from the more general priority assigned to political power over forms of social power based in other social institutions: in gender and seniority (patriarchy), in language (rhetoric), or in markets (property).

In sum, by employing the argument by analogy between microeconomics and the balance of power in the way that he does Waltz is driven toward an uncomfortable but perhaps unnecessary choice between two Realist dogmas: the centrality of state power and the organizing principle of anarchy.

It has seldom been clear in Realist accounts whether the continuing emphasis on international politics as a distinct domain or field of studies is a separatist or an imperialist ploy. If "Hobbes" is right and state supremacy makes politics a kind of master-social-science, then the analogy with microeconomics is spurious because of the contingent character of the anarchy displayed by markets. (Any superiority of economics as "developed science" might well arise only from the limited extent of its scope and therefore be non-transferable.) But Waltz's insistence on the market analogy and a pervading recognition of the variety of sources and expressions of social power in the broader Realist tradition suggest that something closer to "Rousseau" may offer space for a reformulation of the economic analogy, with its undoubted heuristic value, while retaining an emphasis on the distinctive, rather than overweening, nature of state power. The trade-off directs attention toward an issue that has already received attention in Section I, and to which this Section turns in its final chapter, namely the aggregation of power. Our argument there proceeds from the observation that the multi-sectoral approach of Structural Realism resonates with disaggregated state power, argued for in Section I, since states exercise each of their distinctively distributed capabilities not only in their relations with one another but also in their relations with non-state actors whose core activities may be economic, cultural, or coercive.

ANALOGY AS CONFIRMATION

The second methodological point referred to at the start of the previous subsection also relates to the permissibility of the economic analogy. It has to do with Waltz's view of the role that reasoning by analogy can play in the confirmation of theory. Confirmation may, on his view, be achieved in two ways. One is by the formulation and testing of hypotheses, and attention has already been drawn to problems in that procedure. But Waltz goes on to argue that "structural theories . . . gain plausibility if similarities of behavior are observed across realms that are different in substance but similar in structure. . . . This special advantage is won: International-political theory gains credibility from the confirmation of certain theories in economics, anthropology, and other such non-political fields" (Waltz 1979:123).

There is a certain amount of truth in this. Formally similar axiomatic systems might surely be developed in tandem. But Waltz, if he once admits the problem of getting any grip on the world for purposes of testing theories by the stratagem of developing (synthetic) hypotheses from (analytic) axioms, seems to have only three routes open to him. One would be to admit that any theory is simply a set of analytical truths and is empirically vacuous. Structural similarity between theories then in turn disappears into empirical vacuity. It may persuade people, although it is hard to see why; it certainly confirms nothing. The second alternative might be to seek to ground theory in the world through the rationalist device of essential or real definitions. A variant, rather closer to our own pragmatist position, would be to call an orderly retreat in the face of the difficulties confronting any such attempt to ground knowledge, opting instead for a causal account of reference. This would accept a closer relation between different bodies of discourse and the discrete areas of social practice of which they form a part than prevails between the several and distinct discourses which, traditionally, are regarded as forming a single coherent natural language (Schwartz 1977).

If this pluralist strategy is adopted, and if structural similarities then emerge between one social science and another, it will certainly be a matter of interest and may well change one's view of both fields, but it is hard to see how it will *confirm* either theory. In the first case, confirmation would still make sense, but only within bounded areas of social action. In the second case, the very notion of confirmation dissolves. Instead of being seen as a more or less accurate *representation* of action, discourse—including theoretical or meta-discourse—comes to be regarded as part and parcel of that action. It cannot ground or confirm it.

In any case, the procedures laid down by Waltz for testing a theory, which presumably are to be applied equally when employing analogy in its confirmatory role, are deficient. Describing his procedures for testing a theory, Waltz lays out seven steps. The theory must first be stated. Hypotheses must be inferred from it. They are next subjected to tests, care being taken throughout to employ the definitions and terms of the theory. (This begs the questions of definition, reference, and the bridging from analytic to synthetic, with which we have been concerned in this chapter). Exogenous variables must be eliminated or compensated for, and crucial tests sought. The last step urges the scientist, in the event that a test is not passed, to "ask whether the theory flunks completely, needs repair and restatement, or requires a narrowing of the scope of its explanatory claims" (Waltz 1979:13).

Here is a procedure crying out for criteria. On what basis is one to make these important decisions? It is never entirely spelled out, and to judge by later descriptions of tests it seems that common sense is to be our guide, which is a polite way of conceding that here, as with his account of the intuitive origins of theory, Waltz is content to accept practical limits to reason. To Hollis and Nell, as realists, this feature of pragmatism seems more like an abandonment of reason. They spell out the extent to which it makes a sham of any pragmatist claim to stand at the tribunal of experience. "When experience conflicts with expectation," they insist, "pragmatism always offers the scientist a choice of how to pay the bill. Our objection," they continue, "was that universal choice includes choice of whether to pay the bill at all, and that statements of the 'price' of revisions [i.e. what belief must be sacrificed if another is to be adopted] should, for the sake of consistency, themselves be revisable" (Hollis and Nell 1975:163).

CONCLUSION

The analogy running throughout Waltz's *TIP* has been used in this chapter as a diagnostic tool to discover some of the breaking points of his formulation of Realism. Many of the contradictions have been hinted at, but not yet fully explored. It has, for example, been claimed that traces of positivist positions on theory and testing in *TIP* do not sit well with more pragmatist attitudes on epistemology and methodology in the early chapters. It has been suggested that Waltz does not confront the tension between rhetorical purpose and scientific objectivity as squarely as other (less honest) figures in the Realist tradition, such as Carr. It has been suggested that the pervading comparison between the balance of power and oligopolistic markets, with its nostalgic casting of economics as the most objective of social sciences, exposes a central difficulty of Realism concerning the relation between state power and other forms of social power. Presenting contradictions in this way always leaves open the rhetorical strategy, used to such great effect by both E. H. Carr and Hedley Bull, of suddenly pulling a middle way, a splendid compromise, out of the hat. But compromise or reconciliation of apparently contradictory views is not the only way of having cakes and eating them. Indeed, it is often achieved at the level of policy prescription only by leaving epistemological and methodological issues unresolved, storing up problems for the future. Another strategy is to seek ways of effacing the compromises, leaving the formerly contradictory positions intact, still in conflict one with another, perhaps, but at least in a creative and self-conscious conflict. The view taken here has been that many of the apparent contradictions in Waltz stem from inconsistent, inadequately developed, or mistaken epistemological and methodological positions. The remedy, therefore, would appear to be to establish alternative, less vulnerable foundations. No one builds directly on ground known to be treacherous because of old mine workings beneath it. Instead, it is common practice to build on a concrete raft. No builder mistakes a raft for bedrock, yet the artificial may in these circumstances provide a surer ground than the natural. So next we build a raft.

199

CHAPTER ELEVEN

Analogy and Metaphor

At this point the argument moves from an agenda set by the traditional epistemological mission of much modern British and American
philosophy to an agenda explored until the last twenty years or so
almost exclusively by literary critics and by philosophers in the Continental tradition. It is time to firm up our portrayal of rhetoric, or "the
study of how people persuade" (McCloskey 1986:29).

RHETORIC AND METAPHOR

Now that the attempt to locate the analogy between balance of power
theory and microeconomics within a positivist logic of testing and
confirmation of theory-as-knowledge has been exposed as incoherent,
an alternative path deserves to be explored, in which the relation
between economics and international politics is characterized as metaphor. It makes much better sense of Waltz's view of theorizing and
explanation as creativity or intuition. It reformulates the difficult question of how, for the pragmatist we take him to be, international
theory, microeconomic theory, or any other social theory relates to
reality. It fits his views about language as outlined in the previous
chapter. It also offers solutions to two abiding weaknesses of political
Realism identified in the opening paragraphs of this section: the problem of relativism, identified by E. H. Carr building upon the work of
Karl Mannheim in the 1930s, and the all-pervading question of the
relationship between science and policy, analysis and prescription.

Here is a theory of metaphor to which we do *not* subscribe. Normally, people use literal language. Sometimes they embellish in order
to gain attention, as a form of shorthand, to focus on some special
aspect of our subject, or simply to dazzle. We may speak of "the
Eagle" and "the Bear" instead of the United States and Russia. But
such figures of speech are optional. We can do without them, and it is

always possible, though it may be cumbersome, to spell out literally what is conveyed for ease and pleasure through metaphor or by some other figurative use of language.

A corollary of this view is that when we wish to speak with precision, as in scientific inquiry or where great issues are at stake, we are best advised to eschew metaphor. Thomas Hobbes was very much of this view. He is best known, especially to students of international relations, for his claim that social order could not be maintained except by a central authority backed by force. But he also offered, as a further reason why men and women could not live in ordered self-regulated anarchy, as bees did, that mankind had the ability, through language, to deceive intentionally. The way to suppress deceit in human affairs, he argued, was to avoid metaphor. Counsellors, for example, in assisting the deliberations of princes, were to avoid "all metaphoricall Speeches, tending to the stirring up of Passion, (because such reasoning, and such expressions, are useful onely to deceive)" (Hobbes [1909]:199). Again, in his attack on the temporal pretensions of the Church, Hobbes criticized clerics' deceitful use of terms referring to "incorporeal substances" to mystify the faith. "Satan," he claimed, was simply a word meaning "the enemy." The personification of demons, one of his favorite targets, arose from leaving abstract terms untranslated (Hobbes 1909:354).

The irony of later metaphorical extensions of Hobbes's treatment of individual persons in a state of nature to apply to relations between states in an anarchical system will be apparent. But the immediate point of referring to Hobbes has been to make clear the historical, and hence relative, character of the emphasis placed in modern Europe on the literal. Earlier writers had used metaphor extensively. But a reaction had set in during the second half of the sixteenth century. The task undertaken by Hobbes had already been begun by Peter Ramus, who had produced a revised taxonomy of traditional rhetoric conducive to a separation of content from form, argument from embellishment, the literal from the metaphorical (Hawkes 1972; McCloskey 1986:29–30). He may be seen as redeeming rhetoric for the time being by advocating the combination of logical analysis and rhetorical expression, argument, and embellishment. But in making the distinction between the two so clear he has been seen as paving the way for the rationalist correspondence theories of language of the eighteenth century.

This move, Hawkes argues, coincided with a privileging, facilitated by the new technology of printing, of the written over the spoken word. It coincided also with the parallel tendency, facilitated by the development of printing, for codified law more and more to replace the deliberative processes of king in council and customary or common law and for printed notices to take the place of spoken announcements or judgments (Jones 1987). Writing began to be regarded as more precise, more permanent, and less swayed by the passions than spoken language. Writing took language half way towards Euclidian geometry, which provided an ideal of precision and certainty for the seventeenth century. Hobbes finally codified these new approaches to language so persuasively that for most of the modern period people of European descent have been sharply distinguished from their Muslim contemporaries by their willingness, whether believers or not, to read the Christian scriptures as metaphorical works, variously looking for richnesses of meaning in them through their metaphors, dismissing them as meaningless because metaphorical, or else, rather feebly, claiming that they possessed a different, and more or less privileged, kind of meaning than literal texts, but always accepting a duality which would be regarded as deeply offensive by Muslims if applied to the Qur'an.

This consensus, and the beginning of its downfall, are both evident in a remark made by Immanuel Kant in the preface to the first edition of the *Critique of Pure Reason,* published in 1781. Kant, and this particular work of Kant's, is referred to here because it provides at one and the same time the most powerful summation of the epistemological mission of Western philosophy and the seeds of a dissolution of this project to be achieved by German philosophy over the following hundred and fifty years. To epistemologists it still provides the most complex statement available at the very end of the European Enlightenment of the tension between empiricism and rationalism. It represents in short the apogee of the philosophical tradition in which Waltz places himself. Yet it can also be interpreted as a Romantic work offering, as does political Realism, the possibility of a radical break with the epistemological project. This makes Kant's remarks on rhetoric and politics of more than passing interest.

In the first critique Kant admits the heuristic value of examples and illustrations, but feels that "such assistance is not required by genuine students of the science, and, though always pleasing, might very well in this case have been self-defeating in its effects." Too often, he continues, "the bright coloring of the illustrative material intervenes to cover and conceal the articulation and organisation of the system, which . . . chiefly concerns us" (Kant [1933]:13). It seems a clear enough opting for the literal. But why on earth should Kant choose to make the point metaphorically, seeming almost to deny his commitment to the truth of the proposition by the way he expresses it? The long locked door between content and expression begins to open. Why else, in the work that follows, do metaphors abound, and abound most freely in the treatment of error in the Dialectic? If metaphor is a source of confusion and error, should it not be eschewed most of all in a treatment of the errors to which human reason is subject? Why, above all, is the Dialectic, explicitly concerned with human reason and knowledge, shot through with *political* metaphors? And why, finally, do those political metaphors, on examination, turn out to refer to a multiplicity of mutually inconsistent constitutions and plots? It is hard to resist the conclusion that no text can achieve its rhetorical or political objective without at some point compromising the truths it purports to convey. There is always more than one audience, and in an anarchic world one at least of the audiences must be lied to if truth is to prevail? Realism proceeds by the taking off and putting on of masks.

A ROMANTIC ACCOUNT OF METAPHOR

This is not the time to spell out detailed answers to these questions. The short answer is that Kant's linguistic practice is indicative of a moment in which the supremacy of the literal was beginning to be challenged. A strain of thought about language running from Vico, through Herder and the English Romantic poets was giving rise to a new attitude towards metaphor, summarized neatly by Terence Hawkes. For the Romantics, he suggests, "metaphor cannot be thought of as simply a cloak for a pre-existing thought. A metaphor is a thought in its own right." As a corollary, "there is . . . no way in which language can be 'cleared' of metaphor' " (Hawkes 1972:55).

An extension of this revival of rhetoric has been the widespread substitution for language-as-representation of language-as-metaphor in characterizing the relation between language and the world. This removes the stress from a whole family of concepts including theory, measurement, accuracy, approximation, and truth and places it instead on creativity, richness, elegance, exploration, inquiry, suggestion, interaction, conversation, and success in the general characterization of what scientists are about when they do science. It will readily be seen that there is a family resemblance here between literalist views of language and empiricist characterizations of knowledge on the one hand, romantic theories of language and pragmatist epistemology on the other.

For many contemporary philosophers, even those writing in the Anglo-American analytical tradition, things have now come full circle. Willard Van Orman Quine captured the reversal of view very neatly, affirming that "it is a mistake . . . to think of linguistic usage as literalistic in its main body and metaphorical in its trimming. Metaphor or something like it," he continued, "governs both the growth of language and our acquisition of it. Cognitive discourse at its most dryly literal is largely a refinement rather, characteristic of the neatly worked inner stretches of science. It is an open space in the tropical jungle, created by clearing tropes away" (Quine 1960:188). ("Trope," meaning "turn," is the term used by rhetoricians to describe figurative uses of language.).

To get a sense of the far-reaching implications of the Romantic approach to metaphor the student of International Relations need only consider that most familiar of metaphors in the field, the personification of the state. It is customary to discuss the rights and obligations of states, to speak of international society, and also to point out the limits of the metaphor: states are not so easily killed as individual persons; they have no natural point of physical maturity; they are much more unequal in (physical) power than are individuals; etc. (Bull 1977). There can be few better examples of a metaphor which, far from expressing felicitously an existing state of affairs, creates a reality and a set of obligations that would not otherwise exist. As Carr once put it: "There is a world community for the reason (and for no other) that people talk, and within certain limits behave, as if there were a world community" (Carr 1939:206).

A literalist approach to metaphor might concede this act of linguistic and social creation, but would surely wish to maintain that it was rooted in a fundamental use of the language of personality, obligation, and rights relating to individual persons. The Romantic approach takes a further step, revealing the literal as already metaphorical.

How is this done? In the present example the path leads to the treatment of personality provided by Marcel Mauss. By means of comparative anthropology Mauss set out to persuade his reader that the relationship between the self and the person was not everywhere and always as close as in modern European culture. Mauss observed the manner in which a proper name together with social roles and obligations pertaining to it would be assigned to an individual within some indigenous American cultures for a lifetime, passing on the death of that individual to another carrier. Personality of this kind had a continuity extending beyond any single life and was clearly distinct from one's more primitive sense of being-just-here, of being oneself and not some-*body* else. He went on to claim that in the West it was only during the classical period that the concept of personality as something superimposed upon individuals began to be extended to "the individual, with his nature laid bare and every mask torn away." Here, surely, was an act of linguistic construction of reality every bit as audacious as the later personification of the state or the partial substitution of political argument for physical battle (Carrithers 1985; Mannheim 1936:34).

And if anyone recalls that Mauss himself preserved the literal even while exposing the conventionality of notions of personality when he noted how a distinction still remained, after this superimposition of personality on the individual, between "the sense of what is the innermost nature of this 'person' (*personne*), and the sense of what is the 'role-player' (*personnage*)," it can be conceded that what was true of Mauss was true also of other neo-Kantian theorists of language, metaphor, and consciousness for whom the transcendental deduction, with the burden which it placed on selfhood, remained the most alluring yet problematic passage in the *Critique of Pure Reason* (Müller 1887, 1889). All that can be said here is that any claims for universality of a human selfhood beneath the socially constructed personality is itself vulnerable to attack through social-constructivist approaches to the emotions and the most basic facets of rationality, or, more comprehensively, through philosophical strategies such as that of Nietzsche, which portray the self as created, not discovered (Harré 1986; Murray 1978; Rorty 1989).

It was not until the historical transition described by Mauss, in which personality changed from an incidental to a seemingly essential—even a natural—attribute of each human individual, had taken place: that is to say, it was not until our current "literal" sense of "person" had taken firm root that its metaphorical use to describe corporations, states, universities, and other "moral persons" could develop. And indeed, Mauss dates the emergence of this most significant usage precisely to the early Christian period (Carrithers 1985:19). Further developments take place, which can hardly be traced here. Yet it must be noted, because it is of such great consequence for the original formulation of the current social sciences, that Hobbes, with his stress on the force of human passions rooted in the material, corporeal individual, participated in a materialistic and individualistic revolution in the concept of personality every bit as fundamental as, and parallel to, his assertions of the primacy within language of the literal and the written over the metaphorical, or of positive over natural law. The image that best captures the whole process is of the gradual development of a coral reef in which successive generations of dead metaphors provide the habitat for new tropes.

To sum up, it is not the case that personality, as a quality of human beings, is a clear and uncomplicated foundation on which to build a second-order, metaphorical, more shadowy or conditional notion of group personality. Personality attaching to individual human beings is itself a social institution that may post-date human society and has certainly undergone change over time. Yet this very lack of certainty at the foundation of the metaphor may make it more effective. If we have no trouble handling the dead metaphor of ourselves-as-persons, may not the trouble we encounter with the metaphor of states-as-persons stem from nothing more than its novelty and lack of familiarity?

THE RELFEXIVE NATURE OF REALISM

One common reason given by for resisting adoption of the sort of attitude to language and tropes advanced here is that it is held to be subversive of rationality itself. If the literal base (microeconomics). of which much of Waltz's discussion of the balance of power is a metaphorical extension is not in some way more solid than that extension, if it has no superior authority, then what precisely is the force of the metaphor? The argument is first cousin to that employed by empiricists against the sociology of knowledge and glanced at briefly in the opening subsection of the previous chapter. Since this approach to knowledge entered the study of international relations early on, as we have seen, through Carr's reading of Mannheim, it will be best to consider the two arguments in tandem.

In brief, two approaches to a sociological explanation of knowledge may be discerned, roughly parallel to the literalist and Romantic accounts of metaphor. The first holds that error requires causal explanation while truth is guaranteed by the reasoning that leads to it. Error is a deviation from truth just as metaphor is a deviation from the literal. The so-called "strong" position, by contrast, holds that all knowledge is caused, whether it is true or mistaken, including those rational procedures such as mathematics and logic so often considered universal and foundational (Bloor 1976). Here truth is put in question in a manner precisely analogous to that in which the literal is exposed as metaphorical in romantic theories of metaphor. Our contention, recalling the closing paragraph of the previous chapter, will be that awareness—a public awareness—of this problem of reflexivity is a raft offering as much support as the romantic Realist can hope for. The raft is to be preferred when the supposedly solid earth beneath is quaking.

Carr deploys a sociological approach to knowledge in the early chapters of *The Twenty Years' Crisis*. His critique of idealism or utopianism depends substantially upon this argument. "The outstanding achievement of modern Realism—he writes—has been to reveal . . . the relative and pragmatic character of thought itself" (Carr 1939:87). In brief he notes that thought is generally conditioned not only by the concerns and position of the thinker but also by intention. He then moves swiftly to consider the reflexive character of this criticism, noting "our promptness to detect the conditioning or purposeful nature of other people's thought, while assuming that our own is wholly objective" (Carr 1939:92). Wholly consistent Realism, Carr suggests, would require Realists to accept that their own emphasis on continuity, the power of structural causes, or the inevitability of determined historical change is an index of their own conservatism and cannot therefore place them in a superior position to those idealists whom they criticize (Carr 1939:113). Indeed, Realists generally break their own rules, as they must, when acting in the public sphere, by pragmatically "assuming an ultimate reality outside the historical process" in which to ground their preferred policies (Carr 1939:114).

This argument is neat. If you expose the principles advanced by others as the merest cloaks for interest you expose yourself to the same charge. If you try to claim that all language is metaphorical, you cease to be able to make sense of metaphor, which can only be defined by reference to the literal. If you regard truth as a matter of coherence rather than of the accuracy of knowledge claims you destroy any basis for the defense of your own beliefs. A pragmatist approach to politics has plainly to address reflexive arguments of this form if it is not to inhibit effective action by those who adopt it.

It is helpful to realize, first of all, just what Carr is up to when he turns on Realism after using it to demolish idealism. His book is based entirely around a set of dichotomies: between power and morality, determinism and freedom, practice and theory. The structure of the argument is dialectical: thesis (utopianism), antithesis (Realism), synthesis (principled acquiescence in history). The dialectical structure was calculated to appeal at one and the same time to the Left, who would have recognized it as a distinctively Marxist strategy, and to the British Conservative policymakers it was chiefly intended to influence, who, by and large, would have taken it simply as a somewhat high-falutin' exercise in reasonableness and compromise. To the first audience Carr is saying "The Soviet Union, too, is a revisionist power." To the second: "Ought we not to behave more reasonably to the Germans, who are, after all, our cousins?." Carr would have known well and might have chuckled over the preface to Lenin's *Imperialism*: "The careful reader will easily substitute Russia for Japan, etc." (Lenin 1939:2).

In short, the reflexive argument purporting to confound thorough-going Realism is deployed by Carr as part of a *really* Realist strategy aimed at effective persuasion of policymakers. For Carr, as for any Realist, persuasion comes higher than truth, rhetoric than methodology, action than theory, and the point is never more effectively proved than through this attempt to dissociate himself from Realism. The apologist of Realism, like the prince, "should appear to be . . . faithful to his word . . . And indeed he should be so. But his disposition should be such that, if he needs to be the opposite, he knows how"

(Machiavelli [1961]:100–101). Once again, the taking off and putting on of masks.

Carr, the Realist, surely knew how. He had doubtless seen in Karl Mannheim's work, to which he draws special attention in his preface, a possible escape from the paradox with which Carr, the man of sound common sense and compromise, subdues Realism. The argument goes like this. Understanding how someone came to hold a particular view does not demolish that view. Nor does the fact that the sociological approach may be applied to one's own knowledge claims (or Mannheim's) demolish the sociology of knowledge. On the contrary, understanding the determination of one's own views enhances one's rationality. "What seems to be so unbearable in life itself, namely to continue to live with the unconscious uncovered, is the historical prerequisite of scientific critical self-awareness," writes Mannheim. He continues, closely following the trail already blazed by Dilthey: "Man attains objectivity and acquires a self with reference to his conception of his world not by giving up his will to action and holding his evaluation in abeyance but in confronting and examining himself." He draws attention to the underlying paradox, that "the opportunity for relative emancipation from social determination increases proportionately with insight into this determination" (Mannheim 1936:42–43; Rickman 1961:ch.6).

Reflexive arguments do not defeat pragmatist Romantics; they simply defer "the literal," "truth," and "certainty" indefinitely, allowing the unresolved tensions of the dialectics of metaphor and literal, fiction and truth, subjective and objective, theory and action, to be sustained. We are not, in the end, all liars, trying to convince each other of our particular fantasies. Why not? Because these dialectics, opened up as they are by pragmatism, provide evident means to discriminate between those "lies" and "fantasies" which are able to command sustained assent and those which are not. Hackneyed it may be, but you really can't fool all the people all the time.

SOME IMPLICATIONS OF METAPHOR

If all of this were accepted and the analogy between the balance of power and microeconomics seen as metaphorical in character, to do with creation and political action rather than the testing of knowledge claims, what difference if any would it make? Adopting a neo-Romantic approach, the big difference turns out to be that both the tenor (literal) and the vehicle (embellishment) are transformed by metaphor; it is not a matter of learning from a better developed science (economics) but of seeing what happens to both international politics *and* microeconomics when they are compared one with another. What was billed as a lecture by professorial microeconomics to neophyte international politics turns out instead to be an interactive seminar.

The resultant conversation is also much more noisy and unruly than that reported by Waltz because there are other participants. Scanning the wave-bands, the well-rehearsed antiphonal exchange between balance of power theory and oligopoly theory suddenly gives way to what sounds like the rehearsals of an amateur orchestra. Four or five principals are playing a recognizable piece. Different groups can be discerned: the play of authority systems against self-regulating anarchic systems, the political against the economic. But some instruments plainly don't quite know quite which group to play with. States and firms are now with one group, now with another. It is not clear whether there is a conductor or not. From time to time there is a snatch from some familiar melody: the theory of the firm, public goods theory, imperfect competition, hegemony, or game theory. Can that be Waltz, on timpani, playing from a score? The others seem to be improvising, but it is hard to tell because the audience are talking a good deal as they move in and out of the auditorium, plainly excited by undisclosed events taking place in the city outside. While the concert has been going on Stalinism has collapsed, Latin America has been humbled, and the disaster of United States arms in Southeast Asia redeemed, so it might appear, in the Gulf.

The methodological conformity with which Waltz needlessly burdens himself restricts international political economy to the application of established wisdom deriving from economics, a rather narrow diet of well-established theory of imperfect competition. The revision proposed here makes it much more reasonable to bring in insights that are perhaps more peripheral or less universally agreed within economics and to try them for size against the structure of the international anarchy. Conversely, it suggests that economists might carry home some fresh insights were they seriously to apply their techniques of analysis to competition between states.

It does not matter that there is no space to do more than scratch the surface of these opportunities here, because to a large extent what is being proposed is simply an overarching framework or methodological rationalization for a great variety of work of the past two decades that has already advanced quite far and has come to be known as international political economy. But to illustrate the nature and breadth of the conversation it may help to look briefly at recent approaches that challenge the quantity theory of competition employed by Waltz, and at the confluence of game theory and public goods theory as applied to international relations.

The standard view of competition which Waltz shares with neoclassical economists holds that "the number of firms and their size distribution [Waltzean distribution of capabilities] is crucial in determining the extent of competition in an industry" (Jenkins 1987:44). Although determination is incomplete, and there will be abberant cases for game-theoretic reasons, it will generally be the case that as the number of firms approaches unity, or as the number of dominant states approaches unity in the bipolar world favored by Waltz, so competition reduces and socialization through imitation becomes more important.

This image of competition is consistent with the idea that concentration of capital through the emergence of dominant multinational corporations in, say, the world motor industry, represents a *reduction* in the level of competition. But recent attempts to revive the classical concept of competition have challenged this. "Mobility of resources rather than the number of firms in a particular market becomes the crucial determinant of the degree of competition" (Jenkins 1987:45). Competition may be heightened for any given size distribution to the extent that effective concentration of authority over resources *within* the competing units enables anticipation to substitute for retrospective response to market change, and cost-reduction for the raising of barriers to entry as a competitive strategy. Translated into Structural Realist terminology, differentiation of function may produce very different outcomes at two successive periods in the history of the international anarchy even when the distribution of capabilities appears, arithmetically, to be the same.

In short, some economists—a minority to be sure, but a persistent minority—have been challenging from their side of the fence the simple idea, already challenged in earlier Sections of this book, that competition, even in a necessarily anarchic system, entails units of like function. And by doing so they have, by implication, cast doubt on the notion that a given structural disposition of the international political system will ever determine outcomes, even in the limited sense of shoving in a predictable direction.

In the world of firms it is with the giant—often transnational—corporation that mobility of resources is perfected, and this has led James Clifton to argue that the world economy has become more, not less, competitive with the concentration of capital in giant corporations and the development of oligopolistic world markets. "Capital is always searching out its highest reward at all stages of capitalist development," Clifton concludes. "The fact that it is typically the modern corporation rather than the independent capitalist that pursues this search today does not at all imply a lessening of competition in the capitalist economy" (Clifton 1977:150).

Jenkins, too, stresses the dynamic character of this approach to competition, emphasizing the systematic alternation over time of competition and monopoly. "TNCs," he writes, "give rise to increased mobility of capital between industries and countries. But an important part of competition between TNCs is the search for surplus profits which frequently involves the creation of quasi-monopolistic positions and attempts to protect such positions which are under threat from other TNCs" (Jenkins 1987:58).

What this talk of the mobility of capital achieved by large well-administered firms means is that large firms increasingly face an array of markets (sometimes both as buyers and sellers). including the markets for factors of production, for intermediate goods, for new technology, and for each of their main products. They are able to scan this array searching for opportunities to secure rents which may, in turn, enable them to enhance their competitiveness in less secluded markets. In addition, firms constantly face the issue of internalization, first identified by Coase. What is the limit of advantage to be had from further extension of the administrative grip of the firm? Where is the frontier beyond which the market will provide cheaper solutions? Furthermore, it is apparent that in reaching decisions firms have to anticipate the decisions that their competitors will make, and that subsequent decisions of each competitor will be influenced by past decisions of the others, any series of which is rapidly interpreted as a strategy. Whatever may be the attractions of elegance and simplicity in theory-building, there is always the counter-attraction of a model that retains formality even while incorporating further complexities. Here, the appropriate formal image seems to be of a number of kinds of player simultaneously engaging in a series of multiplayer reiterated variable-sum games.

Translating this into the world of international competition, it may readily be seen that there are indeed several multiplayer games going on between overlapping, though far from identical, groups of participants. States have their games, many of which, like arms racing and reduction, may be modeled in the formal terms of game theory; national economies (represented chiefly by constituency representatives in the legislature, trade union leaders, and employers' organizations) have theirs; truly transnational firms have theirs; publicists have theirs. Players from any game may intervene, either occasionally or habitually, in a game primarily played out between one of the other groups. The winning strategy may not be the same in each group. Deciding how much attention to give to each of the various games is itself a game in which all players participate. Some get this wrong either in the short term (ITT in Allende's Chile) or in the long term (the East India Company). Others get it right (Virginia, perhaps, in its translation from company to state?).

The internalization game may also be quite readily transferred from the world of firms to the world of states. Just how great a range of functions can a state perform with economy and across how wide a territory? The answer has varied greatly across time with changes in interaction capacity stemming from new techniques of transport, communications, and warfare. It has varied also, for individual states, according to the relative speed and success with which they and their rivals have adopted new techniques and with the extent to which they were able to give attention to this, as well as to the many other games states play.

The relationship between the British state and British-based capital will provide an illustration of what may variously be called the internalization game, Coase's game, or, when played by states, "Public and Private." In brief, the weak and impecunious state under the Tudors and Stuarts gladly delegates political authority to groups of British merchants operating abroad, allowing them to set up courts, raise troops, engage in diplomatic relations with other sovereigns, and behave as quasi-sovereign entities. At home, the same state attempts centralization and places ever more emphasis on statute law but remains perpetually dependent on local Justices of the Peace and on the customary framework of common law for the maintenance of social order. During the eighteenth century a drift towards more effective central control takes place. Better and cheaper communications and transport progressively remove the barriers to entry which had formerly protected local centers of British power, both at home and abroad. Toward the end of the nineteenth century, during a period of temporary strategic overextension the British once again delegated imperial power, this time to land-based trading organizations in Southern and East Africa.

At the same time that it was being played out territorially, the internalization game was also being played out by states within their boundaries as popular pressure and the need to be able to operate an effective war economy together brought an expansion of state intervention in the economy, the family, local government, and, indeed, every facet of civil society.

These developments, at home and abroad, were clothed in a victorious ideology of welfare or compensatory liberalism. A succession of writers were able to redefine the public realm to embrace many matters of local government or commercial behavior formerly regarded as private. Here, a number of games played out by publicists, businessmen, and politicians came into synchronization in a manner nicely captured in Gramsci's notion of "hegemony" (Gill and Law 1988:64).

It has been argued that one of the first fruits of the replacement of positivist talk of analogy as a form of testing or confirmation by a Romantic view of analogy as metaphor might be to open up the possibility of a fruitful conversation between the two elements of the metaphor—economics and international politics—to which each may contribute and by which each may be changed. But preliminary discussion of the gains to be had from this methodological transformation is dangerously exposed so long as the issue of the scope of state power remains unresolved. It therefore plainly becomes critically important to return to a question anticipated in chapter 10, when the issues of contingent versus necessary anarchy and of the implications of the analogy between microeconomics and the balance of power were first raised. Resolution hinged on the extent to which varieties of social power were ultimately dominated by or dependent upon state power. The question now recurs. Must the kind of elaborate multi-game model sketched just now form part of a viable international theory or does it represent a needless sacrifice of theoretical elegance? Is social power essentially dispersed or is Waltz literally correct in his assertion that "the economic, military, and other capabilities of nations cannot be sectored and separately weighed" (Waltz 1979:131).

CHAPTER TWELVE

Vertical Sectors and
Disaggregated Power

This chapter returns to the Neorealist project of aggregating state capabilities into a single concept of power, already discussed in Section I. The intention here is to build on this earlier discussion and relate it to our proposal for a division of the international system into vertical sectors. These issues are pursued through further consideration of the relationship between the economic and the political, though now of a more practical character than in the previous chapter. The exercise also provides a preliminary opportunity to reflect upon our own use of metaphor in the exposition of the earlier sectoral development of Structural Realism and, in doing so, to spell out in a little more detail what is implied in the "idealism" or "utopianism" of Realism, referred to earlier, and to begin to suggest how the rhetorical turn of chapter 11 may be contained within a Structural Realist approach.

A first step must be to toss into the ring, precisely in order to dismiss them, some proposals for what might be termed "strong sectoring," in which different arenas of international power are inhabited by quite distinct sets of actors. Strong sectoring is subsequently abandoned in favor of the more muted form of sectoring proposed in Section I, in which international relations are perceived of as less than the totality of social or inter-human relations, centering rather on the performance of states in relation to each other *and* to non-state actors in a multiplicity of differently ordered sectors or modes—coercive, political, ideological, and economic—each of which has, besides states, its own distinctive actors, its own structural logic, and its own meta-discourse or science. But here the importance of metaphor in reinforcing this bare statement, left implicit in the original outline of our position, is more clearly spelled out. A brief coda does little more than hint at the close support this Structural Realist account of the vari-

216

ety and fungibility of international power can provide for empirical studies.

A SYSTEM OF FIRMS?

From Waltz comes a clear but sparse picture of the structure of the international political system to which we and many others have already suggested revisions. The question to start from is, "Can a similar picture be drawn of an international economic system, or of other global systems such as those we referred to in Section I as societal, strategic, etc.?" This idea will be entertained with particular reference to the possibility of a rival global economic structure, even though this will not in the end be accepted.

There are two reasons for proceeding along this path. First, demonstrating the grave difficulties that lie in the way of expressing such alternative structures in common terms, which is to say in a single conceptual vocabulary permitting discussion about, for example, the effects of the world economic system on the world political system, may help sustain our general case for the importance, indeed the power, of language. It has become conventional, in presenting international political economy to students, to admit this problem by distinguishing at the outset a number of incompatible ideological frameworks—Marxian, liberal, etc.—*within* which such questions may be answered and by frankly accepting the value of eclecticism, even while making clear the authors' own final positions (Gilpin 1987:25; Gill and Law 1988:17–24; McKinlay and Little 1986). Distinct disciplinary discourses, able to be distinguished from ideological differences though related to them, are perhaps equally incommensurable, but it is generally the ideological differences that have been of primary importance to students of international relations, being at one and the same time a chief object of study and a major impediment to consensus.

The second reason is that, because of this objection and others, there is good reason to argue against multiplication of structures as a way of softening or liberalizing structuralism, opting instead for the method, implicit in Section I, of admitting the de facto primacy of a single global system of sovereign states in the modern international

217

system, while proposing a multiplicity of interpretations of this structure (and indeed even the playful positing or entertainment of alternative structures) as utopian rhetorical strategies for overcoming the least satisfactory characteristics of the prevailing system. This admission amounts less to a privileging of states than an open recognition and proclamation that states have seized and are seized of privileges; the Realism it countenances acts less as ideology than as critique. But it is distinct from the more radical neoliberal critiques in resisting the temptation to attack the state directly and generally.

Returning, then, to the project of building a global economic structure to rival the international system, units are first of all required. A first impulse might be to look for avowedly "economic" units or actors. Very large business corporations seem the obvious choice. This, indeed, is what Lenin went for in his structuralist (*pace* Waltz) account of the international system at the turn of the century. States had by 1900 acquired all the non-European territory available and had turned from relatively amicable division to hostile redivision of the world. Analogously, the major capitalist trusts had expanded into all available markets and could now only compete for market share. The easy phase of expansive growth had ended circa 1900 for giant firms as for states. In Lenin's terminology, competitive capitalism had given way to a more aggressive form, monopoly capitalism, competition without a safety valve. The move from an open to a closed system had produced a system change (Lenin 1939).

This kind of comparison has a certain allure, not least because it chimes in with the analogy to which Waltz resorts so frequently, and which we have discussed extensively, between the balance of power and oligopolistic competition.

But it is the wrong picture. It is wrong in its own terms because it is premised on what has already been exposed in chapter 11 as a naive understanding of competitive processes. Much more important, it can also be regarded as methodologically flawed because, owing to the legal subordination of the firm to the state, it collapses back so easily into a story about a single, political, international system of the sort favored by Waltz. Firms, it would be argued, do not together form more than a contingently anarchic system; each is an agglomeration of units formed under and constrained by national law. They may fight battles with states and win some. But the resources at their disposal and the terms on which the battles are fought are ultimately determined by states.

This is not the end of the story, because a Marxist might respond that all this talk of the supremacy of the state is sheer mystification, and that law is used here to conceal the naked truth, that *ultimate* social power under capitalism rests with the owners of capital, and, under monopoly capitalism, with the controllers of massive bureaucratic business corporations, which do, therefore, constitute a necessary anarchy. But in opposition to this view it could easily be claimed that the Marxist account of society with its talk of class "war" and economic "power" is essentially figurative, shot through with metaphors parasitic on more fundamental, common sense uses of language that derive from politics, and therefore implicitly admit its primacy. In turn might come the almost Nietzschean response that the pretense that is so clearly evident in recent and evidently utopian metaphorical systems such as the Marxist or Freudian accounts of the world is there just the same in the dead metaphors that pass for sober description of the world. The supposedly literal ground of political discourse could doubtless also be picked apart and exposed as a tissue of dead metaphors, simply hallowed by time.

There is no way of settling this argument; attempts to do so will founder on the broad incommensurability of two elaborate discourses. But before abandoning the notion of giant corporations as autonomous actors in an international economic anarchy or world market, it may be worth considering two ways, Marxist and liberal, in which the story might be elaborated, simply because of the way in which each claims to recognize real structures underlying the appearance conveyed in our ordinary talk about the social world, perhaps reifying what begin as conceptual differences?

It is clearly possible to construct a Marxist story in which the capitalist state functions as the executive committee of the bourgeoisie. To be at all plausible these days, the story would have to concede, as Marxists did increasingly beginning in the middle 1970s, the relative autonomy of the state. This can be told (though it is hardly kosher to do so) as a public choice story about why leaderships don't do what members want. It is, if you like, Marx crossed with Mancur Olson. Broadly, the state is allowed enough autonomy from its paymasters to recognize the collective interest of capital and act against the perceived interest of powerful sectors of the bourgeoisie in collaboration with foreign capital or popular elements in domestic society. When individual corporations or industrial sectors complain that they have been hurt by such policies, the public-choice Marxist replies "You are simply understating your true demand for the public good of long run social order. You hope to free ride. But we know better. Unless you are willing to take on the onerous task of running the executive committee yourself you had better shut up and pay up!"

But though the state has this much autonomy it remains fundamentally representative of capital. Its broad strategy is to ensure the smooth running and reproduction of a system of which a bourgeoisie, composed now of controllers as much as legal owners of capital, are the chief beneficiaries. The primary purpose of this system is extraction of surplus through the production and exchange of commodities. The most efficient organizational forms for achieving this objective are determined through the market, and it is in market relations and hierarchical relations within firms, and in the way in which the mode of production is constantly transformed through the process of reproduction of the economy, that the basic dramas of social power are constantly played out. But because so exploitative a system could hardly endure if it were once fully understood by the exploited, a vast and elaborate edifice of statehood, law, religion, and pre-capitalist social custom, much of it centuries old, has been retained, albeit in a poor state of repair—the roof leaking, rot in the timbers, vermin in the larder—to house and comfort the masses. Through the filthy and distorting windows of false consciousness the lineaments of reality are scarcely decipherable.

Now for the liberal version, or, better, *a* liberal version. Here the story would start with Tom Paine or someone of the sort telling us how well civil society can manage in the absence of the state. When the American colonists rose against the British there was for a time no effective government in parts of North America. This did not unleash a torrent of antisocial behavior that had been lurking there, waiting for the state to relax its vigilance. Instead, the story goes, the persistence of order in anarchic conditions demonstrated that it is the state itself that represents social violence imposing itself, parasitically, upon a civil society that neither needs nor wants it, yet that cannot evade capture without forming, in its own defense, something state-like of its own, to be kept in the dark fastness of a liberal constitution lest it taste blood and turn savage.

Radicals in this tradition would, of course, have been appalled at the growth of scale of firms since the early nineteenth century and the emergence of transnational corporations. The main line of their critique seems to be a conservative one. Civil society, once threatened by militaristic and dynastic states, reached the verge of a successful constitutionalist revolution only to fall victim to a new threat, this time from a diseased form of capitalism which destroyed customary work practices, replacing them with patterns which, even if they were less exploitative in a merely pecuniary sense, were culturally corrosive, and quite clearly incompatible with those affective and family relationships so essential to social solidarity and the living of the good life.

This story runs easily into a North American, populist, muckraking kind of a tale in which the watchdog down in the dungeon, pluralist beast that she is, is fundamentally trustworthy, but needs to be observed with special care when ready for a male to make sure that she does not couple with the wild corporate and sectional dogs clustering around the castle gate.

Laying *some* of the metaphors aside for a moment, it will be recalled that in this version of events the constitutional state, artificial though it may be, is permitted because it is the only way of protecting natural civil society against *un*-civilized coercion. What is originally objectionable about the unconstitutional state is its militarism and the injustice supposedly embodied in its hereditary principle. Later, the emphasis moves from coercion to enlarged scale or self-consciousness, or both, as the antonym of civility or naturalness. Populism is about small people—often small capitalists—who see themselves as the foundation of civil society, facing impersonal, remote, bureaucratic, knowing, conspiratorial, overgrown institutions—whether public or private.

Back to the watchdog. She must, above all else, be kept from impregnation by the trusts, lest she grow big with their progeny, which is the antipopular uncivilized state that the Marxists say already walks the earth. She looks pretty fat, down in her dungeon; her bureaucracy grows. Is she pregnant? Perhaps it is just the enforced lack of exercise in this confinement which she endures to avoid the feared confinement. So long as she is undefiled there is hope. And so long as she is untouched the transnational corporations may surely be seen to constitute a distinct, rival, and antidemocratic world system. This, translated into the world of contemporary politics, represents the Global Reach approach to transnationals. It is the view held by liberals who believed, in the 1970s, that transnational corporations operating in oligopolistic markets posed a serious exogenous threat to the state system and that this was bad news because states were, on balance and for all their sins, our best hope of responsible and autonomous political institutions.

Plainly these people are not Realists. They think there are good states and bad states; that some states are more natural than others. They surely would not accept Rousseau's view that, since all states are unnatural and can judge power only relative to one another, all are governed by the logic of the security dilemma, so that the best that can be hoped for is that each may be kept in relative isolation. Although they appear to agree with (some) Marxists on the substantive issue of the centrality of giant firms in the international economic system, the agreement is an empty one, since they differ in their conceptions of the state, of class, and of civil society and its natural development. In short, language is not and cannot be a medium of agreement, supporting their superficially common position on the importance of giant firms, since it is so clearly, as it is bound to be, an instrument of each larger political program.

A SYSTEM OF NATIONS

Returning, notwithstanding these considerations, to the story. Let us say that we were, for the sake of argument, to accept the earlier dismissal of large corporations from the scene on the ground of their legal dependence on sovereign states. There would then remain just one other candidate to be the archetypical actor in a world economic system. This is the national economy: civil society itself in its workaday clothes.

Here is another liberal story. Finding it deeply implausible I daresay I shall not tell it very well. Giuseppe Mazzini, with his thesis of a division of labor between whole nations, would manage much better. It starts by accepting Ricardo's theory of comparative advantage. It then attacks the existing territorial demarcations between states. It proceeds as follows.

222

Granted a complete absence of tariffs and quantitative restrictions on trade, comparative advantage will yield gains from trade, even though they may be unevenly distributed, regardless of political frontiers. The gains will accrue to all through their free participation in markets. But in this simple model the division of the world into states, and the use of territorially defined national economies as the fiscal bases of rival states, will lead to a system of accounting in which the gains from trade are conceptualized as accruing to national economies, not to an undifferentiated mass of traders. The lack of economic frontiers in this model seems to ensure that global efficiency is maximized. For good measure it will also be assumed that all states rely for their income on a standard method of direct taxation levied at a uniform rate. But if it is allowed that the utility of citizens and their incentive to produce is influenced by the distribution of state expenditure, it will follow that there will be efficiency gains to be had from drawing territorial boundaries in such a way as to maximize global confidence in the probable distribution of the social wage. This may require the dissolving of multinational states, the unscrambling of different religious or ethnic communities, or the breakup of empires; it may correspondingly provoke strong resistance from church, minorities, and empires. For Mazzini, it plainly required the unification of Italy on the ground that nationality was somehow a natural or just basis for political organization and was also a prerequisite for an effective division of labor between states. This would need, of course, to be set against possible welfare losses resulting from possible diseconomies of scale in the practice of government arising out of the initially preferred set of frontiers.

To anyone who thought in this way—a liberally-minded nationalist—the idea of a natural order of national economies as the reality underlying the appearance of the arbitrary system of states could clearly act both as a framework for analysis and the basis for policy. Faced with the Realist's affirmation of the centrality of the state and its ultimate monopoly of coercive power, Mazzini, along with his more patient cousins in Eastern Europe can proclaim: "The state and its power are rooted in our acquiescence and in the taxes we pay. Ultimately, states are dependent on nations, who will only resource them if they are given adequate incentives and conditions." Such forces reshaped Europe in the nineteenth century and are at work again today.

This story, in which national economies figure as the units of a world economic system, yields a distinctive and autonomous anarchic system just as the story about firms does. There are fewer units this time. There might be more than in the existing state system (Croatia, Ukraine, and so on); there might be fewer (the European Community). Some are bigger than others. The system is broadly oligopolistic in character, but less so than the world of corporations. Those who identify with it are clearly intent on pushing and shoving the system of states into consistency with it, just as those who identify more closely with states would hope to pull and shove the system of national economies and identities into conformity with their own preferences. This might plausibly be told in the nineteenth century as a story of class war between rising (nationalist, capitalist) bourgeoisie and established (statist, precapitalist) aristocracy. In the twentieth century it dissolves for two generations into a rather different story about the effective mobilization of industrial resources for war.

Each story, the one about business corporations and the one about national economies, suggests a world economic system that is anarchic in structure. But there the resemblance—between the two of them and between each and Waltz—ends. This is implicit in the discussion of the varieties of microeconomics, aside from traditional theory of imperfect competition, earlier called up by Waltz's invocation of analogy. The economic system in which corporations are units has a vast number of independent economic actors, ranging from individual proprietorships, through small partnerships, to giant transnational corporations, state corporations, even states, when acting as free participants in markets. Individuals may participate in more than one unit. Units have widely differing functions. Capabilities are extremely unevenly distributed, with a few immense units controlling a very substantial percentage of total resources and skills. Competition in specific markets follows a dialectical or oscillatory pattern, resonating with other, related, markets. Similar differences can be provided to distinguish the world of competing national economies from that of states. So while it would be absurd to try to exclude either of these systems from the field of International Relations, they are clearly not closely comparable in organization or in competitive logic with the system of states and, like it or not, have failed to express their power through the same range of media or with anything like the level of effectiveness customarily achieved by major states.

224

These fairy stories have not obviously, if at all, yielded an international economic system offering possibilities of structural comparison through the analogy of microeconomics and the balance of power as reformulated in chapter 11. What, then, has been their point? First of all it has been to suggest that all those views which seriously entertain ideas of a world economic system parallel to, and substantially independent of, the state system—a world economic system in which transnational corporations or national economies are the dominant actors—turn out, on examination, to rest on layer after layer of the remains of earlier intellectual dwellings. Each of the two traditions discussed above perceives the giant firm so differently that there is little hope of consensus, and a large measure of the disagreement results from radically differing conceptions of the state underlying perceptions of giant firms themselves. To throw up one's hands and say simply: "Liberals think this way, Marxists that way, and there is no conclusion to be reached other than within some set of ideological blinkers" is a desperate counsel. We hope to have offered something more eclectic and more fruitful.

Secondly, the fairy stories, though they are caricatures, are sufficiently accurate to carry one critical point, namely that attempts to build descriptions of the economic sector in terms of a single category of non-state actor, just like attempts to describe international politics solely in terms of states, do violence to common experience, and that, moreover, they have in common the desire to create a secure ground from which to attack the primacy of the state. They constitute, in short, rhetorical strategies as much as scientific analyses. This is only to be expected. Our argument is that they are mistaken strategies, because, in restricting the apparent scope of states to the "political," narrowly defined, they opt to marginalize instead of develop an institution that still has tremendous potential for constructive reform in response to the whole range of human needs.

Not long ago, Richard Rorty sketched a new characterization of utopian politics in which "the method is to redescribe lots and lots of things in new ways, until you have created a pattern of linguistic behavior which will tempt the rising generation to adopt it, thereby causing them to look for appropriate new forms of non-linguistic behavior, for example the adoption of new scientific equipment or new social institutions" (Rorty 1989:9). Whatever else they have been doing, the principal schools of International Political Economy have been engaging in this kind of utopianism. The battle will go to whichever group succeeds in winning acceptance for its favored description of international relations; but it will be no victory if the winner helps, however inadvertently, to reproduce a system of states narrowly defined in terms of their coercive functions.

Realists live among the ruins of a very different city; they build in a different style and from a different kind of rubble; they have distinct rallying points; they do not speak the same language. Their vocabularies may sometimes overlap with those of the schematic varieties of liberals and Marxists portrayed here, but this merely misleads. The single advantage they possess is that the state does not intrude, uninvited, into their attempts to describe some distinct global economy in which transnational firms or national economies are the typical actors. Instead Structural Realism, no less involved than the other players described so far in this chapter in the utopian contest for an acceptable description of the international system, allows from the start for an international economic sector in which disaggregated state power facilitates sectorally specific participation by states, even where the typical actor may be a giant firm or a national economy, and the sectoral logic best captured in microeconomic theory. There are the beginnings, here, not of the marginalization, capture, or destruction, but of the taming and humanizing of the state.

REALIST VARIATIONS

To a textbook Realist, the stories sketched so far in this chapter would be unacceptable because that Realist accepts at face value the primacy of the state system, welcomes the privileging of the nexus of law-state-coercion as the supreme expression of social power, and therefore takes entirely literally, not metaphorically, such things as the legal dependence of corporations and citizens alike upon the state.

We find the stories equally unacceptable, but for quite different reasons. They are not referred to as "stories" because we are in any doubt about the possibility of truths, but because none is, as yet, generally accepted. For this reason each retains an air of pretense. We might therefore still resort to the traditional conservative response to the metaphor that has not yet died and become invisible, literal, and "factual," dismissing it as merely fashionable or decadent (Rorty

1989:48). Also, they divorce the state far too emphatically from the international economy, both in principle and in practice.

Like many Realists, we incline toward maintaining some sense of the primacy of the state within the political sphere, but have argued in chapter 10 that this primacy results from the practical and wholly contingent dominance of modern sovereign states rather than any uniquely necessary character of the anarchy of states as compared with the anarchies of a multiplicity of firms or civil societies or belief-systems. It is, moreover, a primacy puffed up by dubious assumptions regarding the continuity of key descriptive terms which, in turn, has permitted excessive claims for an actual continuity of events. Yet it is a useful primacy.

Unlike many Realists, we have tried to suggest, throughout this volume, that Structural Realism is consistent not simply with the reproduction but also with the transformation of structures, including the possibility of a displacement of the state system from primacy among other global systems. Our utopian purpose favors the suggestion of multiple and open possibilities over the determination of some preferred utopia from among them. The project of the modern sovereign state consisted in planting a finger in every pie. It led to totalitarian excess, but it made the state peculiarly central among other social institutions, and that is why we continue to take the view that states, for all their deficiencies, currently offer the best available way of opening conduits between what is unconscious, personal, and customary, and what is self-conscious, public, and legal. We reject the standard utopias, sketched just now, because they propose to idealize or destroy the state, rather than to demystify and humanize it.

To announce this aim might seem self-defeating. This would be true if the only way metaphor could gain acceptance and so make new realities were by creeping unnoticed into currency. But if it is sufficiently attractive, metaphor may be openly proposed and openly adopted. The claim that the state is the ultimate arbiter of social relations while also a pretense—no more than a band of brigands: bastards, but our own bastards—is little different to parallel claims considered earlier with respect to other fields: "The literal (last hope of meaning) is just dead metaphor" or "The self (last hope of Being) is contingent" or "My knowledge (last hope of certainty), just like everyone's, is socially constructed."

Exposure of this sort does not subvert, let alone destroy, the state but, on the contrary, liberates it and opens up the utopian possibility of making out of it a medium in which expression of individual liberty is always possible. Indeed it offers a possible referent for the puzzling Marxist idea of the state "withering away."

Since the first step to this apotheosis, rather oddly, has been a provisional admission of the supreme, if arbitrary, nature of the state, it will pay us to don the old Realist suit for a little, and see how this feels. It seems to be a man's suit. It is well-worn, probably of Harris Tweed though perhaps, having fallen upon hard times, of corduroy, and smelling slightly of pipe smoke. Having tried it on, we might try to describe the international economic system, like the international political system, as a system of states, not of national economies, and certainly not of corporations. We would look, for example, at the size of each state's budget relative to GNP and ask how effective each state is at raising taxes and how dependent on borrowing, from its own citizens and from abroad. We would want to know how much of its resources have to be spent on military forces in order to maintain its position vis à vis other states, how well able its administration was to mobilize the resources of the citizens, and to maintain their support through its influence over religious and cultural institutions, and how open the national economy was, how rich in strategic materials.

Waltz, consistent in his emphasis upon the ultimate aggregation of power within the state, but at odds with his own assertion of the distinctiveness of the political from other social realms, including, surely, the economic, describes just such a system when he treats the functions common to all states, but expands it to embrace those which in most large countries are functions of civil society, not of the state. Contrary to his view, each *state* does *not* ordinarily supply "most of the food, clothing, housing, transportation, and amenities consumed and used by its citizens" (Waltz 1979:96). Elsewhere, again, when arguing for the ranking of states by the distribution of aggregated power, he writes of the "economic, military, and political capabilities of nations," when what are clearly referred to are capabilities of states (Waltz 1979:131).

These slips, even if they are no more than slips, indicate the indifference of Neorealism to the analytical distinction toward which we have been laboring in this chapter, between a global economic system, constituted by firms or national economies, and that aspect of international or inter-human relations, broadly conceived, which is constituted by the behavior of states acting in their economic capacities. The distinction is a very real one, but one that slips through Waltz's fingers. It deserves to be held in mind because it suggests a global system along the following lines. A necessarily anarchic economic sector relates to other equally anarchic sectors, including the international political system. Yet the latter, which is on our account necessarily anarchic, at times appears not to be, because, in its economic (or ideological, or coercive) aspect, it takes on not only a distinct, internally derived distribution of capabilities but also something of the purely reflected color of the logic of relations between non-state actors in the sector in question. This is why international political economy is so slippery, and why it seemed appropriate to circle the airfield, in the first two sections of this chapter, before coming in to land. We hope to have arrived at a formulation of the combined effects of sectoring and the disaggregation of state power that respects the relative autonomy of activity in different sectors of the international system while identifying the chameleon state in each.

SECTORAL METAPHORS

If one way of driving home this position was to recite tales of misleading attempts at strong sectoring in which the baby was thrown out with the bathwater, then another, possibly more effective, may be to examine the metaphors employed in chapter 3, when the sectoral division of the international system was originally put forward. The first was a textile metaphor. "In thinking about any historical event it is difficult to disentangle the economic, political, societal and strategic threads that make up the whole. Because each sector is a partial view of the whole, sectors necessarily overlap and interweave." This is immediately followed by a mapping or territorial metaphor. "sectors are not separated by clear boundaries."

The second of these metaphors offers a spatial model of clarity that is unattainable in practice when trying to subdivide the international system. The first offers a compromise, a way round this problem. Cloth is a single entity made up of a multiplicity of elements (threads) often running more or less parallel to one another, but for it to hold together there must also be threads running across the warp. The metaphor is especially helpful because generally, in the finished cloth, the separateness of the threads is hardly perceived, being overwhelmingly dominated by the cloth itself. The idea of cloth carries, also, notions of richness and texture that help convey what is intended. The metaphor seems to imply what has indeed been the case: that we have been looking for a way of enriching structuralism without fragmenting it.

But a third metaphor in our original discussion of disaggregation enables us to steer well clear of the commitments still implicit in those already examined to multiple systems with distinct sets of actors: firms, states, etc. The metaphor of viewpoints stresses that "sectors do not represent subdivisions of the whole system, but partial views of the whole." Further help comes from the metaphor of the lens. "The partial systems identified by sectors are not subsystems in the normal sense of units located within a larger set, and containing fewer units than the whole. Instead they are views of the whole through some selective lens which highlights one particular aspect of the relationship and interaction among all of its constituent units. . . . Even though the object observed remains the same (ignoring Heisenberg), different lenses highlight different aspects of its reality."

It is hard to think of a more creative metaphor. The language attaching to lenses, filters, X-rays, provides a tremendous resource for working out the issues under discussion here. It offers the possibility that some entities might be visible in one set of circumstances but not in another, and, at the same time, that a set of entities might appear very different at one time than another. Thus it offers a way of finessing the issue of disaggregation in a way in which that term itself, and the physical-mechanical metaphor from which it derives, plainly does not. Any idea of physical separation of economy, society, polity, etc., like so many pebbles or threads, is incoherent. The idea that in some circumstances one is aware only of the political, the economic, or the social because each, say, is of a particular color, and will show up only when viewed through the right filter, is coherent, and, what is more, remains coherent when elaborated to include the possibility that the same entity—the state, for example—may exhibit a distinct distribution of capabilities when each different filter is employed.

Thus, the lens image, pursued and elaborated, offers to facilitate a genuinely plural conception of the world system that sets states, acting simultaneously in their economic, cultural, judicial, and other modes, in a web of tensions with firms, ethnic groups, individuals, and cultures; and it does so without encouraging a stultifying reification of parallel structures and analogous sets of units. In short, there is no need to expect that it should be possible to produce a neat matrix of the kind we offer for the international political sector, extended to cover a number of discrete sectors. Indeed, optical metaphors offer the possibility that it may be impossible to see all there is to see at one and the same time. The very terms "aggregate / disaggregate," "structure," "grid," "vertical," "horizontal," and so on, through the dead spatial-physical metaphors they embody, obscure more than they display.

This leaves an important question. What is tenor to the lens's vehicle? What, putting it another way, is the literal of which "lens" "filter," "viewpoint," etc. are the embellishment? It is, surely, the investigator, and what the metaphor claims is just what was claimed as the heart of the Realist position at the outset, namely that the observer is also a participant, that viewpoint makes a difference to what is perceived, and that far from rendering objectivity unattainable, this participation in the observed world is the very condition of scientific understanding. It is hard to better Dilthey's characterization of the position of the social scientist. "The special character of life is understood by means of categories which do not apply to our knowledge of physical reality. Here, too, the decisive point is that these categories are not applied a priori to life as something strange but that they are part of it. The attitude expressed abstractly in them is the exclusive point of departure for the understanding of life. For life is only to be found in the special relationship between a whole and its parts; and, if we abstract these relations as categories, we find that the number of these cannot be determined and their relations to each other cannot be reduced to a logical formula" (Rickman 1961:105).

The great promise held out by disaggregation of power and vertical sectoring, whatever metaphors are used to convey it, is that they offer a greatly enriched potential for employing structuralist analysis to discuss social change at a cost of a very small, and necessary, sacrifice in elegance. The principal reason for this is that, alongside the structurationist approach of Section II, they point to a possibility of generating change within what otherwise appears an entirely synchronic system. It is as though disaggregation turned off the stroboscope to reveal that what had appeared to be static had in fact been rotating rapidly.

Whatever structural differences might be anticipated between a particular oligopolistic market and a multipolar balance of power, it might be anticipated that each facet of the interstate system would be similar in structure. But we have already seen that each facet can be characterized by a different distribution of capabilities at any one time, and, moreover, each facet may reflect a differently structured world of non-state actors. This yields interesting plays and possibilities of change.

The most obvious example of this possibility of generating change out of a multi-faceted state system, chosen here for its central position in the history of the field, is the opposition of economically declining but politically dominant status quo power and economically vigorous revisionist states outlined by Carr on the eve of the Second World War and discussed again in recent years by Paul Kennedy, Waltz himself, and numerous others in the context of relative United States decline and European and Japanese resurgence. It is plain that relationships of suzerainty, dependence, and even colonization may well respond to the dual logics of the prevailing condition of the balance of power and the relative strength or weakness of different states with respect to civil society within their home territories. Without reifying inelegant structures parallel to the state system, one can still easily see in these past struggles tensions between the balance of power, conventionally described, and the ideological bipolarity of liberalism and communism or the economic hegemony of the United States at its peak. The immediate point is that the claims we have made for the disaggregation of state power, for differentiation of function of actors, for possibilities of system transformation arising out of the mutual constitution of agents and structures, and for discourse about these matters as one among the multiplicity of interacting structures together make possible the discussion of detail and change alongside structure and continuity in a discourse which can claim to be at once practical and, in the best sense, theoretical. In short, they justify the move from an overly restrictive and exclusivist Neorealism to a more complex, operational, and integrative Structural Realism, which is what this book has been about.

CHAPTER THIRTEEN

Summary and Conclusions

The purpose of this chapter is to highlight the main themes from the three sections, and to focus some thoughts on the research agendas to which we think our arguments point. We are fully aware that our pursuit of the logic of anarchy in the preceding pages has opened up more areas than it has in any sense "closed." In moving from a purely structural theory to a more fully systemic one, it is impossible to avoid a very considerable expansion of the subject area.

Our aim has been to sketch out a fairly comprehensive theoretical framework for this larger area, and by doing so to indicate how much of International Relations theory can be integrated. Structural Realism seeks to construct an ordering principle by which the previously dispersed "islands" of International Relations theory can now be viewed as an archipelago. The islands are mostly still separate, but the distance and direction between them is clearer, and the geology and geography that set the conditions for building causeways, bridges, or tunnels (or merely setting up ferry routes) begins to emerge into view. We do not claim that this framework is complete, or that all parts of it are equally well developed.

Like the Neorealists we have focused on the system level, though we hope that we have much expanded what counts at that level. We have ventured more into the rich layers of the unit level than they do, but there is still much there that we have left largely untouched. We have tried to show more clearly than the Neorealists have how the structure and unit levels interplay with each other, first by showing how structural hypotheses can set the framework for unit level analysis, and second by demonstrating how the process of structuration brings system structure and the domestic structure of the units into a strong relationship. Structural Realism is much more open to change than Neorealism, though we hope that we have preserved and enriched the analytical utility of the static power of structure to shape and constrain the behavior of units. Although the main purpose of this exercise has been to expand away from Neorealism we hope along the way to have reduced the level of misunderstanding about it. One advantage of using Waltz's text as a starting point has been to expose just how much misunderstanding of *TIP* (as opposed to mere disagreement about it) persists despite more than a decade of intense debate.

In the summaries that follow, we take the opportunity that we rejected in the main text of starting with methodology and epistemology, and then going on to elaborate the logic of the theory.

In Section III Waltz was accused of a residual positivism inconsistent with the generally pragmatist tone of a majority of his remarks about theory and knowledge. This positivism was especially evident in his treatment of the pervasive analogy between microeconomics and the balance of power, which was couched in the language of hypothesis and testing. Besides, it relied upon what were felt to be unjustified assumptions about the superiority of economics and about the similarity of competition between firms to competition between states.

An attempt was made to ground Structural Realism on pragmatist epistemological foundations. At the level of methodology, an alternative characterization of the analogy as metaphor was proposed. By this strategy it was hoped that some of the difficulties encountered in *TIP* might be circumvented and a clear recognition of the rhetorical force of language restored to pride of place within the Realist tradition without sacrificing the gains of a structuralist, systematic theory of international relations.

What was proposed, in short, was the frank acceptance of language as power, rather than as a transparent medium of investigation. Language, and its use both by statesmen and publicists in deliberations about foreign policy, was put forward as one manifestation of power: a structure, like the balance of power or the market. The point of this was to bring back into a systemic theory of international relations those facets of experience, such as interpretation, symbolism, persuasion, motive, and the unconscious, which *TIP* had seemed to marginalize by its much more sparse definitions of power and state capabilities. It was also suggested that this incorporation of language was bound to strengthen any structuralist Realism in a number of ways, most of all, perhaps, by providing a better understanding of the causes and possibilities of change in the international system than had been offered by Neorealism.

The philosophically trained reader may detect a hankering after scientific realism and a desire to tell truths about things as they are beneath the pragmatism of Section III, frustrated in the end by epistemological resignation. The tension is left unresolved not out of sheer funk, but because this appears to be one of those situations in which some hunches, requiring further empirical work, need to be played before the more abstract issues can be taken much further. In particular, the stress in Section III on language, metaphor, and their spontaneity and power, coupled with the evidently tentative attitude adopted there toward theories of reference and possibilities of *absolute* rather than historically and socially *relative* truths, suggests that the way forward may lie in a close scrutiny of foreign policy debates and diplomatic discourse, transtemporal as well as transcultural, employing the techniques of analysis of the literary critic. It would seem quite unsafe to rest too much philosophical weight on the diplomatic form of life before testing it out a little. As things stand, indeed, the reliance on linguistic spontaneity as a source of change in Section III is no less incautious than Waltz's own resort to intuition in accounting for theory generation. This said, a research program comprising close empirical study of the diplomatic and foreign–policy-making community, its practice and discourse, has this great advantage: it leaves open the passes to sociological theories of reference and to the admittedly somewhat diluted forms of scientific realism which they might permit, though those attempting the route should be sure to carry chains in the trunk.

Research of this sort, aimed at the identification of social entities that might act as the subjects of a Structural Realist theory of international relations, cannot simply go after the best available expert consensus on what was meant by "state," or "war," or any other key descriptive term in this or that culture, language, or period. Not can it go hunting innocently, without its own preconceptions and language. The best that it is likely to be able to supply is an account, based on the utterances of policymakers and intellectuals and phrased in the most open, ironic, and provisional manner possible, of the tensions that have formed around contested concepts, the strategies by which usages of key terms have been established and maintained, and the implications such established usages have had for social action. As a conjecture to guide research, one might regard the development of the kinds of highly reflexive, self-conscious, and manipulative systems of symbols, signs and images that suffuse modern political discourse as an instance of change in interaction capacity of the kind identified in Section I.

What is required, moreover, is not simply empirical groundwork to clear the way for a more precise theoretical statement, but also ways of reporting that work which respect the reflexive, tightly folded character of the object of study in their own mode of expression. There is plenty of space between the style of the best current work on international relations and the much more cunning and playful prose of Nietzsche, let alone the less accessible expressions of Derrida. Some attempts have been made to occupy this stylistic space, but it is still thinly populated, remote, and poorly serviced, though probably fertile.

Another face of the attempt made here to reinstate rhetoric at the core of Realism is the way in which it blurs the distinction between practitioner and observer. The implicated and manipulative politician or statesman can no longer so easily be contrasted with the supposedly objective academic once the latter's utterances are allowed a part, albeit sometimes as no more than the merest eddy, in the flow of policy-making and the reproduction of its terms and procedures. On this view each uses language as much to achieve objectives as to express beliefs. Academics cannot have the satisfaction of naming reason as trumps *and* dealing the cards. Some will find this uncomfortable, but to many it will seem less uncomfortable than the evident positivist lie of scientific detachment and objectivity. Once again, however, the way to deal with this would seem to lie initially in practice, which to academics consists in research, as a way to establish provisional trust. No amount of abstract reasoning is going to help.

All this might seem to amount to no more than a suggestion that careful, theoretically informed scrutiny of the language of public utterances on international relations coupled with an *engagé* approach to the issues of the day are appropriate practices for people who might perhaps better conceive of themselves as intellectuals than academics, and that, diligently pursued, these strategies may pay dividends in clearer theoretical understanding of the practices themselves. The response of many historians and "common sense" Realists, not to mention Marxists, will surely be that they knew this very well already. Maybe. But one defense against this charge of redundancy would be that the trick of maintaining theory and practice in productive tension needs to be constantly re-learned in new circumstances, and, if nothing else has happened since Waltz wrote *TIP,* circumstances have certainly changed.

Indeed, these changes provided a point of departure for our comparison between *TIP* and *LoA* in the Introduction. Section I then provided an exegesis, clarification, and critique of both Waltz and some of his critics. In addition to exploring the logic of Waltz's theory in its own terms, it reconstructed and extended the theory in such a way as to transform it from Waltz's narrow and excessively closed structuralism into the more open theory that we have labeled Structural Realism. The opening of Neorealism into Structural Realism has two consequences. First, it brings the logic of Neorealism into contact with several other areas of international relations theory. In particular, clarifying the boundary between the unit and structure levels of analysis shows how theory at the level of distributional structure can usefully be tied into study of process formations in fields as diverse as Strategic Studies and International Political Economy (IPE). The opening up of the second tier of structure (functional differentiation) under anarchy also points to links with theory of the state, and to possible further links with IPE, some of which were pursued further in Sections II and III.

The other consequence of opening was to undo the excessively static formulation of Neorealism by introducing three elements of change to work alongside its highly durable "shoving and shaping" structures. Waltz's formulation was virtually static except for the distribution of power in which one change from a multipolar to a bipolar system after the Second World War was allowed.

The first element of change is achieved by disaggregating power. Once singular power is disaggregated into plural capabilities the possibilities for change in the distributional structure increase automatically. Economic and ideological polarity can and have changed while military bipolarity has remained more stable. When power is disaggregated, the possibility for change is increased not only by the additional variables in play, but also by the combinations and permutations of how the different types of polarity relate to each other. In turn, the overall pattern of distributional structure has to be related to the shifting contexts (or regimes) of non-state activity within which state capabilities are exercised. This unpacking of power is both supported and made necessary by the use of system sectors as a tool of analysis, a theme explored further in chapter 12.

The second element of change comes from opening the functional differentiation tier of structure within anarchy, which Waltz treats as closed. Once opened, this tier offers opportunities for change not only as between type 2 and type 4 anarchies (respectively, those with like and with unlike units), but also within type 4 as between different classifications of functional differentiation. This opening paves the way for the more comprehensive exploration of Structural Realism in historical application in Section II.

The third element of change came from adding interaction capacity as a new level of analysis enabling Structural Realism to meet the requirements of a full system theory. Because interaction capacity rests on the absolute qualities of attributive power rather than the relative weight of relational power, it is by definition sensitive to a substantial range of ongoing technological, normative, and organizational changes in the international system.

These three elements add considerably to the reach and complexity of structural theory in International Relations. They meet many of the criticisms of Neorealism, but do so without losing touch with its basic ideas about the conditioning effects of international political structure. The theory is nevertheless quite transformed from narrow Neorealism; Structural Realism takes on many qualities not obviously present in Neorealism, and in some cases seemingly opposed to it.

The purpose of Section I was to establish an overview of the transformation of Neorealism to Structural Realism, but there has not been space to work out to the fullest extent all of the implications and consequences of the argument. There is thus a research agenda arising that still needs to be addressed, and it will come as no surprise that this agenda stems largely from the three elements of change introduced into the theory.

Waltz's theory on the distribution of power generated a whole subliterature on the analysis of power polarity. For the most part, this work has reached a dead-end because the variable turned out to be too crude to explain much. The disaggregation of power offers the possibility of reviving this debate on a sounder footing, but it requires systematic rethinking and elaboration of new hypotheses. Several possible lines of development were suggested in chapter 3. It is clear that disaggregation involves not only thinking through the definitions and implications of polarity regarding specific capabilities, but also the new step of thinking through the consequences of different polarities occurring in parallel in different sectors. What happens when military polarity and economic polarity don't line up, as is the case during the 1990s? What is the difference between a situation in which ideological polarity correlates with the location of military power, as during the 1930s, and when it doesn't, as might be one reading of the relationship between Islam and liberal capitalism as state ideologies during the 1990s?

One consequential question arising from these considerations is whether the influence of distributional structure (and thus its explanatory power) declines in relation to unit and interaction capacity explanations when the different sectoral polarities pull in different directions. In other words, is the shaping force of distributional structure stronger when events produce the (Neorealist) condition of aggregated power, and weaker when they do not? A second consequential question: do the prevailing structures of non-state systems in the economic and ideological spheres substantially constrain the shaping force of the distributional structure of state power?

A second area needing further thinking is the clarification of criteria for defining and specifying differentiation of function. Some suggestions are made in chapter 3 and the theme is carried forward in Section II, but this task is filled with hazards as well as opportunities. One tempting, though in the end untenable, reason that Waltz might have given for leaving the second tier of structure closed is that it creates too many problems if opened. Two issues need to be confronted. One is to clarify what counts as functional differentiation and what doesn't. The mistaken desire of some to classify the international roles of states as a function has already been mentioned. Another way of looking at this task is to see it in terms of the need to construct definitions for the structure of states that are as clear as those we now have for the structure of the international system. Once an acceptable range of "function" has been established, the other task is to establish criteria for the extent of change that is to be considered structural in terms of the international system. Setting very broad criteria, as Waltz does for his conception of states as like units, reduces the frequency of structural change. Narrower criteria, such as those suggested in chapter 3 and Section II, make deep structural change more frequent, but have the advantage of linking structural theory clearly and neatly into other areas of theory, particularly theory of the state and IPE. It is conceivable that further work in this still largely virgin territory would expose strong links between differentiation of function and interaction capacity. If so, this might at some point call for a reconsideration of the close linkage between tiers one and two of deep structure as laid out in chapter 3.

The third item on the research agenda of Structural Realism is to develop a fuller conceptual apparatus for handling interaction capacity, and to further integrate this level of analysis into international systems theory. One task is to articulate criteria for differentiating between significant and incidental change in the level of interaction capacity. When does the introduction and spread of a new technology, a new norm or a new organizational network actually produce a step-level change in the functioning of the international system? Another task is to think further about interaction capacity and the definition of system. The arguments in Sections I and II indicate that there are very powerful connections between the level of interaction capacity and the existence and function of structure in the system. Among other things, we need to clarify the criteria for structure in the light of interaction capacity, and to attempt to understand the history of the international system in terms of both the unit-structure and interaction capacity insights of Structural Realist theory. Indeed, one purpose in developing Structural Realism was to equip ourselves with theoretical tools able to address the whole history of the international system.

Section II provided a preliminary foray into this terrain, and ensures that the Structural Realist approach developed in this book is not subject to the charge of ahistoricism. The rise and fall of the Roman Empire was chosen as a historical case study in part because these events are difficult to accommodate within the Neorealist framework and in part because they occur in a very different context to the modern international system. The charge of ahistoricism has often been leveled at Waltz and, indeed, at many social scientists who appear to be working within the confines of positivism. But as was demonstrated in Section III, the claim that Waltz is a positivist is suspect; on closer inspection his epistemology is seen to contain more than a dash of pragmatism. By the same token, the superficial signs of ahistoricism which undoubtedly litter the text of *TIP* mask a clear acceptance on Waltz's part that there is a need to study historical change as well as continuity in the international system. Because Waltz asserts so vigorously that he is interested in continuity rather than transformation, most critics have failed to observe just how much allowance he makes for historical change in his theory. Section II identifies the dynamic features of the theory and then goes on to extend them.

There are two major lines of development and both build on ideas raised in Section I. The first carries forward the inclusion of functional differentiation in the Structural Realist approach. It begins this task by exposing an incipient theory of the state embedded in *TIP*. Critics of Waltz have argued that he treats the state as an ontologically primitive concept. By this they mean that there is no attempt to explain the origin or evolution of the state. In making this claim, the critics have been misled by Waltz's rhetoric. A more sympathetic reading of *TIP* reveals that it operates at the interface of the structure of the state and the structure of the international system. As far as Waltz is concerned, international anarchy presupposes state autonomy: the two are inextricably interconnected. In Waltz's balance of power theory, as a consequence, the structure of the state and the structure of the international system are essentially fused. To ensure that the state survives, its agents have not only to take account of shifts in the pattern of alliances, but also to be prepared to make adjustments to the structure of the state to preserve its relative power position. Waltz is clear, moreover, that international moves to form alliances cannot offset, in the long term, the need to sustain domestic sources of power. The implications of this simple "truth" are examined in Kennedy's controversial account of the rise and fall of the Great Powers in the modern international system. States that fail to emulate successful modes of domestic power formation steadily slip down the power hierarchy.

In Section II we develop Structural Realism by defusing the structure of the state and the structure of the international system. Waltz's fusion of these structures opens the way to the Neorealist prediction about the homogenization of states over time. The defusion by contrast opens the way to our Structural Realist prediction about the potential for functional differentiation within the international system. Agents of the state, it is argued, are sometimes unable to respond to pressure imposed upon them by the structure of the international system because of the strength of the constraints generated by the structure of the state. So while Neorealism presupposes that all states will undergo restructuring, whenever necessary, thereby ensuring that the anarchic structure of the international system is reproduced, Structural Realism presupposes that the internal structure of states in the international system can diverge, and the resulting functional differentiation can be preserved by the external dimension of the balance of power. This defusion of domestic and international structures helps to account for the divergence between type 2 and type 4 anarchies discussed in Section I.

Section II goes on to develop the idea that anarchy can also be conceived as a differentiated phenomenon which is not governed as Waltz indicates by a single logic. The nature of the logic is dictated by the structure of the units in the system. Examples of semi-autonomous units reveal that anarchy does not necessarily generate balance of power behavior. This extension has particularly important ramifications if it is accepted that, until quite recently, the international system consisted of relatively autonomous subsystems that have operated on the basis of different logics of anarchy. Only with the rise of interaction capacity at the global level have these subsystems finally coalesced.

The second development of Structural Realism is designed to build on the idea of an interaction capacity. Reference is made in Section I to the role of societal norms in the process of interaction. Section II further explores the reasons why, contrary to Waltz, cooperation can occur within an anarchy, and give rise to norms and rules within the international system. By opening up this line of thought, contact can be made with a growing body of literature that defines the international arena in societal rather than systemic terms. Ironically, this school of thought also fuses the structure of the state and the system, but in very different terms to those favored by Waltz. Its adherents argue that the sovereign state and the international system are mutually constituted, and it is therefore not possible to conceive of the state as an autonomous entity within an independent international system. Membership of international society is a defining feature of the state with the structure of the state and that of the international society being mutually constituted. So whereas Neorealists argue that there are mutual constraints set up by the structure of the state and the system, the societal school of thought argues that the state and system are mutually constituted.

The difference is not simply one of terminology. Neorealists argue that the autonomy of states is preserved by the balance of power while

242

the societal school argue that the independence of sovereign states is preserved because these states collectively implement a body of rules that ensures the reproduction of a system of states. From a structural realist perspective, however, both of these schools of thought are thinking in terms of the contemporary global system which is made up of units that can be defined in either sovereign or autonomous terms. Structural Realism, as defined in this book, does not seek to adjudicate between these two schools of thought. Instead, it accepts that there have been international systems where power predominates and others where societal norms play a role in the constitution of both the state and the system. But it is also accepted that even in systems where norms play an integral role, the significance of power persists. The quality of anarchy will be very different as between international systems and international societies. Among other things, international society might support type 4 systems, as was the case during the nineteenth century. Developing these ideas further requires the clarificatory work on functional differentiation and the structure of the state sketched above.

In maintaining this position, a number of difficult methodological questions about the relationship between explanations based on causal factors and on the process of reasoning have been glossed over. Scientific realism provides one possible route for reconciling these two different modes of explanation. But as is made clear in Section III, there is, as yet, no solution capable of overcoming all the difficulties. It would be a mistake to presuppose that it is not possible to make any progress until the problems of methodology and epistemology have been overcome. On the contrary, it can be argued that methodologists and epistemologists necessarily follow in the wake of social scientists who are engaged in the practice of trying to understand social reality (Little 1991). This section leads to a conclusion very similar to that of Section III: that progress in the task of understanding international relations will only come about by moving beyond the narrow confines of the modern international system and drawing much more systematically on world history.

Structural Realism, as mapped out in sections I and II, generates an extensive research program. In the first place, the theoretical ideas associated with Structural Realism can be used to trace the broad outlines of how the international system has evolved. It is already clear that these outlines will diverge sharply from what Clark (1989) has called Whig and Tory views of world history. The former depicts world history in terms of the steady advance of civilization, while the latter sees only historical cycles, and sometimes regressive cycles at that (Farrenkopf 1991). Structural Realism, by contrast, focuses on the initial diversity of autonomous subsystems within the international system. Once the range has been identified, it becomes possible to look in more detail at the different structures that maintain these autonomous subsystems. In looking at the detail of these empirical cases, it also becomes both necessary and possible to pay more attention to the kinds of theoretical debates that are examined in sections I and II. Although an attempt has been made to reconcile some of the major theoretical disputes in the literature, detailed comparative research is undoubtedly necessary to make further progress.

Thinking about the meaning of structure in a full historical and systemic context points to the disturbing conclusion that the effects of structure are not constant. Significant variations occur caused by important links between both unit and structure and interaction capacity and structure. Between unit and structure it becomes impossible to avoid the conclusion that units and structures are mutually constitutive, and that the nature of the units therefore affects the consequences of structure. This emerged from arguments in both sections II and III. It is perhaps most visible in International Political Economy in the difference between a system of liberal states and a system of mercantilist ones. The openness of liberal states is what enables an international market structure to emerge, the closure of mercantilist ones directly suppresses market structure. Between interaction capacity and structure it becomes impossible to avoid the conclusion that both the capacity and type of interaction that define the system also affect the consequences of structure. Neorealist theory focuses on a middle level of capacity, and produces a logic of anarchy centered on strategic interaction. At higher and lower levels of capacity the system may be defined principally by types of interaction other than strategic. Such systems will display a logic of anarchy quite different from that sketched by Waltz.

Structure is therefore only one component of a more complex systemic equation. There is not one logic of anarchy but many. This is not a cause for abandoning the theoretical enterprise in despair. It does wreck the fences around Waltz's tidy universe in which a single logic of anarchy prevails. But it leaves intact the powerful theoretical apparatus of structural analysis. Since anarchy remains the great constant in the international system this is no mean legacy.

Structural Realism provides the tools with which one can assess continuity and change in the international system. It offers the possibility of thinking systematically about both the whole history of the international system, and some aspects of its future. To do this, Structural Realists need to equip themselves with a set of lenses through which they can examine all of the sectors of the system. They need to train themselves to interpret the partial picture of the whole that each lens gives, and to be able to see how the different perspectives relate to each other. They need to avoid the illusion that sectors are self-contained universes, and to cultivate an awareness that language is part of the political process. They need to understand that a systems approach necessitates awareness not only of the constraints of structure, but also of the structuration process between units and structure, and of the pervasive influence of interaction capacity on the meaning and significance of system. They need, in other words, to take a very comprehensive view of the traditional wisdom that Realism is about understanding what is. Only with that foundation can one think usefully and responsibly about the potential for purposive change.

When more fully developed, and if used with care and precision, these tools could take us a long way down the road toward an integrative and coherent theory of international relations. There still remains a great deal to do.

References

Adcock, F. E. 1957. *The Greek and Macedonian Art of War*. Berkeley: University of California Press.

Alker, Hayward. 1987. "Fairy Tales, Tragedies and World Histories: Towards Interpretive Strong Grammars as Possibilist World Models." *Behaviourmetrika* 21:1–28.

Alker, Hayward. 1990. "Rescuing 'Reason' from the Rationalists: Resolving Vico, Marx and Weber as Reflective Institutionalists." *Millennium* 19:161–84.

Alker, Hayward. Forthcoming. "The Presumption of Anarchy in World Politics." In H. Alker and R. Ashley eds. *After Neorealism: Anarchy, Power and International Collaboration*.

Anderson, Perry. 1974. *Passages from Antiquity to Feudalism*. London: New Left Books.

Aquinas, Thomas. [1966]. *Summa Theologiae, XXVIII*. Blackfriars: Eyre & Spottiswoode.

Aquinas, Thomas. [1973]. *Summa Theologiae, XXXVI*. Blackfriars: Eyre & Spottiswoode.

Archer, Margaret S. 1985. "Structuration Versus Morphogenesis." In S. N. Eisenstedt and H. J. Helle eds. *Macro-Sociological Theory: Perspectives on Sociological Theory* Vol. 1. Beverley Hills: Sage.

Archer, Margaret S. 1988. *Culture and Agency: The Place of Culture in Social Theory*. Cambridge: Cambridge University Press.

Ashley, Richard K. 1982. "Realism and Human Interests." *International Studies Quarterly* 25:204–36.

Ashley, Richard K. 1988. "Untying the Sovereign State: A Double Reading of the Anarchy Problematique." *Millennium* 17(2):227–262.

Ashley, Richard K. 1989. "Living on the Border Lines: Man, Post-Structuralism and War." In J. Der Derian and M. J. Shapiro eds. *International Intertextual Relations: The Boundaries of Knowledge and Practice in World Politics*. Lexington: Lexington Books.

Ayoob, Mohammed ed. 1986. *Regional Security in the Third World: Case Studies from Southeast Asia and the Middle East* (London: Croom Helm.

Baldwin, D. A. 1980. "Interdependence and Power: a conceptual analysis." *International Organization* 34(4):471–506.

Bhaskar, Roy. 1989 [1979]. *The Possibility of Naturalism: a Philosophical Cri-*

tique of the Contemporary Human Sciences. Hemel Hempstead: Harvester Wheatsheaf.

Blaug, Marc. 1980. *The Methodology of Economics, or How Economists Explain*. Cambridge: Cambridge University Press.

Bloor, David. 1976. *Knowledge and Social Imagery*. London: Routledge & Kegan Paul.

Boardman, John, Jasper Griffen and Oswyn Murray eds. 1986. *The Oxford History of the Classical World*. Oxford: Oxford University Press.

Bozeman, Adda B. 1960. *Politics and Culture in International History*. Princeton: Princeton University Press.

Brecher, Michael. 1963. "International Relations and Asian Studies: The Subordinate State System of Southern Asia." *World Politics* 15(2):213–35.

Briscoe, J. 1978. "The Antigonids and the Greek States 276–196 B.C." In P. D. A. Garnsey and C. R. Whittaker eds. *Imperialism in the Ancient World*. Cambridge: Cambridge University Press.

Brown, C. W. 1987. "Thucydides, Hobbes and the Derivation of Anarchy." *History of Political Thought* 8(1):33–62.

Brown, C. W. 1989. "Thucydides, Hobbes and the Linear Causal Perspective." *History of Political Thought* 10(2):215–56.

Brown, Peter. 1971. *The World of Late Antiquity*. London: Thames and Hudson.

Brunt, P. A. 1971. *Social Conflicts in the Roman Republic*. London: Chatto and Windus.

Brunt, P. A. 1978. "Laus Imperii." In P. D. Garnsey and C. R. Whittaker eds. *Imperialism in the Ancient World*. New York: Cambridge University Press.

Bull, Hedley. 1977. *The Anarchical Society*. London: Macmillan.

Bull, Hedley, and Adam Watson eds. 1984. *The Expansion of International Society*. Oxford: Oxford University Press.

Burton, John W. 1972. *World Society*. Cambridge: Cambridge University Press.

Buzan, Barry. 1984. "Peace, Power and Security: Contending Concepts in the Study of International Relations." *Journal of Peace Research* 21(2):110–125.

Buzan, Barry. 1987. *An Introduction to Strategic Studies: Military Technology and International Relations*. London: Macmillan.

Buzan, Barry. 1988. "People, States and Fear: the National Security Problem in the Third World." In Edward Azar and Chung-in Moon eds. *National Security in the Third World: the Management of Internal and External Threats*. Upleadon: Edward Elgar Publishing. 14–43.

Buzan, Barry. 1991. *People, States and Fear: An Agenda for International Security Studies in the Post-Cold War Era*. Hemel Hempstead: Harvester-Wheatsheaf.

Buzan, Barry, and Gowher Rizvi. 1986. *South Asian Insecurity and the Great Powers*. London: Macmillan. chs. 1 and 9.

Cantori, Louis J. and Steven L. Spiegel, 1970. *The International Politics of Regions: A Comparative Approach*. Englewood Cliffs: Prentice Hall.

Cantori, Louis J. and Steven L. Spiegel. 1973. "The Analysis of Regional International Politics: The Integration versus the Empirical Systems Approach." *International Organization* 27(4):465–94.

Carr, E. H. 1946 [1939]. *The Twenty Years' Crisis, 1919–1939: an Introduction to the Study of International Relations*. London: Macmillan.

Carrithers, Michael, Steven Collins, and Steven Lukes eds. 1985. *The Category of the Person: Anthropology, Philosophy, History*. Cambridge: Cambridge University Press.

Cartledge, Paul. 1977. "Hoplites and Heroes: Sparta's Contribution to the Technique of Ancient War." *Journal of Hellenic Studies* 97:11–27.

Cerny, P. G. 1990. *The Changing Architecture of Politics: Structure, Agency and the Future of the State*. London: Sage.

Chase-Dunn, Christopher. 1981. "Interstate System and Capitalist World-Economy: One Logic or Two?" *International Studies Quarterly* 25(1):19–42.

Choucri, Nazli, and North, Robert C. 1975. *Nations in Conflict: National Growth and International Violence*. San Francisco: W. H. Freeman.

Christensen, Thomas J., and Jack Snyder. 1990. "Chain Gangs and Passed Bucks: Predicting Alliance Patterns in Multipolarity." *International Organization* 44(2):137–68.

Clark, I. 1989. *The Hierarchy of States: Reform and Resistance in the International Order*. Cambridge: Cambridge University Press.

Clegg, S. R. 1989. *Frameworks of Power*. London and Newbury Park: Sage.

Clifton, J. 1977. "Competition and the Evolution of the Capitalist Mode of Production." *Cambridge Journal of Economics* 1(1).

Collingwood, R. G. 1939. *An Autobiography*. London: Oxford University Press.

Cottingham, John. 1984. *Rationalism*. London: Paladin.

Cox, Robert W. 1986. "Social Forces, States and World Orders: Beyond International Relations Theory." In R. O. Keohane ed. *Neorealism and its Critics*. New York: Columbia University Press.

Crawford, Michael. 1986. "Early Rome and Italy." In John Boardman, Jasper Griffen and Oswyn Murray eds. *The Oxford History of the Classical World*. Oxford: Oxford University Press.

Dessler, David. 1989. "What's at Stake in the Agent-Structure Debate?" *International Organization* 43(3):441–73.

Deutsch, Karl, and J. David Singer. 1964. "Multipolar Power Systems and International Stability." *World Politics* 16:390–406.

Doyle, Michael W. 1986. *Empires*. Ithaca: Cornell University Press.

Falk, Richard A. 1978. "Anarchism and World Order." In J. Roland Pennock and John W. Chapman eds. *Anarchism*. Nomos Vol. 19. New York: New York University Press.

Farrenkopf, John. 1991. "The Challenge of Spenglerian Pessimism to Ranke and Political Realism." *Review of International Studies* 17:267–84.

Ferguson, William Scott. 1913. *Greek Imperialism*. Boston: Houghton Mifflin.

Ferguson, Yale H., and Richard W. Mansbach. 1988. *The Elusive Quest: Theory and International Politics*. Columbia: University of South Carolina Press.

Fleiss, Peter J. 1986. *Thucydides and the Politics of Bipolarity*. Baton Rouge: Louisiana State University Press.

Foucault, Michel. 1981. *History of Sexuality*. Harmondsworth: Penguin.

Fox, Edward Whiting. 1971. *History in Geographic Perspective: the Other France*. New York: Norton.

Garnsey, P. D. A., and C. R. Whittaker eds. 1978. *Imperialism in the Ancient World*. Cambridge: Cambridge University Press.

Gellman, Peter. 1988. "Hans J. Morgenthau and the Legacy of Political Realism." *Review of International Studies* 14(4):247–66.

Giddens, Anthony. 1979. *Central Problems in Social Theory*. London: Macmillan.

Giddens, Anthony. 1984. *The Constitution of Society: An Outline of the Theory of Structuration*. Cambridge: Polity Press.

Gill, Stephen, and David Law. 1988. *The Global Political Economy: Perspectives, Problems, and Policies*. Hemel Hempstead: Harvester, Wheatsheaf.

Gilpin, Robert. 1981. *War and Change in World Politics*. Cambridge: Cambridge University Press.

Gilpin, Robert. 1987. *The Political Economy of International Relations* Princeton: Princeton University Press.

Goffart, Walter. 1989. *Rome's Fall and After*. London: The Hambledon Press.

Goldmann, Kjell. 1979. *Is My Enemy's Enemy My Friend's Friend?*. Lund: Cultural Indicators, The Swedish Symbol System, 1945–1975, Report No. 1.

Gourevitch, Peter. 1978. "The International System and Regime Formation: A Critical Review of Anderson and Wallerstein." *Comparative Politics* 10(3):419–38.

Grafstein, Robert. 1988. "The Problem of Institutional Constraint." *Journal of Politics* 50(3):577–99.

Grieco, J. M. 1988a. "Realist Theory and the Problems of International Cooperation." *Journal of Politics* 50(3):600–24.

Grieco, J. M. 1988b. "Anarchy and the Limits of Cooperation: A Realist Critique of the New Liberal Institutionalism." *International Organization* 42(3):485–508.

Haas, Michael. 1970. "International Subsystems: Stability and Polarity." *American Political Science Review* 64(1):98–103.

Haas, Michael. 1974. *International Conflict*. Indianapolis: Bobbs-Merrill.

Halladay, A. J. 1982. "Hoplites and Heresies." *Journal of Hellenic Studies* 102:94–103.

Halliday, Fred. 1989. "Theorizing the International." *Economy and Society* 18(3):346–59.

Harré, Rom. ed.. 1986. *The Social Construction of the Emotions*. Oxford: Blackwell.

Harris, William V. 1979. *War and Imperialism in Republican Rome 327–70 B.C.* Oxford: Clarendon Press.

Hawkes, Terence. 1972. *Metaphor*. London: Methuen.

Herodotus (1987). *The History*. Trans. David Grene. Chicago: University of Chicago Press.

Hinsley, F. H. 1963. *Power and the Pursuit of Peace*. Cambridge: Cambridge University Press.

Hobbes, Thomas 1909 [1651]. *Leviathan*. Oxford: Clarendon Press.

Hollis, Martin, and Steven Nell. 1975. *Rational Economic Man: a Philosophical Critique of Neo-Classical Economics*. Cambridge: Cambridge University Press.

Hollis, Martin, and Steve Smith. 1990. *Explaining and Understanding International Relations*. Oxford: Clarendon Press.

Hollis, Martin, and Steve Smith. 1991. "Beware of Gurus: Structure and Action in International Relations." *Review of International Studies* 17:393–410.

Holsti, K. J. 1985. *The Dividing Discipline. Hegemony and Diversity in International Theory*. Boston: Allen & Unwin.

Ikenberry, G. John, and Charles A. Kupchan. 1990. "Socialization and Hegemonic Power." *International Organization* 44(3):283–315.

Immerwahr, Henry R. 1966. *Form and Thought in Herodotus*. Cleveland: Western Reserve University Press.

Intrilligator, Michael, and Dagobert Brito. 1979. "Nuclear Proliferation and the Problem of War." Center for Arms Control and International Security, UCLA.

Jenkins, Rhys. 1987. *Transnational Corporations and Uneven Development*. London: Methuen.

Jones, Charles A. 1987. "Prudence: Reply to Garver." *Social Epistemology* 1(4):311–20.

Jones, Charles A. 1992. "British Capital in Argentine History: Structures, Rhetoric and Change." in Alistair Hennessy and John King eds. *The Land That England Lost*. London: British Academic Press.

Jones, R. J. Barry. 1981. "Concepts and Models of Change in International Relations." In Barry Buzan and R. J. Barry Jones, eds. *Change and the Study of International Relations*. London: Frances Pinter. ch. 1.

Kant, Immanuel. 1933; [1781, 1787]. *Critique of Pure Reason.* London: Macmillan.

Kaplan, Morton A. 1979. *Towards Professionalism in International Theory.* New York: Free Press.

Keohane, Robert O. 1984. *After Hegemony: Cooperation and Discord in the World Political Economy.* Princeton: Princeton University Press.

Keohane, Robert O., ed. 1986. *Neorealism and its Critics.* New York: Columbia University Press.

Keohane, Robert O., and Joseph Nye. 1977. *Power and Interdependence.* Boston: Little Brown.

Keohane, Robert O., and Joseph Nye. 1987. *"Power and Interdependence* Revisited." *International Organization* 41(4):725–53.

Keohane, Robert O., and Joseph Nye, eds. 1972. *Transnational Relations and World Politics.* Cambridge: Harvard University Press.

Keppie, L. J. F. 1984. *The Making of the Roman Army: From Republic to Empire.* London: Batsford.

Kindleberger, Charles P. 1973. *The World in Depression, 1929–39.* Berkeley: University of California Press.

Kindleberger, Charles P. 1981. "Dominance and Leadership in the International Economy." *International Studies Quarterly* 25(2/3):242–54.

Knorr, Klaus. 1970. "The International Purposes of Military Power." In John Garnett ed. *Theories of Peace and Security.* London: Macmillan. ch. 2.

Kratochwil, Frederick V., and John G. Ruggie. 1986. "International Organization: A State of the Art and an Art of the State." *International Organization* 40(4):753–775.

Kratochwil, Frederick V. 1989. *Rules Norms and Decisions.* Cambridge: Cambridge University Press.

Lane, F. C. 1966. *Venice and History.* Baltimore: Johns Hopkins Press.

Lane, M. 1970. *Structuralism: A Reader.* London: Jonathan Cape.

Lapid, Y. 1989. "The Third Debate: On the Prospects of International Theory in a Post-Positivist Era." *International Studies Quarterly* 33:235–54.

Layder, D. 1981. *Structure, Interaction and Social Theory.* London: Routledge and Kegan Paul.

Layder, D. 1990. *The Realist Image in Social Science.* London: Macmillan.

Lenin, V. I. 1939 [1917]. *Imperialism: the Highest Stage of Capitalism.* New York: International Publishers.

Levi, Margaret. 1988. "The Tranformation of Agrarian Institutions: An Introduction and Perspective." *Politics and Society* 16:2–3:159–71.

Little, Richard. 1985. "Structuralism and Neo-Realism." In Margot Light and A. J. R. Groom eds. *International Relations: A Handbook of Current Theory.* London: Frances Pinter.

Little, Richard. 1991."International Relations and the Methodological Turn." *Political Studies* 39(3):463–78.

Lukes, Steven. 1974. *Power: A Radical Approach*. London: Macmillan.

Luttwak, Edward. 1976. *The Grand Strategy of the Roman Empire from the First Century A.D. to the Third*. Baltimore: Johns Hopkins University Press.

Machiavelli, Niccolo. [1961] 1514. *The Prince*. Harmondsworth: Penguin.

Malinowski, Bronislaw. 1922. *Argonauts of the Western Pacific*. London: Routledge.

Mandelbaum, Michael. 1988. *The Fate of Nations: The Search for National Security in the 19th and 20th Centuries*. Cambridge: Cambridge University Press.

Mannheim, Karl. 1936. *Ideology and Utopia: an Introduction to the Sociology of Knowledge*. London: Routledge & Kegan Paul.

Manning, C. A. W. 1962. *The Nature of International Society*. London: G. Bell and Sons.

Mann, J. C. 1979. "Force and the Frontiers of the Empire." *The Journal of Roman Studies* 69:175–83.

Mann, Michael. 1986. *The Sources of Social Power, Vol 1: A History of Power from the Beginning to A.D. 760*. Cambridge: Cambridge University Press.

Markham, Jesse W. 1968. "Oligopoly." In *International Encyclopedia of the Social Sciences* 11:283–89.

Mastanduno, Michael, David A. Lake and G. John Ikenberry, "Toward a Realist Theory of State Action." *International Studies Quarterly* 33(4) 1989: 457–74.

Mayall, James. 1990. *Nationalism and International Society*. Cambridge: Cambridge University Press.

McCloskey, Donald. 1986. *The Rhetoric of Economics*. Brighton: Wheatsheaf.

McKinlay, Robert D., and Richard Little. 1986. *Global Problems and World Order*. London: Frances Pinter.

McNeill, William H. 1963. *The Rise of the West: A History of the Human Community*. Chicago, University of Chicago Press.

McNeill, William H. 1979. *A World History*. Oxford: Oxford University Press.

Mearsheimer, John J. 1990. "Back to the Future: Instability in Europe After the Cold War." *International Security* 15(1):5–56.

Millis, Walter. 1971. "The Uselessness of Military Power." In William Coplin and Charles Kegley Jr. eds. *A Multi-Method Introduction to International Politics*. Chicago: Markham.

Milner, Helen. 1991. "The Assumption of Anarchy in International Relations Theory: A Critique." *Review of International Studies* 17(1):67–86.

Modelski, George. 1978. "The Long Cycle of Global Politics and the Nation-State." *Comparative Studies in Society and History* 20:214–35.

Morgenthau, Hans. 1978. *Politics Among Nations,* 5th ed. New York: Knopf.

Morrow, James D. 1988. "Social Choice and Social Structure in World Politics." *World Politics* 41(1):75–97.

Müller, F. Max. 1887. *The Science of Thought.* London: Longmans, Green.

Müller, F. Max. 1889. *The Science of Language.* London, Longmans, Green.

Murray, Alexander. 1978. *Reason and Society in the Middle Ages.* Oxford: Clarendon.

Nicholson, Michael. 1985. "Methodology" in Margot Light and A. J. R. Groom eds. *International Relations: a Handbook of Current Theory.* London: Pinter.

Niou, E. M. S. and P. G. Odershook. 1991."Realism versus Neoliberalism: A Formulation." *American Political Science Review* 35(2):481–511.

North, Douglass C. 1981. *Structure and Change in Economic History.* New York and London: W. W. Norton & Co..

Olson, Mancur and Zeckhauser, Richard J. 1966. "An Economic Theory of Alliances." *Review of Economics and Statistics* 48:266–79.

Onuf, Nicholas G. 1982. "Comparative International Politics." *Yearbook of World Affairs* 36:197–212.

Onuf, Nicholas G. 1989. *World of Our Making: Rules and Rule in Social Theory and International Relations.* Columbia: University of South Carolina Press.

Onuf, Nicholas, and Frank F. Klink. 1989. "Anarchy, Authority and Rule." *International Studies Quarterly* 33(2):149–73.

Oye, Kenneth A. 1985. "Explaining Cooperation Under Anarchy: Hypotheses and Strategies." *World Politics* 38(1):1–24.

Posen, Barry. 1984. *The Sources of Military Doctrine.* Ithaca: Cornell University Press.

Pouncey, Peter R. 1980. *The Necessities of War: A Study of Thucydides' Pessimism.* New York: Columbia University Press.

Price, Simon. 1986. "The History of the Hellenistic Period." In John Boardman, Jasper Griffen, and Oswyn Murray eds. *The Oxford History of the Classical World.* Oxford: Oxford University Press.

Przeworski, Adam. 1985. "Marxism and Rational Choice." *Politics and Society* 14(4):379–410.

Putnam, Hilary. 1977. "Meaning and Reference." In Stephen P. Schwartz, ed. *Naming, Necessity and Natural Kinds.* Ithaca and London: Cornell University Press.

Quine, Willard van Orman. 1960. *Word and Object.* Cambridge: MIT Press.

Rapkin, David P., William R. Thompson, and Jon A. Christopherson. 1979.

"Bipolarity and Bipolarization in the Cold War Era." *Journal of Conflict Resolution* 23(2):261–95.

Rickman, H. P. ed. 1961. *Meaning in History: W. Dilthey's Thoughts on History and Society*. London: Allen and Unwin.

Robey, D. 1973. *Structuralism: An Introduction*. Oxford: Clarendon Press.

Rorty, Richard. 1980. *Philosophy and the Mirror of Nature*. Oxford: Blackwell.

Rorty, Richard. 1989. *Contingency, Irony, and Solidarity*. Cambridge: Cambridge University Press.

Rosecrance, Richard. 1963. *Action and Reaction in World Politics*. Westport: Greenwood Press.

Rosecrance, Richard. 1969. "Bipolarity, Multipolarity, and the Future." In J. N. Rosenau ed. *International Politics and Foreign Policy*. New York: Free Press. pp.324–35.

Rosecrance, Richard. 1982. "Exchange of Letters." *International Organization* 36:679–85.

Rosenau, James N. 1990. *Turbulence in World Politics: A Theory of Change and Continuity*. Hemel Hempstead: Harvester Wheatsheaf.

Rosenberg, Justin. 1990. "What's the Matter with Realism?" *Review of International Studies* 16(4):285–303.

Ruggie, John G. "Continuity and Transformation in the World Polity: Towards a Neorealist Synthesis." In R. O. Keohane, ed. *Neorealism and its Critics*. New York: Columbia University Press.

Russett, Bruce M. 1967. *International Regions and the International System*. Chicago: Rand McNally.

Schelling, Thomas C. 1960. *The Strategy of Conflict*. London: Oxford University Press.

Schwartz, Stephen P. ed. 1977. *Naming, Necessity, and Natural Kinds*. Ithaca and London: Cornell University Press.

Singer, J. David. 1961. "The Level of Analysis Problem in International Relations." In Klaus Knorr and Sidney Verba eds. *The International System: Theoretical Essays*. Princeton: Princeton University Press.

Skinner, Quentin. 1985. *The Return of Grand Theory in the Human Sciences*. Cambridge: Cambridge University Press.

Skocpol, Theda. 1979. *States and Social Revolutions*. Cambridge: Cambridge University Press.

Snidal, D. 1985. "The Game Theory of International Politics." *World Politics* 38(1):25–57.

Spegele, Roger D. 1987. "Three Forms of Political Realism." *Political Studies* 35:189–210.

Strange, Susan. 1988. *States and Markets: An Introduction to International Political Economy*. London: Frances Pinter.

Strange, Susan. 1989. "The Future of the American Empire." *Journal of International Affairs* 42(1):1–17.

Sylos-Labini, P. 1987. "Oligopoly." In John Eastwell et al. eds. *The New Palgrave: A Dictionary of Economics*. London: Macmillan. pp. 701–5.

Taylor, Michael. 1989. "Structure Culture and Action in the Explanation of Social Change." *Politics and Society* 17(2):115–62.

Thompson, William R. 1973. "The Regional Subsystem: A Conceptual Explication and a Propositional Inventory." *International Studies Quarterly* 17(1):89–117.

Thompson, William R. 1986. "Polarity, the Long Cycle, and Global Power Warfare." *Journal of Conflict Resolution* 30(4):587–615.

Thucydides. 1954. *History of the Pelopponesian War*. Trans. Rex Warner. Harmondsworth: Penguin.

Uberoi, J. P. Singh. 1962. *Politics of the Kula Ring*. Manchester: Manchester University Press.

Väyrynen, Raimo. 1984. "Regional Conflict Formations: An Intractable Problem of International Relations." *Journal of Peace Research* 21(4):337–59.

Waever, Ole. 1989. "Conflicts of Vision: Visions of Conflict." In Ole Wæver, Pierre Lemaitre and Elzbieta Tromer eds. *European Polyphony: Perspectives Beyond East-West Confrontation*. London: Macmillan. pp. 283–325.

Walbank, F. W. 1981. *The Hellenistic World*. London: Fontana.

Walker, R. J. B. 1987. "Realism, Change and International Political Theory." *International Studies Quarterly* 31:65–84.

Walker, R. J. B. 1989. "History and Structure in the Theory of International Relations." *Millennium* 18(2):163–83.

Wallerstein, Immanual. 1974. *The Modern World System* Vol 1. New York: Academic.

Walt, Stephen M. 1987. *The Origins of Alliances*. Ithaca: Cornell University Press.

Waltz, Kenneth N. 1959. *Man, the State, and War*. New York: Columbia University Press.

Waltz, Kenneth N. 1962. "Kant, Liberalism and War." *American Political Science Review* 56(2):331–40.

Waltz, Kenneth N. 1964. "The Stability of the Bipolar World." *Daedalus* 93(3):881–909.

Waltz, Kenneth N. 1970. "The Myth of National Interdependence." In Charles Kindleberger ed. *The International Corporation*. Cambridge: MIT Press. 205–20.

Waltz, Kenneth N. 1971. "Conflict in World Politics." In S. L. Spiegel and K. N. Waltz eds. *Conflict in World Politics*. Cambridge: Winthrop.

☐ REFERENCES ☐

Waltz, Kenneth N. 1979. *Theory of International Politics*. Reading: Addison-Wesley.
Waltz, Kenneth N. 1986. "Response to My Critics." In R. O. Keohane, ed. *Neorealism and Its Critics*. New York: Columbia University Press.
Waltz, Kenneth N. 1990. "Realist Thought and Neorealist Theory." *Journal of International Affairs* 44(1):21–37.
Ward, V. 1991. "Regime Norms as 'Implicit' Third Parties: Explaining the Anglo-Argentine Relationship." *Review of International Studies* 17(3):167–93.
Warmington, B. H. 1964. *Carthage*. Harmondsworth, Pelican Books.
Warriner, H. 1957. *The Political Philosophy of Hobbes: His Theory of Obligation*. Oxford: Oxford University Press.
Wendt, Alexander E. 1987. "The Agent-Structure Problem in International Relations Theory." *International Organization* 41(3):335–70.
Wendt, Alexander E. 1990. "Sovereignty and the Social Construction of Power Politics." Yale University, unpublished ms., May.
Wendt, Alexander E. 1991. "Bridging the Theory/Meta-theory Gap in International Relations." *Review of International Studies* 17:383–92.
Wendt, Alexander E. Forthcoming. "Anarchy is What States Make of It: The Social Construction of Power Politics." *International Organization*.
Whittaker, C. R. 1978. "Carthaginian Imperialism in the Fifth and Fourth Centuries." In P. D. A. Garnsey and C. R. Whittaker eds. *Imperialism in the Ancient World*. Cambridge: Cambridge University Press.
Wight, Martin. 1977. *Systems of States*. Leicester: Leicester University Press.
Wittgenstein, Ludwig. 1961. *Tractatus Logico-Philosophicus*. London: Routledge & Kegan Paul.
Wittgenstein, Ludwig. 1969. *On Certainty*. Oxford: Blackwell.
Zacher, Mark W. 1987. "Trade Gaps, Analytical Gaps: Regime Analysis and International Commodity Trade Regulation." *International Organization* 41(2):173–202.

Index

Academics, 236
Adcock, F. E., 123
Aeotolian League, 153
Agent-structure relationship: Dessler on, 151–52; Structural Realism and, 83, 102–13; Walker on, 4; Waltz on, 136, 156
Aggregated capabilities, 54–56, 62–63
Aggressive states, 48
Agriculture, 123, 130, 163
Ahistoricism, 240–41
Alexander the Great, 125, 126
Alker, Hayward, 138
Alliances, 62, 118, 129–30, 137, 153
American Empire, 100, 134, 179; *see also* United States
Analogies, 178–80, 186, 197–99, 200–215
Analysis levels, *see* Levels of analysis
Anarchy, 132–54; competition and, 117, 138, 167–68; complexity of, 89; cooperation and, 242; deep structure and, 46, 87, 89, 138; distribution of capabilities and, 51; economic, 194, 195; empires and, 92; functional differentiation and, 89, 131, 146, 166; hierarchy and, 38, 39, 166, 168; interaction capacity and, 77, 78; Onuf on, 5; self-help and, 50; state power and, 196; three-tier political structure and, 36; unit likeness and, 41–42, 119–20
Anderson, Perry on: Athens, 145; Delian League, 144; Greece, 122, 123; Macedonia, 125; Rome, 129, 164; slavery, 130
Anthropologists, 138, 139
Antigonids, 126

A priori knowledge, 182, 188
Aquinas, Thomas, 183
Archer, Margaret S., 104, 105, 109, 111, 136
Aristocracy: Greek, 122–23, 124, 129; Macedonian, 125; Roman, 129, 163, 164, 165
Aristotle, 122, 125
Arms racing, 61
Ashley, Richard K., 3, 25, 133–34, 135
Asia, 40
Athens, 91, 123–24, 144–45
Attributive power, 67–68, 90
Autonomous civilizations, 74, 93, 94–96
Autonomous states, 89, 241, 242–43

Balance of power, 86, 87, 118–19; in chains of states, 157; cultural equilibrium and, 96; decentralized power and, 146–47; functional differentiation and, 131, 146, 242; imperialism and, 92; microeconomics and, 180, 183, 194, 206–7, 209–10, 234; Roman Empire and, 98–99, 147–50; in type 4 system theory, 45
Barbarians, 95, 153–54, 155, 162–63, 164–65
Bhaskar, Roy, 152, 173
Bipolarity: duopoly and, 179; economic, 58, 59, 62; from multipolarity, 118; to multipolarity, 13; to unipolarity, 53
Blaug, Marc, 193
Boundary definition, 92–93, 96
Bozeman, Adda B., 93–94
Briscoe, J., 148–49
British Empire, 91, 92, 93, 179
British government, 213–14